Sport in the Global So

General Editor: J.A. Mangan

RAIN STOPS PLAY

SPORT IN THE GLOBAL SOCIETY

General Editor: J.A. Mangan

The interest in sports studies around the world is growing and will continue to do so. This unique series combines aspects of the expanding study of *sport in the global society*, providing comprehensiveness and comparison under one editorial umbrella. It is particularly timely, with studies in the political, cultural, anthropological, ethnographic, social, economic, geographical and aesthetic elements of sport proliferating in institutions of higher education.

Eric Hobsbawm once called sport one of the most significant practices of the late nineteenth century. Its significance was even more marked in the late twentieth century and will continue to grow in importance into the new millennium as the world develops into a 'global village' sharing the English language, technology and sport.

Other Titles in the Series

Cricket and England
A Cultural and Social History of the Inter-war Years
Jack Williams

Sport in Australasian Society
Past and Present
Edited by J.A. Mangan and John Nauright

Australian Beach Cultures
The History of Sun, Sand and Surf
Douglas Booth

Amateurism in Sport
An Analysis and a Defence
Lincoln Allison

Flat Racing and British Society, 1790–1914
A Social and Economic History
Mike Huggins

Soccer in South Asia
Empire, Nation, Diaspora
Edited by Paul Dimeo and James Mills

Shaping the Superman
Fascist Body as Political Icon – Aryan Fascism
Edited by J.A. Mangan

Scoring for Britain
International Football and International Politics, 1900–1939
Peter J. Beck

Sporting Nationalisms
Identity, Ethnicity, Immigration and Assimilation
Edited by Mike Cronin and David Mayall

The Games Ethic and Imperialism
Aspects of the Diffusion of an Ideal
J.A. Mangan

The Race Game
Sport and Politics in South Africa
Douglas Booth

Rugby's Great Split
Class, Culture and the Origins of Rugby League Football
Tony Collins

Making the Rugby World
Race, Gender, Commerce
Edited by Timothy J.L. Chandler and John Nauright

The First Black Footballer
Arthur Wharton 1865–1930: An Absence of Memory
Phil Vasili

RAIN STOPS PLAY

Cricketing Climates

ANDREW HIGNELL

Foreword by John Kettley
Introduction by Christopher Martin-Jenkins

FRANK CASS
LONDON • PORTLAND, OR

First published in 2002 in Great Britain by
FRANK CASS PUBLISHERS
Crown House, 47 Chase Side, Southgate,
London, N14 5BP

and in the United States of America by
FRANK CASS PUBLISHERS
c/o ISBS, 5824 N.E. Hassalo Street
Portland, Oregon 97213-3644

Website: www.frankcass.com

© 2002 Andrew Hignell

British Library Cataloguing in Publication Data

Hignell, Andrew
    Rain stops play: cricketing climates. – (Sport in the global society; no. 27)
    1. Cricket 2. Cricket – Social aspects 3. Global warming – Social aspects
    I. Title
    796.3'58'09

ISBN 0-7146-5173-7 (cloth)
ISBN 0-7146-8186-5 (paper)
ISSN 1368-9789

Library of Congress Cataloging-in-Publication Data

Hignell, Andrew.
    Rain stops play: cricketing climates/Andrew Hignell.
        p. cm. – (Sport in the global society, ISSN 1368-9789; no. 27)

    Includes bibliographical references (p.   ) and index.
    ISBN 0-7146-5173-7 – ISBN 0-7146-8186-5 (pbk.)
    1. Cricket–Regional disparities. 2. Cricket–Political aspects. 3.
    Cricket–Cross-cultural studies. I.Title. II. Cass series–sport in
    the global society; no. 27.
    GV917 .H54 2002
    796.358–dc21
                                            2001008546

Typeset by FiSH Books, London in 11 on 12.5pt Times
Printed in Great Britain by MPG Books Ltd, Bodmin, Cornwall

Contents

List of Illustrations

List of Diagrams

List of Tables

Foreword

Cricket and the weather are two of the great British institutions which are often inextricably linked. Andrew Hignell has combined original thinking with exhaustive research to produce a book for the academic and cricket enthusiast alike. There is plenty to digest and many items jog the memory. This is not a book to read in haste, but to pore over and imagine, for example, what the state of domestic and international cricket will be in fifly years' time. When I passed my driving test I learned to drive. When I passed my forecasting course I began to understand the weather. When I read this book I realised what a complex sport cricket is – and how much I didn't know! In many ways *Rain Stops Play* is a refreshing break from the plethora of autobiographies and the brilliant annual cricketing bible that is *Wisden*.

ᴗI spent my formative years at Todmorden in the Pennines where east meets west, or more accurately Yorkshire meets Lancashire. Oflen known as the border town, it boasts two cricketers who later won international honours, namely Derek Shackleton and Peter Lever. For as long as I can remember cricket has been my first love but the meteorological extremes of the Pennines sowed the seeds of my future career. In my teenage years a good friend offered me some timely advice when he suggested that you should never make your hobby your profession. That was the end of voluntary weather observations at school but I have continued to follow cricket, simply the greatest game in the world.

Philip Eden's summer index, which has been included in chapter 7, is a very useful guide to the weather across all the English counties. It incorporates temperature, sunshine, rainfall frequency and rainfall amount in equal proportion to reveal how good the summer was. It is worth noting that Surrey has the highest average and Durham the lowest, so whilst congratulating Chester-le-Street for gaining Test status I do implore the authorities to consider the weather, which can be disappointing in early summer.

The following chapter assesses the impact of rain on each county with particular reference to 1998. I found this most interesting because 1998 was (and still is) the warmest year globally since comprehensive temperature data were first collated back in 1860. In 2001, the second warmest year globally since records began, Lancashire lost the first eight days of the season at Old Trafford because of the weather. Not good news for English cricket then!

A memorable occasion where cricket and the weather joined forces was the infamous snowfall of 2 June 1975 at Buxton. On the second day of the County Championship fixture between Derbyshire and Lancashire, an Arctic blast brought an inch of snow, with considerably more on the hills around. Admittedly the ground stands at an altitude of 300m but this was a remarkable event and it probably came as no surprise when the inclement Buxton weather helped persuade Derbyshire to abandon the venue in 1986. Ironically a nation-wide heatwave followed just a few days later!

Who will ever forget The Oval 1968, England versus Australia in the Fifth Test and the days of uncovered wickets? It was all hands on deck as the crowd and officials came to the aid of England following a spell of torrential rain. After hours of wringing sponges and sweeping gallons of water off the playing area Derek Underwood bowled out the Aussies to share the series.

If we are to believe that global warming is occurring, with El Nino being a contributory factor, I can readily see the cricket seasons around the world being adjusted (within commercial constraints). If the past 14 years are anything to go by, we can expect to lose more Test Matches to the weather; there have been four in total since 1988.

On a final note of irony, the weather has proved too much for the incomparable Dickie Bird on two separate occasions. Who else could possibly have been officiating when the water main blew at Headingley and when the sun stopped play at Old Trafford as its rays reflected off an open window?

Will we ever be able to trust the weather – especially on the cricket field?

John Kettley
February 2002

Introduction

I doubt if the expression 'six and out' means anything to anyone outside Britain. To players of my generation at least it was such a familiar adaptation to the laws of cricket that it seldom had to be mentioned. All schoolboys knew that a ball struck into the next garden, or over the wall of the street, or into the hedge at the back of the school playground, meant instant bathos. First the gratification of striking the ball in the middle of the bat; then the horror of seeing it land out of bounds and the consequent dismissal from the crease, lost ball or not.

All cricketers are shaped by their environment. Those habitual six-hitters of Somerset and England renown, Arthur Wellard and Ian Botham (perhaps they were brought up in large gardens – they certainly had inviting straight boundaries at Taunton) were exceptions to the rule that English batsmen are by nature cautious.

This restriction on space for most young cricketers in the UK has surely had something to do with it. They don't have to worry about these things in Australia, where a large playing field is round the corner from most people; or Barbados, where one boundary for the impromptu schoolboy game is often the sea and where, therefore, the harder and higher the hit, the better. No wonder they produced Gary Sobers, the first man to hit six sixes in a first-class over.

Clive Lloyd, another left-hander with a high backlift and mighty bat, hailed from across the sea in Georgetown, Guyana. He once attended a class for advanced coaches in England. All of them were asked to demonstrate the stroke they would play to a fast rising, short ball on the off stump. To a man, the English coaches put their back foot across the imaginary wicket, and played back-foot defensive strokes. Lloyd essayed a vivid hook over square-leg.

It is remarkable, in fact, how Georgetown produces any cricketers of note at all, because with one exception – an interesting one in the era of global warming – it has always rained in torrents when I have been there. The town lies below sea level but it was ingeniously laid out by the Dutch to remain more or less dry by means of a system of sluices. Bourda, the handsome home of the Georgetown Cricket Club, a British introduction, naturally, is the only place where I have seen fish swimming round the outfield.

The last time that an England team visited, in 1998, however, there was a drought throughout Guyana and the Test match was played in hot sunshine, without interruptions. Andrew Hignell refers to this unlikely event in connection with the El Niño phenomenon, one of many angles from which he discusses the effect of the weather on cricket in this, the most exhaustive study ever conducted on a question fundamental to every match ever played out of doors.

Cricket is not only the most profound and satisfying team game ever invented, it is also the cruellest and least fair. Timing is everything and the weather can intervene every bit as unjustly as the umpire or a freakish piece of brilliance by an opponent. I write as one who was just starting to feel confident at the crease when it began snowing in a final trial at Cambridge University. On that occasion it is true that nobody wanted to continue playing except me, but generally speaking nothing is more depressing to cricketers than rain, unless it is making nought, dropping a catch or getting hit for 15 in an over.

A serious look at the relationship between cricket and physical geography was therefore overdue. It is a relief, for example, to receive confirmation of what every player knows (but scientists have sometimes claimed to disprove), namely that weather affects batting and bowling conditions. In a nutshell, the ball swings more when it is moist and it is much easier batting when it is dry and sunny.

It also intrigued me to read in these pages that there is growing evidence, in the age of global warming, for the belief that it rains more in England and Wales in April and May than it does in September. Quite apart from the effect on professional cricket that is the author's chief concern, this is bad news for schoolboys. It is always particularly sad when rain ruins matches for the fortunate few who still play cricket at their schools. The summer term gets shorter, it seems, by the year as exams increasingly bear down upon teachers and pupils alike. For years it has been appreciated by all who care for cricket that more needs to be done to foster the game in schools. Here, surely, is compelling evidence in favour of the proposed six-term year, provided, of course, at least two of them allow for cricket as the main sport in the curriculum. The second of them would offer at least two advantages over the status quo: no imminent exams and better weather.

Whether or not the young get a better deal in future, partly as a result of the evidence presented here that drier Septembers and wetter Mays are both likely to become more common in Britain, the cricket authorities would do well to heed the advice of a schoolmaster of Andrew Hignell's reputation when it comes to the game that is played for money as part of the entertainment business. He makes the case well for paying more attention to the weather during the creation of what is always a complex fixture list. Many factors go into the ECB's computer before the list is produced each year, but they do not include the table that suggests that to get the best of the weather in each locality the correct order for Tests to be staged on the established grounds should be Headingley (starting on June 1), Edgbaston (15 June), Lord's (13 July), Trent Bridge (27 July), Old Trafford (24 August) and The Oval (7 September.)

The snag, of course, is that professional cricket in England and Wales evolved: it was never part of a master plan. Attempts to fine-tune it according to the weather are, therefore, no easier than the frequent attempts to change it according to technical and commercial changes in the game, usually driven by forces from overseas. If a domestic programme were to be drawn up for the twenty-first century for the purposes of making a profitable game and of creating an England team that is as strong as possible, the designers of the template would certainly not start with 18 county teams.

It is the main thesis of this work that the ECB cannot afford, as the author expresses it, to 'wallow in nostalgia and ignore the fundamental changes to the geographical environment, both physical and human, in which the games are played'. Of course not, but the game would have to generate very much more income than it does to come up with a definitive answer to the menace of rain stopping play. Given unlimited funds the solution, of course, would be to make cricket purely an indoor sport in years to come, played beneath the retractable roofs that alone offer the only sure answer to the uncertain weather. Even as I write these words a Test is being spoiled by rain in Bangalore, where it simply is not supposed to rain in late December.

Perhaps the reason was that even Indian cities are prone to the extra rain produced by what the author calls 'urban heat islands'. They certainly make rain more likely in England, which is a pity when counties are tending to play a greater majority of their matches at their urban or suburban headquarters for reasons of economy. After explaining in the early stages of his book how the rural pastime of what was once a largely agrarian country has spread to the cities, Andrew finishes his analysis by suggesting that the 18 counties should reinvent themselves as 'city regions' like Birmingham Region or Canterbury Region. Those of us in the know would not be fooled that we were not in reality watching Warwickshire or Kent, but I can see that there might be advantages for counties where the main city also has a football and rugby club in pooling sponsorship and offering joint memberships for all three sports.

In *Rain Stops Play* Andrew Hignell looks at the relation between cricketers and their environment in greater depth and from more different angles than anyone ever has before. His research has been rigorous and his conclusions are illuminating. If this book had been published when I was at school I might, as someone already hopelessly hooked by the simple yet infinite attractions of cricket, have been tempted to do geography as one of my A levels.

Christopher Martin-Jenkins
December 2001

Series Editor's Foreword

At some moment of an undistinguished career, many an exponent of the art of the coarsest cricket has experienced something like what might be called the Newbolt Crisis without, it might be added, Newbolt's tense concern:

> Ten to make and the match to win –
> A bumping pitch and a blinding light,
> An hour to play and the last man in... [1]

Of course, extreme environmental and climatic conditions have made severe demands on more illustrious performers than Newboltian school-boys. Even the brilliant Bradman found form hard to come by on one notable occasion when drought in the wilds of Saskatchewan produced a swarm of grasshoppers on a 'tasty wicket' which made the bounce somewhat unpredictable. [2]

In such conditions there clearly remains a need for the still unwritten opus of the spiritually inclined Mr Opie of *Stamboul Train* fame:

> Suppose you are the last man in; you have put on your pads; eight wickets have fallen; fifty runs must be made; you wonder if the responsibility will fall on you. You will get no strength for that crisis from any of the usual books of contemplation...I aim to supply that man's need. [3]

Interestingly Andrew Hignell – so typically of this Secular Age, doubtless the Archbishop of Canterbury would complain – fails to add this solution to others he posits in response to the challenges of modern cricket in a cold and wet climate.

Cricket conditions made purposefully for pain in the preparation of imperial Spartans and green moving pitches in a land of locusts are in complete contrast to the idyllic pastoral setting for the match between Little Clumpton and Hickory in J.C. Snaith's charming *Willow, the King*.

> It was a perfect morning, flushed with summer. The birds on the boughs were welcoming the young sun; the mists were running before him; the dew on the trees was dancing to him; whilst the drenched meadows and

the cool haze receding to the hills promised ninety in the shade to follow. Evidently Nature, like a downright good sportsman, was going to let us have a real cricketers' day for a true cricketing occasion. Such fragrance made the blood leap. Every muscle seemed electric. To snuff the chill airs was to feel as fit and full of devil as racehorse. By Jove, I felt like getting 'em! There were clean off-drives in the eager brooks, clipping cuts for four in the sparkling grass, sweet leg glances in the singing hedgerows, inimitable hooks and behind the wicket strokes in the cheerful field noises and the bird-thrilled branches.[4]

Such mythical rustic scenes of deepest tranquillity, some claim with the most complete religious conviction, demonstrate that cricket is pantheism and pantheism is cricket – an English religion born of, and unique to, an English climate with its own spiritual sustenance as delightfully described in A. G. Macdonell's *England, Their England*.

It was a hot summer's afternoon. There was no wind, and the smoke from the red-roofed cottages curled slowly up into the golden haze. The clock on the flint tower of the church struck the half-hour, and the vibrations spread slowly across the shimmering hedgerows, spangled with white blossom of the convolvulus, and lost themselves tremulously among the orchards. Bees lazily drifted. White butterflies flapped their aimless way among the gardens. Delphiniums, larkspur, tiger-lilies, evening-primrose, monk's-hood, sweet-peas, swaggered brilliantly above the box hedges, the wooden palings, and the rickety gates. The cricket field itself was a mass of daisies and buttercups and dandelions, tall grasses and purple vetches and thistle-down, and great clumps of dark-red sorrel, except, of course, for the oblong patch in the centre – mown, rolled watered – a smooth, shining emerald of grass, the Pride of Fordenden, the Wicket.

The entire scene was perfect to the last detail.[5]

This is the eternal landscape and climate of English cricketing romantics. In *Rain Stops Play* Hignell reveals himself as an English cricketing realist – a man of the marketing moment – ruthless in pursuit of the requirements of a lean and fit cricketing economy in a cool and dry climate in which tills ring and turnstiles spin continuously. In this pursuit, he has filled an analytical void – no mean feat with the plethora of cricketing books now available. For this he deserves congratulations.

Hignell has a sound sense of timing – the hallmark of the successful marketing man. With climatic change around the corner and the possibility of a warmer (and God forbid) a wetter climate ahead, as he states, 'there could be no better time for a geography of county cricket' (p.xxi).

His close analysis of the game's geographical dimensions, both in the past, present and future, is authoritative, informed and interesting. It is curious, as he remarks, that up to now the chaps rather than the maps have had so much attention. It is even more curious, as he further points out, that in this age of cheque book cricket, profit and places rather than people and places fail to attract due attention. He has changed all that. Not a moment too soon – lads and ladettes now need to be woed and colonels and their ladies have had their day. Shires and narrow access no longer matter; cities and broad motorways now matter. The marketing mogels need a taste for meteorology, for 'while clubs and ECB employ a vast number of commercial executives, marketing consultants and business managers it is remarkable given the fundamental link with the weather, that they do not employ a meteorologist' (p.177). It is thus hardly surprising, comments Hignell, that adequate resources are not yet devoted to 'better mopping "equipment", ground covering or indoor arenas' (p.177). Oddly perverse romantics, it seems, are still to be found in the Country of Cheque Book Cricket, consequently, 'the compromise between catering for profit or precipitation is perhaps one of the most endearing and quaintly English features' (pp.177–8) Endearing! Surely the tongue is lodged firmly in the cheek!

Durhamites will fight for the right to hoist umbrellas; they know all about disastrous Southern Domes, but when Money rules, will they win? Meanwhile, when meteorological records are sufficiently comprehensive and rainfall patterns are brutally clear, will Old Trafford be covered over: 'To an outsider', Hignell argues, 'there seems to be a paradox that at a time when England's administrators are appealing for more sponsorship and investment, they opt to stage five days of Test cricket, plus one (or even two) One-Day Internationals each year at the ground whose county tends to lose more time each season at their home games than any other' (p.184). For outsider read entrepreneur! The bottom line, as Hignell states confidently, is that no matter 'how many reforms are made to the nature of the teams, the format of competitions, and the number of Test and One-Day Internationals each year, cricket will still be, as it always has been, at the whim of the weather' (p.185).

The way ahead is clear: more detailed studies are needed of time lost to weather and where it is lost, if profits are to be protected and, indeed, increased. The only fly in the ointment, of course, is that with changing climatic change ahead, what relevance will present records have to future downpours?

Hignell certainly makes his case, for past casualness and lost profit – and profit maximisation – and pleasure – would seem to demand more adequate meteorological surveys. And indeed, the pursuit of profit could lead to the increase of pleasure – more cricket watched with dry necks. Perhaps with the aid of science, the fictional world of Macdonell and Snaith will become more of a reality – a myth of 'Merrie England' will come closer to idyllic actuality, circumscribed, of course, by chanting lads and ladettes, fast-food litter and ridiculous pyjamas. Of course, to ensure a cool, dry climate of advantage to all – player, official, spectator, sponsor and 'television enthusiast', 'under cover cricket' could be the future. Has anyone told the Prime Minister? Happily, those with quaint and endearing English qualities will continue to play on wet wickets and watch in damp deckchairs for no profit but certain pleasure the length and breadth of England.

This is an absorbing, stimulating and provocative book that makes the case for the importance of meteorology to professional cricket if profit – and pleasure – are to be maximised.

J.A. Mangan
International Research Centre for Sport, Socialisation and Society
University of Strathclyde
February 2002

Preface

This book combines two of the passions in my life – geography and cricket (or should it be cricket and geography?) – and the seeds for the ideas which are expressed in it were sown when I was with my wife – the third passion of my life – on holiday in North Devon during the autumn of 1997. At the time, I was still basking in the glory of Glamorgan's third Championship title. Even though I had been back at Wells Cathedral School, teaching geography for almost two months, their Championship clinching game at Taunton still seemed only a few hours away. Indeed, I had had little time to draw breath and relax, so when our friends Brian and Angela Meyrick, who were working in South Korea, invited us to stay in their delightful cottage at Georgeham in North Devon, the first morning of the Michaelmas half-term saw us quickly heading west down the M5.

Rest and relaxation were at the top of the batting order, and our week consisted of leisurely walks by day along the golden beaches and the rugged, jagged coastline of North Devon, while at night Debra and I enjoyed the sumptuous hospitality at The Rock in Georgeham, before heading back to the cottage to relax by the log fire, put up our weary feet and quietly read, with a glass of fine malt whisky in hand. I had taken with me three books which I had been wanting to read for some time – Peter Wynne-Thomas's *A History of Cricket*, Mike Marqusee's *Anyone, but England* and Peter Haggett's *The Geographer's Art*. This rich diet, both gastronomic and literary, consumed in the peaceful surroundings of Georgeham started to fuel my thought processes and led me to think that if detailed histories of cricket could be written, then why not a geographical analysis of cricket.

I had ventured down this road a few years before when writing *A 'Favourit' Game*, a survey of cricket in South Wales prior to 1914. Rather than adopting a match by match approach to show the increasing popularity of the game, I used a spatial framework, mapping the location of games and the movements of early players. My conclusions were that the game's evolution in South Wales fitted Torsten Hagerstrand's theory of innovation diffusion, with favourable points from which cricket spread, in a fixed and hierarchical way, rather than in a random or chaotic fashion.

By the time we were making our return journey home, I had already made some jottings and a list of 'things to do', but it was a series of coincidences over the next few weeks that stimulated me to put pen to paper in a serious way. Firstly, we were visited in early November by David Money, the eminent geographer and cricket fanatic. David had kindly agreed to speak to our Sixth Form Geographers about global warming, and during his fascinating talk he showed a slide of temperature changes and sunspot activity during the past 150 years. Beside drawing the attention of our pupils to the cyclical patterns, he added that perhaps the fortunes of England's batsmen in the home Test series could almost match these peaks and troughs. Was this a simple throwaway comment, or could he be right? Later that night, I started to delve into *Wisden*, and it was not long before my 'things to do' list spanned several sides of A4 paper.

The second coincidence came in early December when a letter arrived from Dr Eric Midwinter, President of the Association of Cricket Statisticians and Historians. The Association was celebrating its twenty-fifth anniversary with a Conference in Nottingham during the autumn of 1998, and Eric invited me to speak at the conference. He suggested possibly talking about the development of cricket in South Wales, since he knew what I had written in *A 'Favourit' Game* and he wanted a geographical aspect to the Conference. After our week in North Devon and the visit from David Money, there were many other ideas to float. Eric readily agreed to my suggestions, and even added a few ideas of his own, which I quickly added to the ever-growing list of 'things to do'.

The die was now cast, and over the Christmas and New Year holidays of 1997/98, I started to put pen to paper. What follows is the result.

Acknowledgements

A book of this nature could not have been written without the help and encouragement of many people, from both the worlds of geography and cricket. In particular, I would like to thank Professor J.A. Mangan for his support of my initial ideas, and for his encouragement throughout the writing of this book. David Money, John Bale and Dr Eric Midwinter were others who fired my initial enthusiasm, while Mike Hulme and Philip Eden both helped with meteorological advice. Dr David Thornton of UWIC, Dr John Thornes of Birmingham University, and Dr Tony Hoare and Dr Keith Crabtree of Bristol University all gave helpful advice, while Malcolm Walker of the Royal Meteorological Society also provided valuable support.

From the cricket world, I would like to thank Mike Fatkin and the late Byron Denning of Glamorgan CCC, as well as Colin Sexstone, Bert Avery and John Mace from Gloucestershire CCC. Among my many colleagues at Wells Cathedral School, I would also like to thank Elizabeth Cairncross, David Rowley, Nichola Touhey, Charles Cain, Duncan Gowan and Kris Robbetts, together with many sixth form students who have acted as guinea pigs as I have floated my ideas about the link between the weather and cricket. A host of members of the Association of Cricket Statisticians provided rich food for thought, and in particular, I would like to thank Peter Wynne-Thomas, Pete Griffiths, Philip Bailey, Les Hatton, Charles Oliver, William Powell, Bob Harragan and David Jeater, who all provided helpful data and ideas.

David Smith, Duncan Pierce, Rob Steen and Bryn Jones all deserve a big thank you for other helpful comments. I am also very grateful for the help of Paul McGregor in providing some wonderful photographs, as well as the staff from the following Libraries and Record Offices in providing other local information and population data – Lewisham Local Studies Library, Gloucester Record Office, Bristol Record Office, Horsham Library, Bedford Library, Huntingdonshire Record Office, Middlesbrough Borough Council, Cambridge Library, Folkestone Library, Blackpool Library, Pontypridd Library, Blaenau Gwent Borough Council, Taff Ely Borough Council, Wiltshire Record Office, Middlesex Record Office, Tring Library, Staffordshire Record Office, Nottingham Library, Somerset Record Office, Abergavenny Library and the Worcestershire Record Office.

Lastly, but by no means least, my thanks go to Jonathan Manley of Frank Cass for his guidance in the completion of the final manuscript, and to my wife Debra for her support throughout this fascinating project.

Andrew Hignell
Wells, Somerset
February 2002

Introduction:
The Need for a Geography of Cricket

Sir – There is a foolproof method of forecasting the weather in England which can be used whenever our national cricket team is playing at home. If, after the first day's play, the team has established supremacy, four days of rain and poor visibility are on the way; should our players be on the rack, the sun will shine until Tuesday. The validity of this method is supported by the team's results in the Caribbean and the Southern Hemisphere, where the weather is always sunny.[1]

In September 1998, John Walliker of Dadlington, Warwickshire, wrote the above letter to *The Daily Telegraph*. Whilst he may well have had his tongue firmly in his cheek, there is no doubting that cricket is affected by the weather. Interruptions to county and Test matches through rain or bad light have been an integral part of the summer game, and in some people's eyes, the phrase 'Rain Stopped Play' goes hand in hand with English cricket.

It is not just the United Kingdom where such a link occurs between cricket and the weather, as briefly explained by Philip Eden in a short essay in the 1999 edition of *Wisden*. The well-known BBC Radio weather expert showed how the reversal of ocean currents in the Pacific Ocean, known as El Nino, disturbed weather patterns in many countries and had a major impact on playing conditions in Australia, South Africa and the Caribbean. In the case of the latter, El Nino coincided with England's winter tour of the West Indies and the Guyana Test was played in a drought, whilst at Bridgetown, the Barbados Test saw almost two months' worth of rain fall in just 48 hours.[2]

This association with the weather is just one way in which cricket has a link with geography. Another occurs at the commencement of games, when prior to hopefully winning the toss, the captain has to be aware of meteorological conditions, as well as the state of the wicket. Opting to bat in humid conditions could be an unwise move, as could choosing to field first on a very dry wicket, likely to favour the spinners as the game progresses. Despite the high stakes, most county captains are likely to base their decisions on hunches, the views of the local groundsman or a brief weather forecast on breakfast television or in a tabloid newspaper. By its very nature, there are other spatial aspects to English cricket, with elevens representing places, whether they be villages, cities, counties or the country itself. Cricket therefore has a fundamental geographical dimension.

Numerous tourist organisations and promotional agencies have projected images of a cricket field as part of the English way of life, yet the summer game has largely been ignored by geographers, who have devoted their attention to almost every other aspect of the English environment and landscape. There has been a veritable mountain of geography books devoted to an analysis of land use, settlement patterns, the nature of the soil, the type of bedrock, the occupational habits of the residents, the transport networks which developed, the geomorphology of a region and the micro-climate existing over it, yet no books detailing the geographical dimensions of cricket have so far been published – a remarkable oversight given the words of Neville Cardus, the doyen of cricket writers, who in 1977 wrote 'in every English village, a cricket field is as much part of the landscape as the old church'.[3]

Some attention has been paid in a rather basic way to the locational dimensions of the county game. These include Aylwin Sampson's *Grounds of Appeal*,[4] William Powell's *Wisden Guide to Cricket Grounds*[5] and George Plumptre's *The Homes of Cricket*.[6] Delightful and thorough as each of these books are, they are of a literary and journalistic nature, designed more for the coffee table of a sports enthusiast or the shelves of a cricket lover, rather than a worthy place in the library of a professional geographer.

Some of cricket's leading historians, such as Rowland Bowen[7] and Peter Wynne-Thomas,[8] have used simple maps in their excellent accounts of the game's evolution, but as the emphasis in each case was on the people and key dates rather than the patterns, it is the chaps, rather than the maps that get detailed attention. Other historians have analysed the diffusion of the game within English society, but the very nature of its geographical spread has been ignored, leaving many questions unanswered about the spatial dimensions of the game's evolution.

Cricket has proved to be a most fruitful field for academic research, and many other dimensions of the game have been covered. The demographic aspects have been well researched, with social scientists looking at the class barriers which both encouraged and discouraged differing status groups from taking part.[9] They have also investigated the forms of acceptable behaviour and moral codes which cricket embraced, whilst economic historians have looked at what determined who was able to play or watch the county game. Ric Sissons[10] has investigated other economic aspects of the county cricketer's lot, especially how much the professionals were paid and how their status changed over time.

Keith Sandiford has made a detailed analysis of the impact of professionalisation on the post-war English game, and he has shown how commercial interests have affected the structure of the game. His findings are in stark contrast to his research with Wray Vamplew on the economics of English cricket before 1914, a time when profit maximisation was certainly not part of the English game.[11] Jack Williams has followed up this work with an excellent study of the historiography of cricket between the wars, looking at many diverse cultural and social aspects of the county game in the inter-war period, including its structure, participants and spectators.[12]

All of these academics have reached a consensus on the way cricket came to be regarded as a powerful metaphor for Englishness, a symbol of the nation's Christian and cultural values, and of English moral worth.[13] Yet the actual patterns on the ground have been largely ignored – the questions 'when', 'why' and 'who' have been more than adequately answered, but few people have asked the question 'where', leaving many important and fundamental questions unresolved about the actual geography of county cricket.

The chief exception has been John Bale,[14] who has already paid brief attention to the potential of such an approach using a human geographical framework, whilst meteorologists and climate scientists such as Mick Hulme[15] and John Thornes[16] in their surveys of the way the weather has interupted the county game have identified basic links with environmental processes, and shown how cricket is an example of the fundamental interplay between the human and natural environment which lies at the heart of the subject of geography.

This lack of detailed study on the geography of English cricket is mirrored in the wider world of sports geography, where the English games have, until recently, received little detailed attention from sports geographers. The works published in the early 1980s by such sporting academics as Tony Mason[17] on association football between 1863 and 1915 and J.A. Mangan[18] on athleticism in Victorian and Edwardian public schools were early beacons which have subsequently sparked off some interest from geographers,[19] yet we can still echo the words of John Rooney written back in 1974 that 'there is much to be done if we are to realise the vast potential inherent in the geographic study of sport'.[20]

The discipline of sports geography is, according to John Bale,[21] concerned with the following three areas:

1. analysing sporting activity on the earth's surface and the changing spatial distribution of sport over time,
2. the changing character of the sports landscape and the symbiosis between the sports environment and those who participate in it, and
3. the making of prescriptions for spatial and environmental change in the sports environment.

All three areas are very attractive for meaningful and innovative research, yet Bale[22] is the only major author covering English sports. In part, this paucity of research might be due to the fact that more fruitful sporting fields of analysis lie in other, possibly more commercially attractive, team games, especially football, both in its British and North American codes. Yet as John Rooney, the pioneering voice in the field of sports geography stated, 'there is a geography of every game and a sports geography of every region'.[23]

It has to be asked therefore why geographers should be interested in English cricket, and for that matter what extra insights could geographers bring to the already sizeable mass of academic studies on the English summer game. To answer these questions one can turn, once again, to Bale who believes that 'by using the tools of analysis and the conceptual framework of the geographer, new and hitherto unperceived insights on sports may be obtained and new patterns exhumed which, besides being of intrinsic interest, are highly relevant to an understanding of the significance of sport in society'.[24]

Bale also believes that there are natural links between sport and geography as 'both are concerned with space and the way it is occupied; they both focus on the way people and objects move and interact in geographic space; regions form a central feature of the organisation of sports; places are the means of identification for many sports teams; sport is affected by, and increasingly affects, both the environment and the landscape; sport is a world of hierarchy and territoriality. In short, sport – like geography – is a science of space.'[25]

This ignorance of the geography of county cricket is certainly not caused by a lack of data. Cricket has a veritable minefield of statistics, both individual and collective, published on a daily basis in the national newspapers, in the media, and on the Internet. There is also a treasure trove of historical data in *Wisden* and *Lillywhite*, dating back to the middle of the nineteenth century, whilst each of the English (and Welsh) counties produce an annual yearbook, outlining the on-field and off-field action on an annual basis. If ever there was an example of the phrase 'information rich and knowledge poor', one case would be the current knowledge about the geographical dimensions of English cricket.

It is the aim of this book is to fill this void, and to attempt a detailed analysis of the game's geographical dimensions, namely its space and place, both in the past, present and future. Attention will be paid to the locations where the folk-game initially began, and how it diffused and subsequently metamorphosed from a tranquil country pastime into an inter-county contest played in large urban centres. These changes in the geography of county cricket mirror the changes that have occurred in English society as a whole, and one of the academic goals of this book is to highlight the key cultural, social and economic factors in the game's evolution from an informal, meadowland contest to a highly organised and complex multinational business. Consideration is also given to global processes and how climatic factors affect the game in other countries. By looking forward, this book will also achieve a practical goal by considering how under a warmer and possibly wetter climate the county game might become increasingly affected by meteorological factors, necessitating further changes in its geography. In fact, with the 1990s having recently been described as the warmest decade on record, there could be no better time for a geography of county cricket.

The Geographical Boundaries of Cricket

The boundaries of the county game

Most team games in the modern era are place-specific, with the participants representing fixed places. In English football, every major team nowadays represents a city, town, suburb, village or conurbation. Modern cricket is fundamentally different from football in that it is based around a county framework, rather than just one fixed point, even though some of these counties no longer exist on the map.

Even so, there was a place-specific element to earlier forms of the game, as some of the earliest major matches involved games between town sides and a so-called county eleven. Among the earliest entries in Volume 1 of Frederick Lillywhite's *Cricket Scores and Biographies* are reports of games in 1746 between Kent and All-England and in 1771 between the Hambledon Club and Surrey.[1] These earliest county elevens were not fully representative county sides, as formalised county organisations only became widespread during the nineteenth century. In 1895 a fully constituted County Championship was inaugurated and, over 100 years later, this competition remains at the heart of the English game, despite a recent shift from a three-day format to one based around four-day contests.

Over time the counties have also become the governing unit of the English game, which for many years was administered by the MCC. In January 1904, the MCC Secretary wrote to the counties suggesting the formation of an Advisory County Cricket Committee, which would liaise with the MCC over the running of the first-class game. The committee was duly set up, with a representative from each of the first-class counties, but the chairman was a member of the MCC. The Marylebone club therefore still retained its power, and the lack of a national governing body was highlighted in the 1963 Wolfenden Report called *Sport in the Community*.[2] Eventually, changes took place and in 1968 the Test and County Cricket Board (now known as the England and Wales Cricket Board) was created to act as a representative governing body to oversee the first-class game. At the same time, the National Cricket Association was established to administer the recreational aspects of the game below first-class level.

As well as being the basic playing and legal unit, the geographical space covered by each county was the area from which their players were drawn. The county boundaries have been used in the recruitment and registration of players, as each county, in general terms, tried to attract, coach and retain the promising young players from within their geographical boundaries. Changes took place after the Second World War as many counties trawled outside their catchment area and scouted in other counties. But an approach to a young player living and/or born in another county could only be made after obtaining the permission of that particular county club. To avoid poaching, most counties today have a lengthy list of registered players and no county is permitted to approach registered players. Those who are not registered, as well as those born in a 'minor county', plus those born outside the United Kingdom and holding British passports are 'free game' for the talent scouts from the first-class clubs.

At the micro-level, clear geographical boundaries also exist in the modern game, with all the county grounds having an absolute location with advertising boards surrounding the playing area. Yet the geographical space which cricket initially occupied was infinite, reflecting a game of which the origins, however hazy, lay in unbounded rural areas. Boundaries were not even included in the Laws of the game until the 1870s and before then all hits had to be fully run. There was no such thing as a four or a six, and if the ball went into the crowd, they simply moved aside so that the fielders could gather the ball.

Nor were there many restrictions from the point of view of time, unlike the fixed halves in games of football and rugby. Yet in cricket, the earliest fixtures were played out over two, three, four or even five days – simply as long as it took for one of the teams to bowl the other side out twice. The game's subsequent evolution and move into an urban arena has resulted in the establishment of more precise temporal boundaries, yet their placing has ironically meant greater interference from the weather. County games have had to be held at a fixed location, and play has therefore been abandoned when ground conditions were poor, rather than moving to another drier area, or to another ground in another settlement.

This spatial immobility in an age of increased personal mobility and the shrinkage of distance is another of county cricket's geographical idiosyncrasies.

Counties not shires

An important question to ask is why competitive cricket developed using the county as the real unit, rather than around urban areas as with football and rugby, especially given the nature of nineteenth-century industrial and urban expansion. This is an issue that also perplexed the eminent cricket historian Rowland Bowen. In 1970 he wrote 'why did great cricket become centred on the counties in a period when the counties certainly meant a great deal socially, but when travelling conditions must have made county cricket an extremely difficult enterprise to organise. The answer appears to lie in the rise of the great patrons of the game.'[3]

Representative games in the eighteenth century were organised drawing on the finest players of the area. In this pre- and early industrial society, the majority of the English population was rural, so the county boundary, as opposed to the urban one, was the natural way to subdivide an area; another was entomological.

The answer lies in the use of the word 'county' rather than the Anglo-Saxon 'shire'. The term is derived from the Latin *comitatus*, meaning a body of companions or retainers, and later a feudal retinue. Indeed, this was precisely what the early county teams were – a group of eleven men, in some cases hired specifically by a patron or assembled for a contest with another team, raised by an individual, rather than an organised club.

The county boundaries were also used as administrative and political divisions, and although a host of urban centres mushroomed during the second half of the nineteenth century, the county boundaries retained their importance as natural units, despite many reforms and boundary changes. In some cases, their role was enhanced by legislation, as with the Local Government Act of 1888. This created 62 county councils, and severed the shires from the larger urban centres with over 50,000 residents, which became county boroughs. Yet despite these changes, the county remained the natural unit of activity.

This form of organising cricket, created in the pre-industrial era, has been inherited by the post-industrial communities, for whom the large urban area, rather than the isolated rural community, was the main unit of settlement. As Mike Marqusee wrote, 'unlike the great football or tennis competitions which came into being at the same time, county cricket did not enter the late Victorian scene as something novel, an internally coherent creation of the age. It was from the outset a compromise – between professional and amateur, local and national, tradition and the market'.[4]

This situation has become a millstone around the necks of the county officials, who, in the cases of the multi-centred or non-metropolitan counties, had to be democratically drawn from the many centres of population and sporting activity within the county. Factions within committees were inevitable and petty jealousies were likely to fester between north and south, or east and west. This was the case in Glamorgan, where an over-sized committee of 36 remained until the 1960s as the side sought support across three major South Wales counties, and had committee representatives stretching from Carmarthen in the west to Monmouth in the east.

This system of demarcation remains even though many of these counties no longer exist on the map, or have been significantly altered in size. To some observers, the continued use of old county boundaries is an anachronism. This is the view held by Eric Midwinter who feels that 'although the county pattern was, and still is, taken for granted, it was neither an inevitable nor a necessary format. Had the English bothered to look about them they would have observed abroad quite different networks of local administration.'[5]

To some observers, one of the strengths of the English game has been the retention of this traditional framework. More radical commentators, such as Rowland Bowen, have taken a different stance, tracing how the continuation of the county-based system started to present problems in the post-war era. 'Having arisen, having established county cricket as the means par excellence of playing a great match, even if only a few counties were, or could be, involved at that time, later comers had to take it for granted that the county was the true basis for the game's organisation and so they have remained into a period when most people in England are not normally conscious of what county they live in, and back their county team, as they might back a football team – not because the team in any way represents where they live, still less the people generally of their area, but because county cricket has acquired an independent existence of its own.'[6]

Little surprise therefore that attendances at county matches have dwindled, especially when the number of place-specific rivals has increased. Youngsters, seeking association with a tangible entity can now support a city's football team, rugby side, ice hockey team or basketball side. They can also proudly walk around the city centre wearing their team's kit or colours, thereby gaining a place-specific identity, shared by others with a like-mind and coloured robes in an increasingly cosmopolitan environment. A clear identity therefore characterises these other urban-based sports whose evolution has seen a move towards standardised rules, regularised competition and thorough commercialisation. All of these have been stimulated by the need to be competitive and attractive to spectators living in the team's immediate sphere of influence.

Yet county cricket retains many features from the age of rural folk-games, and has many 'under-developed' features in an era where sport is full of the modern trappings of commercialism. The county clubs themselves soldier on in their traditional, ways, despite the fact that the games are staged in these urban arenas, with many of the county names being just that, rather than having a spatial identity.

Few people have dared to question the validity of a county-based organisation, and perhaps more importantly, nobody has succeeded in changing English cricket's framework. Some people have suggested a series of regional teams, but the much vaunted *MacLaurin Report* did not consider this as a viable option towards raising the standards.[7] Instead, from the year 2000, there has been a two-divisional Championships, with two divisions as well in a National Cricket League of one-day contests. Some would welcome the use of the phrase 'Premier League' for the top division of this new League showing how many compare the county-based game of cricket with the city-based game of football. A direct comparison is however somewhat inappropriate given these basic geographical differences between the two games.

The mental maps of cricket

The boundaries of the modern county may not be crystal clear on the ground, but sharply defined mental images are conjured up by what many perceive as the quintessential English summer game. These mental maps of cricket have received some serious attention from geographers, such as John Bale, who showed how 'books, essays, plays, paintings, photographs, poetry, cartoons, postcards, postage stamps, bank notes and advertisements communicate the English cricket landscape in a remarkably consistent way as being natural, rural and southern'.[8] Some may argue that Bale has ignored village grounds in northern England, but even these critics would agree that these various forms of media have projected English cricket as a rural pastime.

Indeed, one has to look no further than the widely lauded writings of John Arlott and Neville Cardus to find such stereotyped descriptions of village cricket. In *The Noblest Game* England's finest cricket writers describe the game as being 'set against a background of green trees, haystacks, barns and a landscape of peace and plenty, remote from a world of busy getting and spending'.[9] This rural identity in the mental image of English cricket is important as both Boyes and Howkins have shown in their studies of English culture that during the late nineteenth and early twentieth century, the rural came to be viewed as aesthetically and morally superior to the urban.[10] The perception was that all things rural represented a traditional and cohesive English society, whilst the urban was degenerate and vulgar, and the home of sordid commercialism.

It was therefore within this ethos that the pastoral myth of village cricket was cultivated. At around the same time, the County Championship also came into being and although the vast majority of games were staged in towns and cities, the organisation of the County Championship, upon the shires – the administrative unit of the pre-industrial era – helped to fuel this rural myth of cricket. In more recent times, this iconography has become part of both the nostalgia industry and a collage of images contributing to national identity. Indeed, it was the cricket team which a

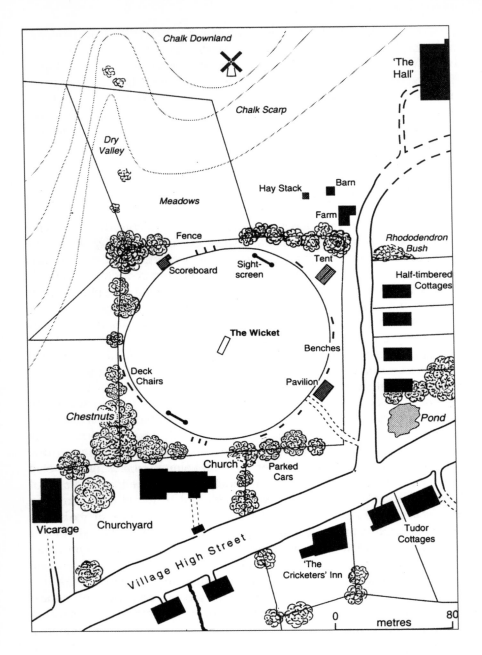

Figure 1 Model of the English cricket landscape ensemble

Source: J. Bale, *Landscapes of Modern Sport* (Leicester: Leicester University Press, 1994), Figure 7.4, p. 158.

person supported that was the yardstick by which Conservative MP Norman Tebbitt notoriously tested a person's nationality.

Bale's simple model of the English cricket landscape ensemble (Figure 1) is typical of the mental map which lies at the heart of the myth of 'Merrie England'. It also forms an intriguing comparison with the modern county game, which now largely takes place in metropolitan venues. With the exception of New Road, Worcester, few of the County Championship games are regularly staged in such picturesque settings. Instead, the majority of first-class games and all home Test fixtures in 1999 have been held in urban stadia, surrounded by brick and concrete. This rural–urban shift has resulted in a blurring of the game's mental image.

Another important change has been the staging of the modern game in artificial surroundings, rather than natural, rustic environs. The county grounds are carefully manicured swards of green turf, with geometrically arranged buildings and precisely measured wickets, boundaries and, in one-day games, fielding circles. Such ordered symmetry was generally lacking in the rural surroundings and the natural, organic feel to the game allowed it to blend into the landscape. In contrast, the green oasis of closely mown grass might seem rather out of place among the brick and mortar, glass, metal and tarmac of the built-up area.

Yet despite this lack of geometrical order, village cricket was a clear image in people's minds and held a firm and distinctive place within village society. In many villages, the fixtures took place on the village green that lay at the heart of the settlement and a broad cross-section of the village population took part in cricketing activity, be it playing, supporting, or making the teas. As a result, cricket had a sharp identity within this pre-industrial landscape. This is in marked contrast to the modern forms of society and settlement. Few county grounds, or even club grounds, currently occupy a nodal location in the towns, cities and conurbations of post-industrial Britain. Moreover, the players who take part in the game do not form a representative cross-section of the socio-economic groups living in the settlement, and moreover, they are drawn from far and wide. It is not surprising that county cricket lacks a precisely defined identity in the minds of the urban population.

This lack of identity is not just a function of location or participation, for cricket has to compete for space, both on the ground and in people's minds. The globalisation of most sports in the modern commercial age has meant that many other pastimes are now on offer during the summer months, whilst a host of new, and glossy, sporting icons are regularly beamed via satellite, cable or the Internet into the home of the armchair supporter.

As Michael Henderson, cricket correspondent of the *Daily Telegraph* recently wrote, 'the game's image has diminished to the point of invisibility in many urban areas, where football often appears to be the only form of human life'. This marginalisation in people's minds was evident in a survey conducted by Surrey CCC in 1997 to find out what The Oval meant to Londoners. The county (hopefully to their horror) discovered that most people thought it was a station on the Northern Line. As Henderson wrote, 'the ground where Hobbs batted and Laker bowled is part of the social history of the capital, yet to thousands of commuters, The Oval is simply the stop before Stockwell!'[11]

The erosion of cricket space

The rural mythification and mystification of cricket could, in theory, be a strength for the county game in the future, as counter-urbanisation rather than urbanisation becomes the dominant process in the settlement geography of twenty-first century Britain. Over the past thirty or so years, rural retreating has taken place with people opting to move out of urban areas to live in more tranquil surroundings in commuter villages in the rural–urban fringe, or more remote rural areas.

This exodus into the countryside has helped to raise the membership of some village cricket teams, but in many, the rise in the resident population has not seen cricket flourish. Whilst these villages may have the architectural trappings of 'Merrie England', in the form of half-timbered, mock Tudor, or thatched buildings, their occupants have other values, and the move into leafy suburbia has certainly not been the result of a search for rural pastimes.

Moreover, the occupants of these metropolitan villages have brought with them their urban values and recreations. Indeed, the vast majority of residents in these dormitory suburbs are still urban-orientated, obtaining their services at edge-of-town retail parks rather than the village shop. So in the same way that Sainsbury's has a greater lure than Mr and Mrs Smith's Village Store, supporting the football team in the nearby city holds greater appeal than the village cricket club.

In addition to the drop in potential support and labour, cricket is facing another threat in the decrease in the number of venues where the game is played. This erosion of cricket space was highlighted by Peter Wynne-Thomas[12] in a survey of the grounds used for recreational cricket in Nottinghamshire between the 1950s and 1990s. As Table 1 shows, there were 398 venues within the county in 1950 where club matches, no matter how humble, took place. Yet by 1999, 219 were disused, with only 179 still in use. Many of these former cricket spaces had reverted to agricultural use, while others have been swallowed up by the urban sprawl and are now used for housing.

However, the greatest decline in Wynne-Thomas' survey was in matches staged in public parks and the examples of Nottingham Forest Recreation Ground and the Nottingham Victoria Embankment Ground epitomise the erosion of this type of cricket space. Both grounds previously had 12 squares, and Forest staged a knock-out competition which was considered a major civic event. By 1999 it only had one pitch, the unused artificial strip which lies between two football pitches. The Victoria ground also had hosted a league competition in the past, but this was discontinued during the 1960s and the park was last used for cricket in 1996. The sheer cost of maintaining these municipal grounds and the loss of a cricket-playing public were major factors behind this loss of cricket space.

TABLE 1
THE NUMBER OF RECREATIONAL CRICKET GROUNDS IN NOTTINGHAMSHIRE, BY TYPE AND DECADE, WHICH HAVE CLOSED, 1950s TO 1990s

Type	Total	1950s	1960s	1970s	1980s	1990s	Total disused	Total in use
Village	103	15	17	4	3	2	41	62
Company	71	3	18	8	13	8	50	21
Urban	63	9	5	6	6	6	32	31
Collieries	38	1	4	5	5	1	16	22
Landed estates	15	1	1	2	1	0	5	10
Public Parks	83	0	9	15	17	15	56	27
School	25	0	1	5	7	6	19	6
Total	398	29	55	45	52	38	21	79

Note: The school grounds are those known to have been used for local club cricket, whilst the public park category includes those where pitches were advertised for hire, rather than the number of public parks

Source: Wynne-Thomas, *Nottinghamshire Cricket Grounds*, p.125.

Table 1 also shows how a significant decline had also taken place among colliery teams, chiefly as a result of the decline in this primary industry within the county and the de-industrialisation process as a whole. Back in 1947 all 36 collieries had sports grounds, and until the 1960s there was a colliery league. By 1999 few coal mines were still in operation and 16 grounds were disused. Once again, financial and demographic factors had played a role in this erosion of cricket space, as the closure of the mines had resulted in the disappearance of both capital and playing personnel.

Of the 71 company grounds in Nottinghamshire, 50 have disappeared since the 1950s, due chiefly to social and economic factors. During the inter-war and immediate post-Second World War eras, the three major companies in Nottingham – Players, Raleigh and Boots – had first-rate grounds used for both club and county 2nd XI matches. Yet by 1999, only the Boots ground still flourished, largely because the county club used it as an overflow facility for second team and youth fixtures. In contrast, the Raleigh ground is now a housing estate. Of the two grounds owned by

John Player, one has been converted for residential use, whilst the other lies derelict. A similar story is true of other 'lost' locations – 11 former company grounds have been used for factory extensions, 13 are housing estates, and 12 lie vacant and disused.

The number of urban clubs has almost halved, and in many cases, sides have merged, such as Forest Amateurs, Notts Forest and Old Nottinghamians, combining to form Nottingham CC. In other cases, clubs such as Lenton United and Bestwood Park have closed due to vandalism, whilst the shortage of people willing to provide the unpaid labour or expertise to maintain the squares has resulted in the disappearance of teams from the map of cricket.

Similar trends have led to the disappearance of recreational clubs elsewhere in the country, with the Stoke Canon side near Exeter failing to secure fixtures for 1999 as they found it difficult to find people who could make decent teas.[13] Whilst the latter comment might be somewhat tongue-in-cheek, there are certainly wider social trends which have contributed to a significant erosion of the cricketing landscape in many parts of the country. These were identified by Christopher Martin-Jenkins who wrote how 'those conscious of the advantages of keeping fit have in many cases, found quicker and more efficient ways of doing so, like spending an hour in the gym, or at a swimming pool. Even many cricket enthusiasts find themselves too busy to fit more than an occasional day of cricket into their fevered lifestyles. Playing cricket for the firm on weekday evenings, or the village or the town at weekends, is no longer the socially acceptable thing for large numbers of sports-minded folk.'[14]

2000 – A cricketing watershed

It is against this backdrop of socio-economic, cultural and demographic influences, that county cricket entered the new millenium. The year 2000 was a real watershed for the county game with the advent of a two divisional County Championship – the first significant change to the format of the premier county competition since it was formalised in 1895. In contrast, there have been dramatic changes to other types of recreation and the world of professional sport in Britain has witnessed significant changes in recent times. There has been a strong whiff of revolution in the corridors of power of many other games, such as football and rugby. Clubs and their controlling bodies have attracted considerable investment, and they have adapted to the demands of an increasingly sophisticated and cosmopolitan public, as well as the 'invisible' television audience, watching on terrestrial channels or via satellite.

A commercial revolution has taken place in many sports, and as Robert

Matusiewicz stated 'soccer has survived because of its mass appeal, benefactors, banks, city institutions and the seductive power of satellite television. Cricket is not in such a fortunate position. The constitution of many counties as members' clubs is anachronistic and a barrier to the development of the professional game. Will cricket survive in either its current or proposed format? Can the Test match grounds justify the continued investment in spectator facilities that are fully utilised for perhaps only four or five days each year? Perhaps the crucial question is how precarious are the finances of the counties? Unless the majority of the counties are financially stable, there is no long-term future for the professional game. The fact that many clubs have celebrated their centenary is no guarantee of future success or even survival.'[15]

Many critics have argued that the county game needs a fundamental change from a members' club to a business culture. History certainly has its place and careful lipservice definitely needs to be paid to the great feats of the past. But sport is now a business, and the socio-economic forces which are guiding the decision-makers in other sports, need to be considered. One long-term goal might be for all counties to develop commercial organisations, with autonomous funds. At present many rely heavily on annual subsidies from the English Cricket Board. Yet even within the ECB itself, there has been until recently no detailed or comprehensive financial strategy, requiring a finance director to produce five-year business plans to allow careful planning for the financial future. Some believe that without this counties might disappear.[16]

Not everyone agrees with this doomsday scenario painted by marketing men such as Matusiewicz, or even with such commercially orientated solutions. Even so, it is widely agreed that county cricket cannot afford to stand still and bask in the reflected glory of the many great feats of English players in both Championship and Test cricket over the past century. The game which began as a folk-game, with its roots in the rural meadowlands of southern England, has become transformed into a game staged on an urban, multinational basis, with participants drawn from all over the world. The socio-economic space in which the county game is being played is very different to that in which the game first acquired its modern format, whilst the values, needs and habits of the people in this modern post-industrial landscape have also fundamentally changed.

Cricket is not alone in facing a need for change, as these socio-economic forces have redefined many other aspects of the geography of the United Kingdom. For example, the industrial map of the country in 2000 looks very different from that of 1900. The previous industrial heartlands, with heavy manufacturing, are now either brownfield locations or swathed under light industry. Many of these new, spatial phenomenon have been carefully analysed and explained by a host of geographers and the time has come for the geography of cricket to be critically evaluated under a new space-economy, dominated by multi-plant multinational organisations.

This study of the geographical evolution of county cricket within a changing spatial framework, has therefore an important practical dimension, and the following analysis should help to pinpoint key spatial patterns and trends, addressing important questions which have been raised about the best way the game of cricket should develop in the future.

The Growth of English Cricket:
A Development Stage Model

Brookes' model

There are two fundamental questions which must be asked at the outset of this geographical analysis of county cricket. Firstly how, and why, did certain county teams emerge? Why, for instance, did Surrey and Middlesex emerge as the main county teams in the London area, rather than Buckinghamshire, Bedfordshire or Berkshire? Secondly, we need to know exactly how, and where cricket developed – was it a random process, or was it in a clear and distinguishable form? To answer both these questions, we need an historical framework on which to analyse the game's evolution.

However, one must proceed with a certain amount of caution, because as Christopher Brookes observed 'accounts of its evolution from folk-game to modern sport have tended unfortunately to be based more on perception and prejudice than fact'.[1] It is not the purpose here to get embroiled in the heated debate over the precise origins of the game, but if a clear spatial picture is to be painted, it is important to have accurate emulsion, otherwise some of the gloss will be taken away from the explanation, no matter how wide the canvas may be.

Perhaps the best sequential model was the one proposed by Brookes:

1. the age of the folk-game,
2. the era of the aristocracy and gentry,
3. the era of the professional elevens,
4. the apogee of amateurism, and
5. the business years.

The latter stage, according to Brookes, began in 1945, but as it is over 20 years since Brookes proposed his model, we could identify a new sixth stage called 'international consumerism' with the Packer revolution, England hosting the 1975, 1979 and 1983 World Cups, day–night matches and a host of well-known overseas players and budding Test stars playing for the county teams.

Brookes' approach was that of a historian, so he did not investigate any spatial patterns. It is the purpose of this chapter to adapt Brookes' historical timescale within a geographical framework, from which a development stage model can be devised.

The origins of cricket

Like most sports, cricket began as a folk-game, but there is no known date when it was first played. Many arguments have taken place over this, chiefly because written records are so scarce, and cricket historians have been hunting for clues. Their search, however, has been largely in vain as the rural games went largely unrecorded in those pre-industrial days. In fact, some researchers feel that this search will be in vain, as nobody actually invented cricket, with the game evolving from other ball games and country pursuits.

Its hybrid origins were traced by Pycroft to the thirteenth-century game of club-ball, with strikers hitting a ball bowled along the ground with a curved club while protecting a wooden gate.[2] Other cricket historians, most notably Rowland Bowen, point to a reference dated 1299–1300 when Prince Edward, the King's son, was playing *creag*.[3] Bowen believed this to be an alternative early spelling for cricket, but as Peter Wynne-Thomas has shown, there is no Latin dictionary which provides a meaning for this word. Wynne-Thomas also exploded the myth about club-ball showing that no known document listing ball games mentions club-ball before the seventeenth century. Wynne-Thomas instead believes the earliest reference to be a Latin translation circa 1180 attributed to Joseph of Exeter which says 'the youths at cricks did play, throughout the merry day'.[4]

While historians still argue over these scattered crumbs, thankfully there are few doubts as to the geographical origins of English cricket being south-east of a line drawn from The Wash to the Isle of Wight (Figure 2).

The earliest centre of cricketing activity prior to 1675 was close to The Weald, and Wynne-Thomas believed that this culture hearth ran in a crescent shape from Selsey and Sidlesham in West Sussex, then north to Richmond in Surrey and then east towards Cranbrook and Ruckridge in South Kent.[5] A mass of written evidence has subsequently been unearthed to support Wynne-Thomas' assertions about the geographical centre for these unorganised or spontaneous games. For example, a document exists referring to a court case over a piece of land held in Guildford in 1598 with cricket being played on the land by schoolboys about 50 years previously.[6]

It is likely however that there were regional variations in the form of the game throughout the area defined above. These ball games were very parochial in the pre-industrial era, and it is probable that there were innumerable variations, at a time when the game's participants did not even imagine themselves to be part of a larger, national community, with a common culture. There were probably children's versions as well as the

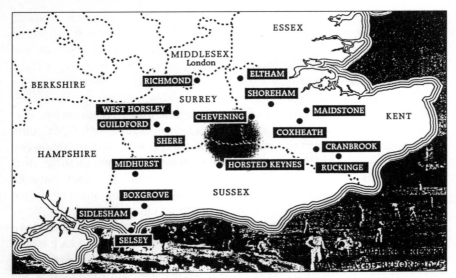

Figure 2 Places where cricket is known to have been played before 1675. The pattern suggests that the game took its present form in The Weald near the point where the three counties of Kent, Surrey and Sussex meet, and spread outwards from there.

Source: P. Wynne-Thomas, *The History of Cricket from The Weald to The World* (HMSO, 1996), p.5.

adult formats, staged at times of holidays or feast-days, as determined by the agricultural or liturgical calendars. Cricketing games were just one of many traditional folk-games and were part of medieval village life, with rules and traditions being passed on from one generation to the next by word of mouth.

Subtle variations were therefore inevitable for the dimensions of the pitch, the size of the bat, or local rules about the number of balls in an over, in the way that there are many variations of the unorganised and spontaneous ball games that young children currently play in their junior school playgrounds. If games are being played against a wall, there will be no runs behind the wicket, whilst there might be rules such as 'hit and run', or even 'six and out'. Some might be single wicket contests with just one batsman, whilst others may have two, yet if you change school there are enough similarities between the variants for a child to continue playing. It seems likely that the early folk games of cricket were akin to these modern playground games.

The earliest fixtures

The next stage in the game's evolution was the playing of fixtures for which one geographical element was vital – enough people good enough to take part in a game and represent the village or small town. Once again, there may have been a few regional variations in the number of people in each team, and the duration of games, but demography was important, and the next stage in cricket's development must have taken place at fixed points, where village clusters had evolved at easily accessible locations.

Wynne-Thomas believes that some early industrial factors contributed to the game's transformation from a rural pastime into a village game.[7] The Sussex Weald was the centre of the iron and glass industry in the sixteenth and seventeenth centuries, and these industries were labour intensive, based around workshops rather than factories. Consequently, this industrial activity would have attracted people into the area and the threshold population of cricket players would have risen sufficiently for teams of between six and twelve members to be chosen.

But if a challenge was going to be made against another village or small town, another factor had to be considered, namely transport. Once again, the growth of industrial activity played a role and assisted the staging of games. With foundries demanding raw materials and fuel from nearby, the transport infrastructure would have improved, resulting in the movement of iron ore, limestone, charcoal and timber by road and track. With more people and better forms of communication, the staging of cricket matches became easier, and there are hosts of records of games taking place in The Weald and Sussex during the late seventeenth and early eighteenth centuries. It was not just the places at the end of the roads which benefited, since the improved routes passed through, or near, smaller settlements, allowing them to stage matches as well. In fact, there are references in the diaries of Thomas Marchant of Hurstpierpoint and Thomas Turner of East Hoathly to inter-village cricket matches, in addition to special games on village feast days and challenge matches organised by the local gentry.[8]

The spread to urban areas

Cricket's subsequent evolution from a poplar rural pastime into an inter-county contest, staged in urban centres, was part of a complex and wider process during which many other games and pastimes emerged. It is also a process which was closely related to changes in the structure and geography of the country's society and economy. The initial culture hearth in The Weald and Sussex played a key role, as it was from this rural centre of gravity that the more advanced form of the game spread to other parts of the country and also to London, the settlement at the top of the hierarchy.

An early reference to cricket taking place in London came in a notice in *The Post Boy* of 28–30 March 1700 advertising a game on Clapham Common.[9] Within a few years, there was a multitude of games taking place on the open spaces in the capital city, as cricket moved from a rural to an urban stage. It also moved into the social world of London, with the game becoming an accepted recreation among the higher echelons of society. According to Brookes, the reasons for the court-based nobility, accustomed to a sophisticated, urbane existence suddenly developing a liking for a rural folk-game can be explained by factors associated with land ownership. He believes that the gentry were probably introduced to the game by the workers on their large country estates – 'It is not necessary to delve too far into the realms of fantasy to imagine a situation in which the lord of the manor comes across some of his servants playing cricket and being stirred by the prospect, decides to try it out for himself.'[10]

Others with yeoman backgrounds, who had purchased landed estates before the Civil War, were also keen to continue with the pastimes of their mundane past, and now with money and time at their disposal, it would not have taken much to persuade them to play cricket. In addition, the chance to play cricket and other folk-games gave an opportunity to escape temporarily from the somewhat claustrophobic predictability of court life. Brookes believes that there were four reasons why the gentry started to arrange fixtures against teams from other estates or sides assembled by other gentlemen:

1. a chance for the squire to impose his presence and authority,
2. to renew old friendships and to keep up-to-date with the latest gossip, scandal and intrigue,
3. to act out personal rivalries without the deadly risk of duelling pistols, and
4. as a means of entertainment, exercise and excitement.

Mike Marqusee describes these factors as 'sentimental ruralism', with the upper class, who lived a town or city-based life, following patterns and models of behaviour which were intrinsically rural. 'With residences (and financial interests) in both the country and city, it was natural for the landowning elite to bring the country game of cricket into the city and there remake it according to their needs.'[11]

These factors helped to explain the emergence of cricket as a fashionable sport amongst the upper classes, but other demographic factors should not be forgotten. The cricketing population in the capital city also rose during the late seventeenth and early eighteenth centuries. Many of the sons of the merchants, industrialists and landed gentry in Surrey, Sussex and Kent were educated at public schools such as Eton, Harrow, Winchester, Westminster and St Paul's, before going to university in Oxford or Cambridge. In each case, cricket was one of the popular pastimes at these seats of learning. With such a base of cricket-playing gentry in the south-east counties, and the sporting activities of upper class boys and undergraduates, the city became the second centre of cricketing in the early 1700s.

Town and county

There was clearly both an urban and a rural dimension to cricket in the early eighteenth century, and with this town and county structure, the next developments saw the emergence of county games, and special challenge matches between the urban elite and their rural counterparts. Indeed, in 1709 the first inter-county match took place between Kent and Surrey at Dartford.[12] The involvement of a team from Surrey was not a surprise given its proximity to the culture hearth, while Kent had become one of the areas where organised forms of cricket had grown in popularity. In fact, by the early 1720s Kent had overtaken Sussex as the centre of gravity for cricket, as shown in the writings of the Earl of Oxford. As he was travelling through Kent in 1723, the Earl noted how 'the men of Tonbridge and the Dartford men were warmly engaged at the sport of cricket, which of all the people of England, the Kentish folk are the most renowned for and of all the Kentish men, the men of Dartford lay claim to the greatest excellence'.[13]

Another important development was the emergence of teams organised by wealthy patrons and the landed gentry. These gentlemen started to finance their own elevens in both town and country, with one of the most influential patrons being the second Duke of Richmond, the grandson of Charles II. The Duke was brought up at Goodwood House in West Sussex, and from the 1720s onwards, he organised grand matches at his country seat.[14] He also employed men to work on his estate, purely because of their cricketing ability, and part of the terms of employment was that the men should also play for Slindon, the village on the edge of the Duke's estate. The presence of these talented players helped to raise the standard of play, and by the 1740s Slindon had one of the finest sides in England – a remarkable feat for a village with a few hundred inhabitants.

Further west, a new growth point emerged in the Hampshire village of Hambledon. Established in 1767 by the Reverend Charles Powlett, their ground on Broadhalfpenny Down became the country's first major venue as the Hambledon side played host to, and defeated, almost every leading side in the country.[15] They were fortunate to have the services of many Oxbridge-educated gentlemen, as well as Richard Nyren, the talented nephew of Richard Newland, the former captain of the Slindon side. They also secured the support of influential patrons such as the Duke of Dorset, Sir Horatio Mann and the Earl of Tankerville, who were delighted to see their team defeat sides from much larger settlements, and even representative elevens. As John Nyren wrote 'Little Hambledon pitted against All England was a proud thought for the Hampshire men. Defeat was glory in such a struggle. Victory, indeed, made us only a little lower than angels.'[16]

Other special challenges took place as sides from the rural areas travelled up to London to play scratch teams drawn from the urban centre, an example being the contest in 1731 between Eleven Gentlemen of Sevenoaks and Eleven Gentlemen of London.[17] These matches were often staged in the public parks or on common land in the suburbs of London, and were held to coincide with the visits to town by country gentlemen in pursuance of their social or political careers.

Members of the nobility also assumed an active role in promoting the game in London as it became *the* socially acceptable recreation for gentlemen and leaders of society. Even members of the Royal Family became involved, including HRH Frederick Louis, the Prince of Wales, who first attended a match in 1731 between London and Surrey.[18] The Prince as well as 'many other persons of distinction' were present at the Artillery Ground in London on 18 June 1744 for what was billed as 'the greatest cricket match ever known' as Kent played against All England. While being another example of a grand challenge match, this game also confirmed the predominance of Kent as the leading cricketing area, as the county side won the contest by one wicket.

The game further afield

By the mid-eighteenth century, games of cricket were being played in front of quite large crowds both in the London area and further afield in Sussex, Hampshire, Kent and Surrey. Its popularity in metropolitan areas was also the result of wagers being struck by opponents, and gambling, the major hobby of the Georgian peerage, was also being indulged in by spectators. With money to be made from such matches, it seems likely that some teams were formed purely for financial reasons.

Elsewhere, cricket was being played in isolated pockets, still in a rural format, rather than the urban form and in some areas, still at the folk-game stage. It was a move forward when special games took place on the country estates of the landed gentry, as many of the wealthy gentlemen who were in business in London retreated to their country seats for the summer months. They acted as cricketing missionaries by helping to spread the gospel of bat and ball besides amusing themselves and their house guests by inviting friends to play in these special games. A few local dignitaries were also invited to take part as the gentlemen reinforced their social position within the country set.

An example of this 'missionary diffusion' took place during the late eighteenth century in South Wales, where there had been many forms of folk-games involving ball-hitting. But it was not until 4 August 1783 that there are references to a formal game of cricket[19] with a contest on Court Henry Down near the county town of Carmarthen. It involved a challenge match between two gentlemen's elevens, organised by J.G. Philipps of Cwmgwili, a member of the local gentry who had been educated at Westminster School and Brasenose College, Oxford. While in England, Philipps learnt the role of a gentleman and in doing so became involved in cricket, before commencing a career as a barrister. He also had an interest in politics, and certainly moved in high circles, both 'in town' and in West Wales, for by the age of 22, he was Carmarthen's mayor and was elected MP for Carmarthen Borough.

No doubt Philipps considered that organising cricket matches for gentlemen, such as the contest in 1783, was in keeping with his lofty position among the social leaders. They were also a suitable way of spending his summer retreats to west Wales, playing cricket and mixing with his social and political acquaintances at the post-match luncheons or dinners. Philipps certainly enjoyed spending time on these convivialities, as there are records that he spent over £15,000 on 'entertainment' during his election campaign in 1803![20]

Philipps was not acting in isolation and he was copying the patterns he had witnessed at first hand growing up in the London area. It is a moot point whether the Welsh gentry would have organised such lavish contests of cricket without knowledge of what was happening in the south-east of England. What is known for certain is that there were plenty of young gentlemen in West Wales, versed in how to play cricket, and with the time and enthusiasm to take part in such challenge games. There was a similar pool of well-heeled participants in other parts of South Wales, with records of games and even clubs being formed in the late eighteenth century in Swansea, Monmouth and Newport. In these towns, there were other cricketing 'missionaries' and by the start of the nineteenth century their actions and social links with London had allowed organised games of cricket to take a firm root in South Wales.[21]

Lord's and the MCC

The eighteenth century, therefore, saw the spread of organised games of cricket to many parts of England and Wales. By the end of the century, there had also been an important geographical shift in the power base of English cricket, away from the countryside of Kent and the village of Hambledon, to the urban environment of London, following the formation and success of the Marylebone Cricket Club. The club's origins stem from the decision by Thomas Lord in 1786 to lease a tavern and an adjacent field in Dorset Square in Marylebone, and then to enclose the field for cricket, and lay a proper wicket. Over time, Lord's became one of the finest grounds in the country, and the MCC became *the* cricket club in the country, organising county competitions and acting as arbiter on the laws of the game as it moved into the next stage of its evolution.[22]

Thomas Lord, the Yorkshire-born son of a labourer, was a wine merchant by trade and through some astute decisions became a gentleman of means. His vision and energy also saw him develop into one of the first entrepreneurs in the game of cricket. In the 1780s the main cricket ground in London was alongside an Islington tavern known as the White Conduit House. During 1786 the Earl of Winchelsea, the Treasurer of the cricket club based at the tavern, told Lord that he and the Duke of Richmond would support Lord if he could lay out a private cricket ground. It was an appealing prospect for Lord, as he was also looking to rub shoulders with possible clients and to exploit new business opportunities. Getting involved with cricket appeared to be the perfect vehicle, especially as the post-match convivialities would give Lord a chance to show off his wares, or even provide free samples!

Like many of the things Lord turned his hand to, the acquisition of the cricket ground was a success. He utilised both his business and cricketing contacts to secure regular patronage of the ground. The popularity of the game among the upper echelons meant that the list of subscribers to the MCC was always expanding, and there was a healthy demand for games and practice matches, as well as challenges with clubs from other areas. Aware of the money to be made, Lord also charged an admission fee of sixpence, and on match days he would hoist a flag high on a pole to let passers-by know that the gentlemen of the MCC were involved in a game.

A measure of Lord's entrepreneurial success can be gained by the fact that as many as 5,000 spectators would turn up to the matches at Dorset Square. Everything was rosy on the business front as well, and by the 1790s Lord was selling wines to the King and other noble houses. He was also making money as a property speculator, buying and selling houses in the expanding city, and by hiring out his ground for non-cricketing activities, including foot races, pigeon shooting, balloon ascents and military parades. Lord's foresight also overcame a problem as the lease ran out on the Dorset Square ground. Aware of the impending difficulties, Lord acquired a lease on land in St John's Wood, allowing the MCC to continue their activities in 1811 when the Dorset Square ground closed down.[23]

The building of the Regent's Canal necessitated another move to St John's Wood Road, where the current Lord's Cricket Ground subsequently developed into the cricketing centre of England, and a permanent urban showground, dedicated to hosting the best games in the country. In the words of Tony Lewis 'the Lord's ground had established itself as a cricket ground without rival. The best players might be members of powerful counties like Kent or Hampshire, but they still liked to have their names on the Marylebone list. It had become almost unthinkable that "great" matches should be played anywhere else.'[24] The MCC also adopted an administrative role, revising the Laws of the game in 1788 and at other times during the nineteenth century. None of this would have been possible had it not been for the business acumen of Thomas Lord and the patronage of the nobility.

The dawn of industrialisation and the emergence of new cricketing centres

With the emergence of the MCC as the premier club, and Lord's as the principal ground, the stage was set at the start of the ninteenth century for cricket to move dramatically forward. But the spread of the game encountered several stumbling blocks around the turn of the century. England faced social problems, in addition to fighting an expensive war with France from 1792 until 1815. People had less time for recreation, and the number of games listed in Arthur Haygarth's excellent *Scores and Biographies* took a sharp decline, with just two a year in 1811 and 1812, compared with 24 in 1799, and no inter-county matches.[25]

Important changes had taken place in the countryside. Whilst the Enclosure of the Commons had benefited some people, others were facing severe economic hardship which prevented them from footing the bill for any special cricket matches. The poor rates system, so prevalent in eastern and southern England, also depressed agricultural wages. These all acted as negative factors, at a time when the newly emerging industrial areas, with their factories, and the prospect of better paid work, acted as positive factors. The net result was the steady drift of people away from the countryside to the new industrial centres. Just as the people moved away from the rural areas, so did cricket, and the early nineteenth century saw the decline of rural areas and villages such as Slindon and Hambledon as the powerhouses of English cricket.

The movement to the industrial cities caused a fundamental change to the geography of the cricket. Up to the 1840s, booming trade in London and the absence of an integrated national transport network meant that the optimal, and only really profitable, location for cricket was in the London conurbation. The Industrial Revolution changed the map of cricket in many ways; firstly, through the development of new cricket-playing centres in booming industrial regions, well away from the eighteenth-century culture hearths in the south-east, and secondly, with the emergence of new promoters as industrial patrons and wealthy entrepreneurs started to finance cricket.

The new cricketing centres included the towns of the East Midlands, especially Nottingham. It gained a greater importance for cricket than the larger industrial centres, where the long hours of work in the heavy industries prevented many of the steelworkers from having enough time to take part in cricket. As Eric Midwinter showed, the labour system was very different in the East Midlands, as 'the small scale nature of the lace, hosiery and allied trades that had developed in Nottingham and its surrounds lent itself to the flexibility of broken time. Piecework at home allowed men choice of time, so that a day away at cricket could be compensated for at another time. Neither the constant demands of agriculture, especially in the summer, nor the unceasing discipline of the full-run factory system was anything like so elastic and obliging.'[26]

The success of cricket in the East Midlands led to rivalry with the earlier centres in the London area. In 1836 Richard Cheslyn, the patron of the ground in Leicester, organised a series between the North of England and the South of England, with one game at Lord's and a return match at his Leicester ground. Other North–South matches took place at the Trent Bridge ground in Nottingham and helped to popularise the game in the region and give the cricketing folk a chance actually to see some of the famous players which they had previously read about, but never seen perform.

These challenge matches between the old and new cricketing centres drew large crowds, and so gave rise to the second feature of this early industrial period – the exploitation of cricket and its spectators for commercial gain. The spectators at the early matches, on common land, racecourses or fields on the edge of towns, had watched free of charge, but during the 1820s, several businessmen took a leaf out of Thomas Lord's book and viewed the game and its spectators as a means of making money. The actions of George Steer of Sheffield were an example of commercial exploitation. He created a ground at Darnall and obtained rents from cricket clubs who used his ground; he also got money from the sale of beer and ground admission from spectators. By 1822 he had raised enough capital to allow him to organise a challenge match between Sheffield and Nottingham, and as his profits increased further, he built an even larger venue in the town, with a grandiose two-storey pavilion and banked seating for 8,000. His commercial speculation met with further reward in 1825 when he paid for a strong England eleven to visit Sheffield for a match against Yorkshire – a contest which drew an estimated 20,000 people each day.[27]

Further commercialisation took place in some of the traditional cricket-playing areas, an example being the investment by James Ireland, a draper who lived in the fashionable seaside resort of Brighton. The town's cricket ground had fallen into disrepair by the end of the Napoleonic Wars, despite having been laid out in 1791 by the Prince Regent, but Ireland took out the lease on the ground, renovated the wicket, built a fives court and added a tea garden. In 1823 he arranged a match between Sussex and the MCC, and two years later organised a fixture between Kent and Sussex. Its success led to a series of inter-county matches and helped Ireland secure a sizeable profit from his investments.[28]

Early county clubs

The spread of the game in the early nineteenth century meant that organised forms of cricket were played by men living in many English

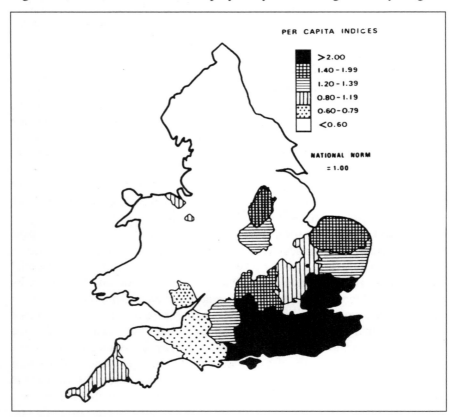

Figure 3   The localisation of cricket in pre-Victorian England

Source: J. Bale, 'Cricket in pre-Victorian England', *Area*, 13 (1981).

counties. John Bale has analysed this pre-Victorian structure by considering G.B. Buckley's 'Fresh Light on eighteenth Century Cricket' and 'Fresh Light on pre-Victorian Cricket.' These contain an extensive and exhaustive listing of games played prior to 1836, and Bale used these lists, together with population data from the 1831 census to devise a series of per capita indices for each county, as shown in Figure 3 and Table 2.[29]

TABLE 2
HIGH-RANKING CRICKET COUNTIES IN PRE-VICTORIAN ENGLAND

County	Per capita index	One club per	No. of clubs
Surrey	6.69	2,040	59
Sussex	5.48	2,373	109
Kent	5.39	2,497	159
Hampshire	4.32	3,165	88
Essex	4.31	3,168	86
Berkshire	2.42	5,642	26
Oxfordshire	1.69	8,040	13
Norfolk	1.54	8,865	42
Buckinghamshire	1.48	9,170	16
Nottingham	1.45	9,391	24
Wiltshire	1.38	9,880	24
Leicestershire	1.32	10,367	19
Suffolk	1.20	11,397	26

Source: Bale, 'Cricket in pre-Victorian England', *Area*, 13 (1981).

In 1831 the population of England and Wales was just below 13 million, and given that 1,017 clubs were listed in Buckley's volumes, it would appear that one club existed for every 13,664 people. Bale used this base number to devise a per capita index, as follows:

$$\frac{\text{number of cricket clubs}}{\text{population}} \div \frac{1}{13,664}$$

which allowed him to see where an above average or below average number of clubs existed. As Table 2 shows, an index of 2.00 indicates a county with twice the national average and 0.5 shows only half the national average. Some critics have wondered if 13,664 was a true threshold, as Buckley listed few games played by women; with many people too old, too young, or too busy to play cricket, Bale has suggested a real threshold population for a club to be nearer 3,400. Even with this readjustment, there were still five counties – Surrey, Sussex, Kent, Hampshire and Essex – where the per capita index was well above average. All of these had a long cricketing tradition and of the well established cores, the only anomaly is Middlesex with an index of 0.32. This could be the result of the small number of exclusive clubs, the lack of space for other decent grounds and the rapid expansion of the county's suburbs.

Bale's work also confirms that a large number of counties had sufficient numbers of men, or a threshold population, playing the game to allow county elevens to be raised. A number of county fixtures were staged in the early nineteenth century, although Sussex was the only formal county club, with elevens properly selected and financed through subscriptions. Many other counties had scratch teams or gentlemen's sides, often playing at country house festivals, with many of these elevens being mustered for one-off challenges, without any formal rules or constitutions.

As far as the formal county clubs were concerned, many were temporary organisations, and most folded. Indeed, of the present first-class counties, the one with the longest consecutive history is Surrey CCC, dating from 1845. Many reasons contributed to the demise of many of these clubs – the first being that the side was chosen by one individual, who despite being a kindly benefactor, was hardly *au fait* with the playing standards throughout an area. The second, and a related aspect, was a rather haphazard selection policy, as shown in these recollections of Herbert Jenner-Fust who in 1834 organised a side representing West Kent for a match with Norfolk. 'I got promises of a full team, but when the day came close those who had promised all cried off. . . I set off to play the county match determined to make a team on the way as best I could. At one place I came across three young men who seemed nice fellows, and as they said they could play cricket I pressed them into service . . . then we went on to Cambridge and I ransacked King's College and found four more men to join me. Two others were met on the ground in Norfolk, and with this strange combination, we won the match.'[30]

A third factor was the selective membership of some county teams. The Monmouthshire club, founded in the 1820s, was a prime example with members drawn from the upper echelons of society. Their membership list read like a local Who's Who, with almost all the wealthy landowners and residents of country houses belonging to the club. For these people, playing cricket was really a form of socialising, and one certainly did not have to have great prowess with either bat or ball to join the club. Like modern freemasonry, if your face fitted and you had the right sort of contacts, you were in! This exclusivity, and at times modest playing standard, deterred other people from joining, and although some young bloods were recruited by the Monmouthshire club, it eventually folded as its founding gentlemen all grew old together.[31]

A fourth and final factor was that nascent county clubs were not attractive to the emerging professionals. Membership of a county organisation such as Monmouthshire was out of the question for social reasons, whilst other county sides were not financially sound enough bodies to offer any guarantees of employment to these paid players. This was in direct contrast to the lucrative offers from the industrial patrons and speculative promoters who were now at the cutting edge of the game's development.

Professional and wandering elevens

In 1846 William Clarke, an innkeeper in Nottingham, formed an All England Eleven and asked sizeable sums for the appearance of his players in special challenge matches against town sides. These games were well attended as the new urban population needed recreation, especially after the introduction of half-day holidays on Saturdays. Moreover, there were many wealthy patrons and newly emerging industrialists who were only too keen to sponsor these games, and with the prospect of seeing the local players pitched against the pick of the country's paid players, a good crowd was guaranteed. Clarke was a shrewd promoter, choosing venues in large industrial centres such as Sheffield, Manchester, Birmingham, Liverpool, York, Newcastle-upon-Tyne and Leeds to play opposing sides, usually with 20-odd local players and reinforced by a guest professional or two. The expanding railway network assisted the movements of Clarke's team around the country, and helped people to travel to these games on a cheaper and faster form of transport compared with the stage-coach.

Within a few years, Nottingham had become, according to Ric Sissons 'the epicentre of professional cricket'.[32] Clarke had even reached a secure enough position to refuse invitations if the guarantees were not sufficiently lucrative. There was such demand for exhibition games that John Wisden, the Sussex cricketer, was able to set up a rival United All-England Eleven. By the mid-1850s, Wisden's side had 15 three-day fixtures, whilst Clarke's team had 24. With such a vast number of fixtures, there were plenty of opportunities for the paid players, and the full-time job of the cricket professional in its modern context was firmly established by 1860. In addition, these exhibition games helped to promote cricket in the newly emerging centres, and as A.A.Thomson wrote, 'their effect in entertainment and emulation over the remoter parts of England was enormous. Indeed, they spread and delighted in spreading the whole art and true spirit of the game.'[33]

Such a role could have been performed by the county clubs, but instead they were left to go their own merry way, and organise matches without the kudos that the exhibition games aroused. Some were fortunate enough to secure fixtures with I Zingari, the all-amateur wandering eleven that had been formed in 1845. They drew heavily on Cambridge graduates, and their fixture list was dominated by games against gentlemen's sides, regimental sides and scratch elevens raised by the landed gentry or local squirarchy as part of the country house 'season'. Such games were an ideal vehicle for public school and university-educated cricketers to play some decent cricket during their summer vacations, and after they had graduated, playing for I Zingari allowed them to remain in contact with their old chums.

Other itinerant elevens and wandering clubs helped to establish an important link between the core and periphery of British cricket. This was the case with the South Wales CC, formed in 1859 by Captain George Homfray, a member of the family from Glenusk which was closely associated with the successful ironworks in Merthyr Tydfil, Ebbw Vale and Tredegar.[34] Although not a great player himself, Homfray was a keen supporter of cricket, and was always ready to dip into his pocket in order to promote a game. In September 1858, he came to an agreement with William Clarke and his Newport club hosted a match between a Monmouthshire side and the All-England Eleven.[35]

This game was a financial success and led Homfray to consider forming a side to represent the whole of South Wales. In 1859 he put his idea to the test by raising a South Wales XXII to play the All-England Eleven, and to Homfray's delight, his side won by 62 runs. Fuelled by their success, Homfray created the South Wales Cricket Club, which during the 1860s, led a nomadic existence travelling to fixtures in the West of England as well as undertaking an annual ten-day tour to London. While in London, Homfray's side played matches against some of the premier clubs such as the MCC, I Zingari, Prince's, Surrey Club and Ground, plus the Gentlemen of Kent and Sussex.

But rather than being an eleven really representative of Welsh players, the South Wales CC was somewhat exclusive. As David Smith observed, 'the composition of the early South Wales teams revealed the blend familiar in regional sides of that period: predominantly gentlemen who had been coached at English public schools, some talented local cricketers and the hard-toiling professionals who were especially welcome for the lengthy bowling stints'.[36] Many reasons explained this – for a start, the gentlemen were the only ones who could realistically afford the time, and money, to play cricket outside South Wales. Secondly, the annual trips to London also satisfied their social and political aspirations, as well as playing alongside old friends and acquaintances. Thirdly, participation with the South Wales club allowed the gentlemen to believe that they were maintaining the gentry's position at the forefront of the game's development and helping its further spread.

Barriers in the valleys

It has been assumed so far that industrial growth gave cricket a boost, but in some of the heavy industrial areas, the long hours of work, low wages and lack of open space were hardly the ingredients for the creation of cricket clubs. This was the case with the valleys of Glamorgan and Monmouthshire, and despite the missionary work of Homfray and his happy band of gentlemen, the spread of cricket into the industrial heartland of South Wales met with several barriers during the middle of the nineteenth century.

These socio-economic obstacles require careful analysis in the overall diffusion process, especially as Merthyr Tydfil, at the top of the Welsh settlement hierarchy during the first half of the nineteenth century, only had one cricket club by 1851. This was a very surprising statistic given that the town was producing 43 per cent of Britain's iron and the wealth created by the ironworks of Dowlais, Cyfarthfa, Penydarren and Plymouth could surely have helped to spawn many more cricket teams. In addition, the town was attracting a flood of migrants, and the roads to the valley town were decent, allowing travel to neighbouring valleys, the coastal strip and mid-Wales.

The ingredients appeared to be the same as in other parts of the United Kingdom, but there were several constraints. The first was time, as many working people on strict shifts at the mines and ironworks could not get time off to practise or participate in games of cricket, or any form of recreation. Secondly, it was expensive to join a club and the annual subscriptions of at least half a guinea were well beyond the means of a person of quite modest means. But the subscriptions were not the only costs, as some clubs levied fines for bad behaviour. One example was at Chepstow CC where members had to pay up to five shillings if they disputed an umpiring decision and 2s 6d for leaving the ground before the game was over, or for throwing down the bat when dismissed.[37]

The situation changed during the second half of the nineteenth century, as a number of industrial philanthropists started to show an interest in organising and promoting working class recreation, thereby breaking down some of the barriers. The patronage of shopowners, businessmen, colliery owners and ironmasters was partly altruistic, believing that they were helping to shape working-class values and providing edifying recreation, with men being kept away from the demon drink. In short, they were providing a form of moral guidance that the clergymen were promoting elsewhere in the more rural locations and smaller towns. Their businesses and companies would also benefit by having a healthy and willing workforce, whilst from a materialistic point of view, their output would be maximised.

One of the earliest patrons in the Welsh valleys was the Guest family, who owned the enormous ironworks at Dowlais. In 1852 Lady Charlotte Guest provided a field to 'enable the young men of the Works and of the town of Dowlais to spend many happy evenings in healthful recreation'.[38] In 1857 Captain Robert Crawshay, the owner of the Cyfarthfa Works followed suit, and by the 1870s, even the notorious Georgetown area of Merthyr Tydfil, renowned for its overcrowded and cramped terraces of houses, also had a cricket team who played on a field provided by the Crawshay family.

The patronage of the industrial leaders therefore helped to break down the barriers that had previously existed. An indication of cricket's diffusion across the region can be gauged by the fact that in March 1869 a meeting was held at The Castle Hotel in Neath at which Glamorganshire CCC was formed.[39] Guided by J.T.D. Llewelyn, a most enthusiastic patron, the Glamorganshire club secured fixtures with Monmouthshire, Breconshire and Radnorshire, as the game in South Wales at long last moved into the next stage of its evolution with the staging of inter-county fixtures.

The growth of organised county clubs

During the second half of the nineteenth century, cricket really started to take off on a county scale. The emergence of these county sides was important as they developed into the growth points for cricket, and a new set of cricketing cores was established in the geography of cricket by the end of the Victorian era. This was a turnround in the status of the county clubs, as for some time the county sides had been out of the cricketing spotlight. The upper classes had been enjoying themselves at country house games, whilst the professionals were earning a lucrative living by playing exhibition games against town sides. For many years, nobody was interested in forming a Championship, but by the 1860s the game had spread to so many parts of the country to make a regional contest a viable proposition.

By this time, there were three different types of county organisation. The first group, which included Sussex, Nottinghamshire and Yorkshire, was supported by lists of subscribers, and had formally appointed secretaries and treasurers who helped to persuade their cricketing friends and wealthy benefactors to make a subscription to finance both home and away games.[40] Over time, a committee was established from the subscribers, and it was these elected officers who selected the teams, fixed salaries and expenses and oversaw the running of the county along similar lines to the modern club.

An alternative route was taken by the second group, which included Surrey and Lancashire, where clubs were formed by groups of cricket enthusiasts.[41] They acquired a ground, built up a fixture list against local clubs and employed professional bowlers for the county side. Their officials then raised representative county elevens, drawing on local talent as well as members of the club itself. The third category was a combination of the first two, with one set of individuals raising a county side via the subscription method, and a second group using an established club. Kent was the best example of this hybrid type, with the cricketing base of the Canterbury club and a looser organisation at Maidstone.[42]

Despite these differences, all three types of county had one thing in common – similar settlement patterns with traditional market towns, with their coterie of landed families, plus sprawling industrial centres with an active urban bourgeoise, eager for social recognition. Membership of the county club provided an ideal vehicle for them to satisfy their social aspirations, as well as keeping in with the gentry. Consequently, the landowners were elected presidents or vice-presidents of the county clubs, whilst the town-based professionals, businessmen and clergy were elected to administrative posts.

In addition to these 'professional' county clubs, the amateur elevens were still in existence, calling themselves 'The Gentlemen of .....', with many being raised by a well-to-do gentleman, frequently for country house games or special exhibition games against I Zingari, the Free Foresters or a regimental side. Most of the counties had both a professional and an amateur side, but it was chiefly through the professional clubs that the County Championship developed.

The emergence of a county championship

The seeds of the formation of the championship had therefore been sown by the middle of the nineteenth century. As the games between North and South showed, there was an element of rivalry between the established regions and the emerging ones. With the popularity of the wandering elevens, the public at large and the media during the 1860s started to take an interest in who was the leading county. Until that time, only Kent, Surrey, Sussex or Nottinghamshire could mount a serious claim to being Champion County. But even then, it was not possible to say accurately who was better than all the others as at no time did any one county play all the others.

During the 1860s, Yorkshire, Middlesex and Lancashire had county clubs of strength equal to the original four, and in the 1870s Hampshire, Cambridgeshire, Derbyshire, Gloucestershire, Buckinghamshire and Somerset all made claims to being amongst the leading counties. However, the picture was very chaotic as there was no co-ordinated programme of inter-county fixtures, let alone a county table. It was often left to the sporting press to make a decision as to who were champions. Yet as Robert Brooke has shown there was no consistency in the methods used to calculate the champions, and there was disagreement over which matches should be included.[43] Whilst some felt that it should be awarded to the county with the fewest defeats, the variation in Table 3 shows that arbitrary decisions or personal choices were made by cricketing contemporaries or publications.

Another problem was the mobility of players, especially the

TABLE 3
POSSIBLE COUNTY CHAMPIONS FOR SEASONS 1864–89

	Bowen	Wisden	John Lillywhite	James Lillywhite	Cricket	WG Grace	Holmes
1864	Surrey	–	–	–	–	Surrey	–
1865	Nottinghamshire	–	Nottinghamshire	–	–	Nottinghamshire	–
1866	Middlesex	–	Middlesex	–	–	Middlesex	–
1867	Yorkshire	–	Yorkshire	–	–	Yorkshire	–
1868	Nottinghamshire	–	–	–	Nottinghamshire	Yorkshire	–
1869	Notts/Yorkshire	–	Notts/Yorkshire	–	Notts/Yorkshire	Nottinghamshire	–
1870	Yorkshire	Yorkshire	Yorkshire	–	Notts/Yorkshire	Yorkshire	–
1871	Nottinghamshire	Nottinghamshire	Nottinghamshire	Nottinghamshire	Notts/Yorkshire	Nottinghamshire	–
1872	Nottinghamshire	–	Nottinghamshire	Nottinghamshire	Notts/Yorkshire	Surrey	–
1873	Gloucs/Notts	Nottinghamshire	Gloucestershire	Gloucs/Notts	–	Gloucs/Notts	Gloucs/Notts
1874	Gloucestershire	–	Gloucestershire	Gloucestershire	–	Gloucestershire	Derbyshire
1875	Nottinghamshire	Nottinghamshire	Nottinghamshire	Nottinghamshire	–	Nottinghamshire	Nottinghamshire
1876	Gloucestershire	–	Gloucestershire	Gloucestershire	–	Gloucestershire	Gloucestershire
1877	Gloucestershire	–	Gloucestershire	Gloucestershire	–	Gloucestershire	Gloucestershire
1878	–	–	–	–	Middlesex	Nottinghamshire	Middlesex
1879	Lancashire/Notts	Nottinghamshire	Lancashire/Notts	Lancashire/Notts	–	Lancashire/Notts	Lancashire/Notts
1880	Nottinghamshire	Nottinghamshire	Nottinghamshire	Nottinghamshire	–	Nottinghamshire	Nottinghamshire
1881	Lancashire	Lancashire	Lancashire	Lancashire	–	Lancashire	Lancashire
1882	Lancashire/Notts	Lancashire/Notts	Lancashire/Notts	Lancashire/Notts	Lancashire	Lancashire/Notts	Lancashire/Notts
1883	Nottinghamshire	Yorkshire	Nottinghamshire	Nottinghamshire	Notts/Yorkshire	Yorkshire	Nottinghamshire
1884	Nottinghamshire	Nottinghamshire	Nottinghamshire	Nottinghamshire	Nottinghamshire	Nottinghamshire	Nottinghamshire
1885	Nottinghamshire	Nottinghamshire	–	Nottinghamshire	Nottinghamshire	Nottinghamshire	Nottinghamshire
1886	Nottinghamshire	Nottinghamshire	–	Nottinghamshire	Surrey	Nottinghamshire	Nottinghamshire
1887	Surrey	Surrey	–	Surrey	Surrey	Surrey	Surrey
1888	Surrey	Surrey	–	Surrey	Surrey	Surrey	Surrey
1889	Lancs/Notts/Surrey	Lancs/Notts/Surrey	–	Lancs/Notts/Surrey	Lancs/Notts/Surrey	Lancs/Notts/Surrey	Lancs/Notts/Surrey

The table includes the opinions of the four major cricketing publications of the 1880s and that of the greatest cricketer of the period.

KEY:
Bowen	Rowland Bowen – cricket historian.
Wisden	*Wisden Cricketers' Almanack.*
John Lillywhite	John Lillywhite's *Cricketers' Companion* (incorporating Frederick Lillywhite's *Guide to Cricketers*).
James Lillywhite	James Lillywhite's *Cricketers' Annual.*
Cricket	Cricket magazine. The details for 1868–72 are as listed in *Baily's Magazine.* The 1878 entry is from *Cricket & Football Times.*
W.G. Grace	List published in 1903 in *Cricket,* edited by H.G. Hutchinson.
Holmes	Rev. R.S. Holmes – his list was first published in *Cricket* 1894. From 1901 until Bowen's revision in 1959 this was accepted as the 'official' list of champions.

Source: Brookes, *A History of the County Championship* (Enfield: Guinness Publishing, 1991).

professionals, some of whom played for more than one side during a season. The only allegiance some of the paid players showed was to the highest bidder, and this somewhat anarchic system was also worrying many county officials. In an attempt to rectify the situation, Surrey CCC called a meeting of the officials of all the leading counties during the winter of 1872/73 in an attempt to standardise the system and draw up a few basic rules. Only Nottinghamshire was not represented at the London meeting where the following points were agreed.

1. A cricketer should not play for more than one county in the same season.
2. A qualifying period of two years bona fide residence should be imposed on any player anxious to change county.
3. In cases of disputes, the MCC would be invited to arbitrate.

One nettle that was not grasped was the format of the Championship itself, and there was no agreement over the standard number of fixtures. Derbyshire, Gloucestershire, Kent, Lancashire, Middlesex, Nottingham-shire, Surrey, Sussex and Yorkshire continued to play an irregular number of games. In 1873 the MCC made an attempt to rationalise matters by introducing an inter-county knock-out competition, but the idea for the Silver Cup failed to take hold, and the Championship continued to be decided in a haphazard way.

In 1882 the county secretaries agreed on a rudimentary system of points for the inter-county games, and in 1887 the County Cricket Council was formed. But the power lay in the hands of the press, as shown in 1889 when the Editor of *Wisden*, Charles Pardon, declared a triple tie between Lancashire, Surrey and Nottinghamshire, despite the latter having lost the fewest games! A second example had taken place a few years before when Derbyshire went through several seasons without winning a game. As E.W. Swanton wrote, the press played a hand in the ostracism of Derbyshire, as 'they fell from favour at the instigation, if you please, of the sporting press in London, with the other counties apparently conniving on the grounds that they had won only one match in four years'.[44]

The county structure badly needed a strong central authority on *all* matters, not just on player qualification. As Christopher Brookes wrote 'the MCC was the obvious choice, but for 20 years the club eschewed this responsibility... the authorities at Lord's preferred to sit back and let the counties try to resolve the problem of the Championship. If they could come up with a viable blueprint, then and only then, would the club agree to reconsider its position. So from 1873, crisis followed crisis as the county clubs tried to agree upon the best way to run the Championship.'[45]

In 1889 the County Cricket Council created a sub-committee in an attempt to solve the unsatisfactory situation, and a partial solution was reached when the secretaries of the major counties met at Lord's in December 1889 to decide on the fixture list for the following summer. A private meeting was attended by representatives of Gloucestershire, Kent, Lancashire, Middlesex, Nottinghamshire, Surrey, Sussex and Yorkshire, at which it was decided to subdivide the counties into three groups:

First-class: Gloucestershire, Kent, Lancashire, Middlesex, Nottinghamshire, Surrey, Sussex and Yorkshire;

Second-class: Cheshire, Derbyshire, Essex, Hampshire, Leicestershire, Somerset, Staffordshire and Warwickshire.

Third-class: Devon, Durham, Glamorgan, Hertfordshire, Lincolnshire, Norfolk, Northamptonshire and Northumberland.

It was also agreed to formalise the order of merit by awarding one point for a win, deducting one point for a defeat, with nothing added or taken away in drawn games. Consequently, Surrey, by virtue of nine wins and three defeats was awarded the Championship in 1890. This was a huge step forward, but the sub-committee, led by Lord Harris, had recommended relegation and promotion between each of the divisions. No decision was reached on this at a subsequent meeting in December 1890, although Somerset, who had won the second-class competition, went ahead with arranging games with the eight first-class sides for 1891.

Arguments continued over whether promotion and relegation should take place, and whether more than eight counties should form the first-class group. The County Cricket Council, at long last, turned to the MCC for help, and in October 1894 they decreed that 'the counties shall be divided into first-class or not, and there shall be no limit to the number of first-class counties'.[46] They also elevated Derbyshire, Essex, Hampshire, Leicestershire and Warwickshire to the County Championship, and left the other counties to their own devices. In 1895 the second-class and third-class clubs formed the Minor County Cricket Association, and inaugurated their own Championship, in an attempt to boost the claims of any other counties for elevation to the first-class arena. In 1899 Worcestershire won promotion, followed by Northampton-shire in 1905, Glamorgan in 1921, and Durham in 1992.

A development stage model

The nature of the County Championship was therefore established in a fairly ad hoc way by the end of the nineteenth century, which had seen important changes to the geography of English and Welsh cricket so that by the outbreak of the First World War, the game had reached what most historians describe as its modern format.

From a sports geography point of view, the county had developed as the representative unit in each area, and the game, in general, had passed through the following stages:

1. An unorganised folk-game.
2. A more formalised game, although still quite primitive with games being staged in villages, market towns and the early industrial centres. Opponents for matches came from the immediate locality.
3. The creation of formal clubs in the industrial centres with standardised rules and regulations. Inter-club fixtures replaced the friendlies and practice sessions, with teams travelling much further to play matches. The leading participants at this time were the wealthy and *nouveaux riches*, although a few professionals appeared.
4. Ad hoc county elevens and wandering clubs were formed, while improvements in schools allowed cricket to spread down the social ladder to the working classes. Better transport allowed players to travel to more distant places for fixtures.
5. Regular county matches were staged by the formalised county sides.

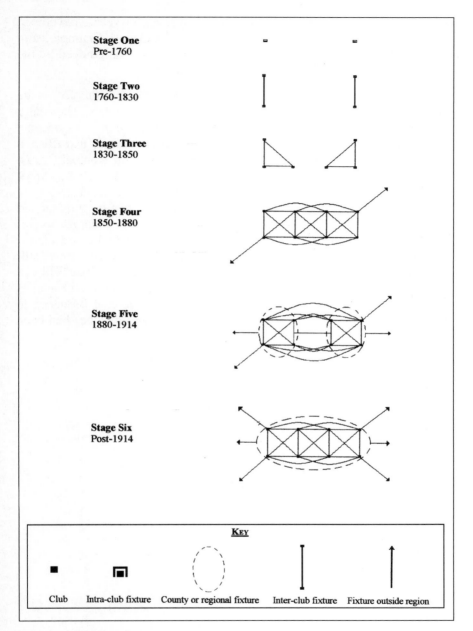

Figure 4   A model of changing geographical characteristics in South Wales

Source: Hignell, *A 'Favourit' Game* (Cardiff: University of Wales Press, 1992).

Professionals became more numerous and intense rivalries developed between clubs and county sides. Over time, a County Championship was established, and at club level, the game was strengthened by the formation of regional leagues and associations.

There were, quite naturally, a few regional variations to this five-stage model, and in South Wales, the process involved six stages. The major difference came when regional rivalries caused the 'county' to become divided. In the case of South Wales, a distinctive east–west split had affected the Glamorganshire club created in 1869. Internal cohesion eventually came in 1888 when Glamorgan CCC was created, uniting the factions from Cardiff and Swansea, and allowing the region to enter a sixth stage.

From a geographical point of view, these changes can be summarised by the sequential model in Figure 4. In Stage 1 the game emerged in two isolated culture locations, before contact began in Stage 2 with new teams. A further expansion took place in Stage 3, although intra-club fixtures still took place, for example, between Married and Single or Over Thirties against Under Thirties. By Stage 4 a complex web of inter-club games existed with players travelling throughout a wide sphere of influence to play games. By Stage 5 a formalised system of county matches had been superimposed on this web.

The Diffusion of Cricket:
A Geographical Explanation

Hagerstrand's diffusion theory

The previous chapter outlined the structural changes that took place during the eighteenth and nineteenth centuries, and this chapter aims to analyse in more detail the spatial patterns on a national scale. A few geographical insights have already been provided by Bale's map in Figure 3, showing the areal importance of each county in the pre-Victorian era. The subsequent spread of the more advanced forms of the game from Stage 2 onwards now require careful analysis, and we can utilise the writings of Torsten Hagerstrand, who developed a number of theories on innovation diffusion, based on the spread of new concepts and methods in Swedish agriculture.[1]

Hagerstrand defined an innovation as the successful introduction of ideas, or artefacts that are perceived as new, into an existing socio-economic system. Hagerstrand believed that their introduction and subsequent spread was neither haphazard nor chaotic, but followed a distinctive pattern over time and space. Using data on the spread of new ideas such as artificial insemination, Hagerstrand showed how initially the number adopting this innovation was small, but as time passed, there was a rapid increase in the use of this new method, before a ceiling was reached when the majority of farmers were using this technique. The exceptions were a small number of laggards who still preferred traditional methods.

When plotted as a frequency curve, the cumulative number of adopters over time approximates to an S-shaped curve, as in Figure 5. Hagerstrand concluded that this sigmoid pattern of adopters was the result of three effects.

1. Neighbourhood: contagious diffusion took place so that the greater the distance from an area of adoption, the smaller the amount of spread. People close to an area of adoption were much more likely to know about the innovation, as information was spread in a private way by word of mouth, rather than publicly through the mass media.
2. Barrier: the spread of ideas was restricted, especially in the early stages, some of the people who heard about the new ideas being

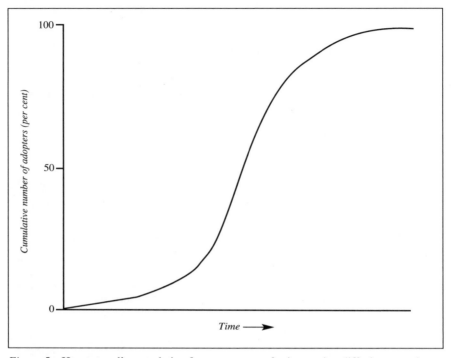

Figure 5 Hagerstrand's cumulative frequency curve for innovation diffusion over time

reluctant to change and forsake their tried and trusted methods. They may also have been reluctant to change due to economic restraints, such as lack of money or machines. There were also psychological barriers, such as not trusting their informant, or topographical ones including hills or marshes, so that areas became isolated and an integrated transport network could not develop.

3. Hierarchical: a new idea spread from the top of the hierarchy, i.e. the most important, or largest, to the bottom, i.e. the least important, or smallest. In Hagerstrand's case study, it was the richest farmers who were the first to introduce new ideas as they could afford to take risks or diversify. The poorest farmers were the last to adopt the new methods.

It is the aim of this chapter to see whether the same S-shaped pattern existed in the spread of cricket in England and Wales, and to find out whether these neighbourhood, barrier and hierarchical effects also played a significant role, using South Wales as a case study.

Diffusion patterns

As far as the national scale is concerned, the record of matches in Volumes 1 and 2 of F. Lillywhite's *Scores and Biographies* can be used as a source of information between 1746 and 1840. These are extensive listings, compiled with the assistance of the zealous A. Haygarth, and together with G.B. Buckley's *Fresh Light on Pre-Victorian Cricket*, they represent the finest source of secondary data for cricket historians researching the 'great' matches of the eighteenth and nineteenth centuries.[2]

Figure 6 shows the cumulative number of games in *Scores and Biographies*. There are several similarities with Hagerstrand's theoretical curve in Figure 5, although the steady increase to 1800 levels off until the end of the Napoleonic wars. There was a steep increase from 1825 onwards as cricket gained in popularity and overall there are close approximations with Hagerstrand's theory at the national level.

Similar curves can also be found for the growth of cricket in the nineteenth century at the regional and local scale, by using South Wales and Cardiff as examples. The data analysed for these localities are the match reports and line scores in the main newspapers which covered the region.[3] As today, not all games that took place were actually included in these newspapers, so those that were covered represent only the tip of the iceberg, and depended on club secretaries to submit details, or the personal whim of editors. Sports news, especially scores in cricket games were likely to be omitted by newspapers during a local election, an outbreak of cholera, during civil unrest or at the time of another major news item.

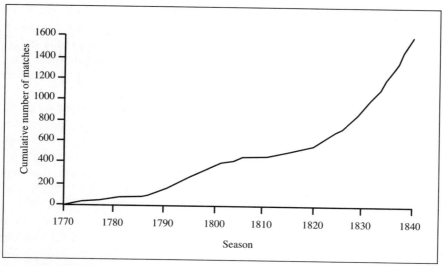

Figure 6   Cumulative number of matches in Lillywhite's *Scores and Biographies*

Even so, like all historical geographers we can only use whatever secondary data is readily available and by trawling through over a dozen different newspapers, an effective survey has been achieved.

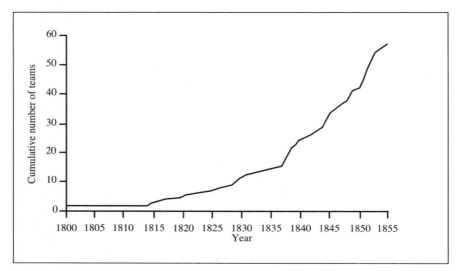

Figure 7   Cumulative number of teams in South Wales, 1800–55

Source: Hignell, *A 'Favourit' Game*, p. 34.

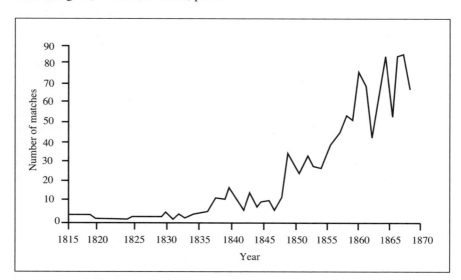

Figure 8   Number of matches reported in the newspapers, 1815–68

Source: Hignell, *A 'Favourit' Game*, p. 74.

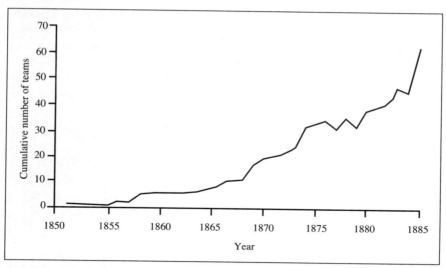

Figure 9 Cumulative number of Cardiff-based teams mentioned in newspapers, 1851–85

Source: Hignell, *A 'Favourit' Game,* p. 130.

Figure 7 shows the cumulative number of teams in South Wales between 1800 and 1855, whilst Figure 8 illustrates the annual number of matches reported from 1815 to 1868 – the year before Glamorganshire CCC was formed. Once again, these two diagrams of the regional level indicate that diffusion also approximated to a sigmoid curve during this pre-county era.

Cardiff can also be used as an example of the diffusion process at the urban scale. Figure 9 shows the number of Cardiff-based clubs recorded by newspapers as staging fixtures between 1851 and 1885. During the 1850s, only half a dozen sides actively played inter-club matches. But as trade from the towns docks rapidly picked up, and a flood of migrants poured into the town, the number of clubs had risen to 20 by 1870, 39 by 1880 and 63 by 1885. Overall, one can conclude that the increase in the number of clubs and matches fits Hagerstrand's diffusion curve on the national, regional and local scale.

Neighbourhood effects

To see if cricket spread by the neighbourhood effect, we have to focus on the developments from Stage 2 onwards. John Bale's map in Figure 3 can also be used as an indication of the culture hearths or cores from which any

spread took place. Some work has already been undertaken by Rowland
Bowen in mapping the spread of the game, based on an extensive trawl of
newspaper reports and using the date of the first recorded match as a
yardstick of the diffusion process.[4] His results can be seen in Figure 10.

Bowen also tabulated the earliest known dates for a match by a side
representing each county, as shown in Table 4. Chapter 2 has already

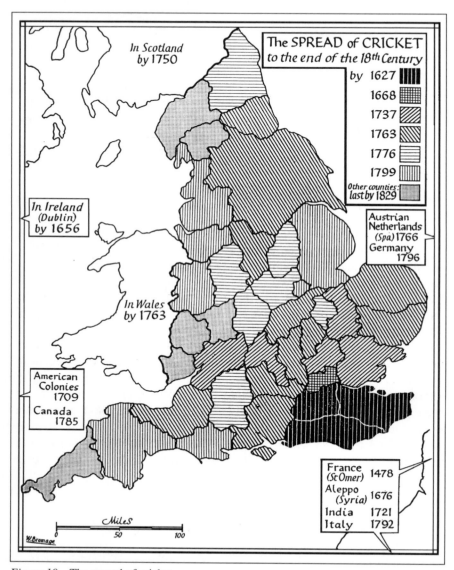

Figure 10   The spread of cricket

Source: Bowen, *Cricket – A History of its Growth and Development throughout the World*
(London: Eyre and Spottiswoode, 1970).

shown how it took time for formalised clubs to develop, and these dates
are evidence of a gradual move from Stages 2 and 3 of the development
model towards Stage 4. Once again, there is clear evidence of a distance
decay effect, with the earliest county games in Middlesex, Essex,
Bedfordshire and Buckinghamshire taking place nearest the culture hearth
of Kent and Surrey, as identified by John Bale and Peter Wynne-Thomas.
The more remote counties furthest from these early cores were among the
last to have a county eleven.[5]

TABLE 4
EARLIEST DATES FOR REPRESENTATIVE COUNTY ELEVENS

pre-1750	
1709	Kent, Surrey
1728	Sussex
1730	Middlesex
1737	Essex
1741	Bedfordshire, Buckinghamshire, Northamptonshire
1749	Hertfordshire
1750–99	
1764	Norfolk, Suffolk
1766	Hampshire
1769	Berkshire
1779	Oxfordshire
1791	Leicestershire
1798	Nottinghamshire, Somerset, Wiltshire, Yorkshire
1800–50	
1813	Cambridgeshire, Cornwall, Huntingdonshire
1814	Rutland
1818	Cheshire, Shropshire
1823	Monmouthshire
1824	Devon
1826	Warwickshire
1828	Lincolnshire
1834	Northumberland
1835	Westmoreland
1836	Herefordshire
1839	Gloucestershire
1844	Worcestershire
1845	Dorset
1846	Staffordshire
1849	Lancashire
post-1851	
1852	Carmarthenshire
1853	Cumberland, Durham
1861	Glamorgan
1864	Denbighshire
1866	Radnorshire
1870	Derbyshire

Source: Bowen, *Cricket – A History of its Growth and Development throughout the World*, pp. 382–3.

Barrier effects

As shown in Table 4, the counties of South Wales were amongst the last
parts of the country to stage county matches and to an extent the area
lagged behind its neighbours on the other side of Offa's Dyke and the
Severn Estuary. Some of the barriers in South Wales have already been
discussed in Chapter 2, namely the lack of a large ruling elite, and time
constraints caused by long shifts. However, other stumbling blocks existed
including transportational and religious factors, which prevented the quick
spread of the game and a rapid move from Stage 2 into Stages 3 and 4 of
the development model.

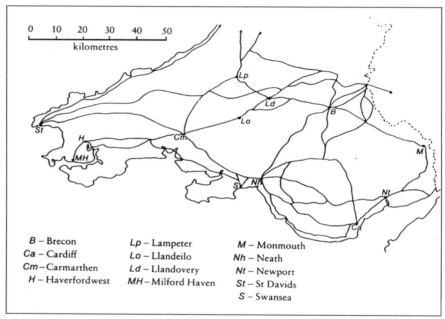

Figure 11   The road network of nineteenth-century south Wales showing the location of
pre-1840 games

Source: Hignell, *A 'Favourit' Game*, p. 44.

An efficient transport network was a necessity if clubs were to host
regular inter-club fixtures on both a home and away basis. The earliest
matches before 1840 in South Wales were held near some of the major
bridleways and drovers routes running from west Wales across the Heads
of the Valleys, into Monmouthshire and the towns on the English borders.
As seen in Figure 11, relatively few inter-club matches took place on the
coastal plain or in the valleys due to the primitive and slow transport by

road. This presented a barrier to the ambitious clubs in Newport and Cardiff, who were eager to expand their fixture list with games against top English sides. To play the Clifton club in Bristol either involved a long and tiring road journey via Gloucester, or catching the 'Bristol Packet' across the Severn Estuary. The latter was the preferred route for the Clifton side in July 1844 for a two innings match with Cardiff. But the crossing was rough and the game was reduced to a single innings contest as many of the visitors had either been seasick or were more than a little weary after their journey.[6]

The Clifton side tried the same route for a match with Newport in June 1845 and this time the boat came to their rescue. They had made only 105, and Newport were on the verge of winning at 100 for 6, when the bell sounding the imminent departure of the packet caused the contest to be hastily terminated to allow the Cliftonians to travel home.[7]

In order to travel to matches before 1840, most teams had to use the stage-coaches or travel by their own horse and carriage. Indeed, some match reports for this period spent as much time describing the grand carriages the team members arrived in, as they did in covering the play. Nevertheless, there were a few hazards to be faced if horses were tethered for a long time in the heat of a summer afternoon. An example occurred during a match in August 1839 as four members of the Raglan side were injured leaving the ground in the Forest of Dean when one of their horses, which had become restless during the long, hot afternoon, bolted and turned over their carriage.[8] At times, it also seemed as if a means of private transport, plus one's own coachman, was as important a playing requirement as proficiency with either bat or ball.

From the 1840s onwards, the cricketing growth points were the coastal towns of Cardiff, Newport, Neath, Swansea and Llanelli – all strategic points on the newly created railway network, and from which lines ran inland up the previously isolated valleys, which were now undergoing rapid industrial growth. The effect of the opening of these lines and their integration into the South Wales Railway from 1850 was nothing short of dramatic, and the removal of the frictional effect of distance can be seen in Figure 12.

The coming of the railways

Between 1837 and 1848 only four matches were played in Cardiff, yet from 1849 to 1855 25 were staged. In the west, Neath saw an increase from one to 16 games during the same period as teams which had previously been too far away in terms of time or distance for a single innings match were now in the catchment area of the new centres on the railway network, and regular fixtures were arranged.

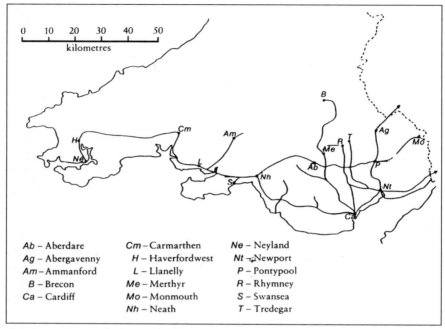

| 0 | 10 | 20 | 30 | 40 | 50 |
| kilometres |

Ab – Aberdare
Ag – Abergavenny
Am – Ammanford
B – Brecon
Ca – Cardiff

Cm – Carmarthen
H – Haverfordwest
L – Llanelly
Me – Merthyr
Mo – Monmouth
Nh – Neath

Ne – Neyland
Nt – Newport
P – Pontypool
R – Rhymney
S – Swansea
T – Tredegar

Figure 12   The railway network in South Wales before 1860

Source: Hignell, *A 'Favourit' Game*, p. 43.

Figures 13 and 14 show how the spheres of influence of the clubs in Cardiff, Llanelli and Swansea widened as a result of these transport improvements. In the pre-railway age Cardiff travelled an average distance of 30.5 km for away games, and in 1847 when they accepted a challenge from Tredegar, they staged the game at a convenient mid-point near Merthyr. Even so, Cardiff's players still travelled further than their counterparts in Swansea and Llanelly, whose mean journeys were 13.2 km and 16.3 km, respectively. Everything changed after the opening of the South Wales Railway, as Cardiff travelled a mean away distance of 47.2 km, whilst Swansea's rose to 41.4 km and Llanelli's to 44.7 km. The lines into Carmarthenshire and Pembrokeshire allowed both Swansea and Llanelli to play Haverfordwest and Carmarthen. Previously, the journey from Llanelli to Carmarthen had taken over three hours by stage-coach on narrow and often rutted roads. Now, Carmarthen was just 50 minutes down the line!

The opening of the railway lines also reduced the costs incurred by the clubs in staging away fixtures, with some of the railway companies

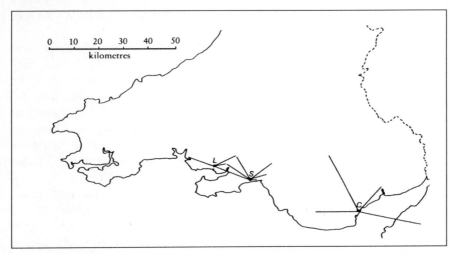

Figure 13 Spheres of influence of clubs in Cardiff, Llanelli and Swansea in the 1840s

Source: Hignell, *A 'Favourit' Game*, p. 45.

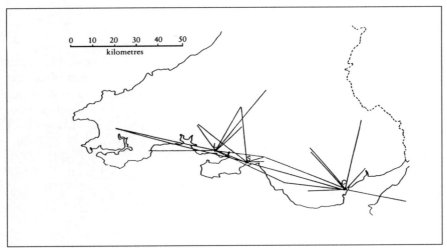

Figure 14 Spheres of influence of clubs in Cardiff, Llanelli and Swansea in the 1850s

Source: Hignell, *A 'Favourit' Game,* p. 45.

running special trains or services with cheap fares, allowing both the team and its supporters to travel. In one example in 1853 *The Cambrian* reported how a special train, courtesy of the Llanelly and Llandeilo Railway, for their match at Tenby 'conveyed a large number of excursionists from Llanelly and other places to witness the rather novel game...which shows a love for the renovating and healthful pastime. Cricket is becoming more and more appreciated.'[9]

As well as the erosion of some of these economic barriers, there were two other effects that these transport improvements created. Firstly, they allowed better communications between the clubs and news could be disseminated throughout the coastal plain and up the valleys. Not only did this facilitate the arrangement of inter-club fixtures, but the spread of weekly newspapers and journals allowed more people to read about the games that took place in the region and beyond. This spread of public information and greater awareness would have reinforced the news about clubs and players that was being spread by word of mouth.

The second effect was that the railways accelerated the contagious spread of the game. No longer were the early Welsh centres of the culture isolated around Carmarthen and Raglan, the railway lines united the region and allowed easier movement within it. In addition, it was now far easier to play games against English clubs, and teams did not have to disadvantage themselves by travelling on the Severn ferry, or spending a long time on the few roads over the hills in order to play the crack English teams.

'The Deadly Sin of Cricket'

Despite the arrival of steam trains and the plethora of new and faster routes, there were still other barriers that prevented the spread of cricket from the coastal plain of South Wales. The major obstacle was a religious one, as many of the migrants moving to the new industrial centres from rural parts of Wales were strict Nonconformists. They held strong views against recreation on the Sabbath instead of bible reading or attending chapel, and they took a dim view of the gambling, drinking and general after-match merriment. They believed that playing any game was vain and inconsistent with the seriousness of life. Playing ball games on the odd Feast Day was just about tolerated, but to play on the Sabbath was, in their eyes, sinful and would result in a greater penance after death, as judged by this inscription on a church wall near Caerwent:[10]

> Whoever hear on Sunday
> will practis playing at ball
> It may be before Monday
> The Devil will have you all.

Pierce has estimated that in 1851 Nonconformity was the preferred religion of around 80 per cent of the population of Merthyr Tydfil.[11] At this time, only 1.3 per cent of the town's population was in socio-economic group I, a mere 4.9 per cent in group II, and 63.9 per cent in group III.

Kenneth Morgan described Merthyr Tydfil as 'a rough, raw frontier settlement, consisting largely of uneducated colliers and ironworkers'. Given such people and their staunch Nonconformist views, it was not surprising to find so few cricket clubs in the settlement at the top of the region's hierarchy.[12]

Another area of Nonconformist opposition existed to the east of Monmouth and close to the Forest of Dean. This area adjacent to the English border could have been a thriving hotbed of cricketing activity, but its religious leaders were strong Nonconformists. In 1851 the Reverend P.M. Procter of Monmouth issued a pamphlet outlining the actions of a miner called Thomas Morgan, who was normally first to arrive at the town's cricket ground and the last to return home. The pamphlet recounted how one Sunday Morgan decided to refrain from his heathen tendencies and drinking habits by going to church instead. He was immediately converted and never went near a cricket ground again![13]

Strong words against cricket were also delivered from the pulpit; the vicar of Tabor Welsh Independent Chapel in Maesycymmer delivered a sermon entitled 'The Deadly Sin of Cricket'. The preacher told the congregation that working men ought not to join themselves with gentlemen, who had more money to spend, and that it was a positive sin for young men to go into a cricket field when they should have been reading their bibles.[14]

These religious barriers were steadily broken down from the 1850s on by the spread of Muscular Christianity and the patronage in sporting activity by industrial philanthropists. The ethic of Muscular Christianity, and the writings of Charles Kingsley, advocating recreation as a means of bodily purification and practical Christianity, helped to break down Nonconformist resistance to cricket. Playing games was now shown to be full of manly virtues, with brute strength being good and godly, whilst physical weakness or lack of exercise was a sign of moral and spiritual inadequacy. Kingsley and his followers believed cricket also taught respect and adherence to regulations, while it strengthened the physique and helped people build up an immunity against a range of ailments, including typhoid, pneumonia and cholera, which caused Victorian society to be in almost mortal fear of illness and disease.

Lessons at school

The removal of the Nonconformist barriers was assisted by reforms in the educational system following the 1847 Commission of Inquiry into Education in Wales. It reported that large numbers of people in the Principality spoke their native language and were ignorant of English. The

Commission believed that this was synonymous with ignorance in general, and they encouraged the introduction of English habits and pastimes instead. The first element of this Anglicisation of the South Wales valleys was the creation of 'Normal' or 'British' schools where the curriculum included gymnastic recreation and military training. The playing of such games as cricket was therefore added to the school routine in the valley communities, and in 1850 *The Cambrian* was 'glad to see the efforts in Merthyr latterly by the schoolmasters in improving the physical structure of their scholars by cricket matches'.[15]

Important changes also took place in a number of colleges and theological centres, as Muscular Christianity was advocated for the students at places of learning such as St David's College, Lampeter. In 1850, the college introduced a rule that the students should spend their spare time in 'healthful exercise rather than in clownish lounging about the shops or market place'. It was no surprise to find that the rule was introduced by the Vice-Principal, the Reverend Rowland Williams, a fellow of King's College, Cambridge, and a fervent supporter of Kingsley's writings.[16]

Welsh grammar schools also emerged as new centres of Anglicisation and also centres for the spread of cricket during the second half of the nineteenth century. Created under the 1840 Grammar Schools Act, one of the most successful to emerge was at Cowbridge, where cricket fixtures were introduced by the Headmaster, the Reverend Hugo Harper in 1849. Within a few years, young scholars were able to challenge the Cardiff club, and by 1857 they were invited by the Nicholl family to take part in their country house fixtures at Merthyr Mawr House.[17]

After catching the cricket bug while at Cowbridge, the young men continued to play while at university and then when taking up jobs on their return home to South Wales. Many of the young scholars took up holy orders, and were therefore in an ideal position to spread the gospel of cricket among the local population. One was Thomas Lister, the Rector of St Mark's, Newport; he had been in the Cowbridge XI during the 1850s, and actively encouraged his parishioners to play the healthy and manly game he had learnt at Cowbridge, he also assembled his own side for an annual challenge with the Newport club.[18]

Another active former pupil of Cowbridge Grammar was the Reverend William David of St Fagan's. He took over the parish, to the west of Cardiff, in December 1856, and in the early 1860s he formed St Fagan's Cricket Club. David was a man of immense energy, and in addition to running the cricket team, he oversaw the rebuilding of the rectory and the parish church. No surprise therefore that by the 1870s, St Fagan's had become one of the leading club sides in South Wales, and David's son Edmund[19] was the captain of Glamorgan CCC in their inaugural county game in 1889.

Hierarchical diffusion

At both national level in the United Kingdom and regional level in South Wales, there is clear evidence of the hierarchical diffusion of cricket from settlements and by leaders of society. Looking first at the way the game spread to, or from, settlements on a national scale, there was not a perfect top to bottom spread. The game began in rural areas and small market towns, before spreading to larger settlements in the eighteenth century, and to the conurbation of London. During the late eighteenth and nineteenth century, there were rapid rates of urban growth and the emergence of crowded industrial centres, allowing the game to trickle down the settlement hierarchy. During the second half of the nineteenth century, the game was introduced into the suburban enclaves and dormitory villages that sprawled into the rural–urban fringe. This was a hybrid example of Mike Marqusee's 'sentimental ruralism', by which the leading figures of urban life sought to establish a new collective identity in the peace and quiet of the rural hinterland where the game had first emerged several centuries before.

If hierarchical diffusion did not take place perfectly from the largest to the smallest settlement, it certainly occurred in an almost perfect way down the social ladder at the regional level in Monmouthshire. This had been one of the earliest centres of cricket in South Wales, with games staged in the early nineteenth century at country houses such as Cwrt-y-Gollen near Crickhowell. In 1824 a gentleman's side called the Monmouthshire CC was established in the market town of Raglan on land behind the Beaufort Arms on part of the Duke of Beaufort's extensive estate. Indeed, one of the leading figures behind the formation of the club and the gatherings at Cwrt-y-Gollen was Lord William Somerset, son of the fifth Duke of Beaufort.[20]

By 1836, the Monmouthshire club had over 100 members, and all political, commercial and social leaders of the area subscribed to the Raglan club. Their matches bore similarities to the present-day Royal Ascot or Henley Regatta, with the *Monmouthshire Merlin* for July 1834 observing how 'numerous carriages of the leading families of the county and many ladies and gentlemen from more distant quarters were on the ground at an early hour'.[21] The club also held lavish annual dinners and formal balls after play in the Beaufort Arms, and the events of the Monmouthshire club were highlights of both the cricketing and social calendar. For some, perhaps, the lure of the ballroom and the popping of champagne corks may have been a greater incentive to be members of Monmouthshire CC than the sound of leather on willow.

During the mid-nineteenth century, the game started to spread down the social ladder as a result of the actions of the landed gentry. The members of the squirarchy enjoyed their involvement so much so that they formed their own teams or organised country house cricket. Among the families to have their own eleven or cricket weeks by the 1860s and 1870s were Charles Crompton-Roberts of Drybridge, the Pelhams of Penallt, the Bosanquets of Dingestow Court, the Rolls of Monmouth, the Curres of Itton Park and the Walwyns of Croft-y-Bwlla. All these wealthy families had previously been members of the Raglan club.

By this time, a number of clerics and industrialists had started to become involved. Many had also been guests at the country house games and knew the benefits of healthy recreation. One of the cricketing clerics who helped to spread the game was the Reverend Griffiths of Trevethin, near Pontypool, who organised a side in 1876 and laid a wicket in the village. He also ensured that the team was composed solely of regular churchgoers in order to highlight the benefits of Muscular Christianity, and no doubt to swell his congregation in the face of strong competition from other denominations.

The entrepreneurs of Monmouthshire also adopted a paternalistic role, a notable example being Capel Hanbury-Leigh, the patron of Pontypool CC. By 1856 the club's membership exceeded 110 and as a result of its success, Hanbury-Leigh allowed them to play in the grounds of his home at Pontypool Park. Other industrialists saw sport as a means of establishing good relations between their white-collar and blue-collar workers. This was the case at Panteg where Samson Copestake, the owner of the town's steelworks, formed a side in 1876. During its early years, the Panteg eleven included several of the labourers and office workers, as well as the Manager and Director of the works.[22]

The industrial boom of the mid-nineteenth century also saw the involvement in the Monmouthshire valleys and coastal settlements of shopkeepers, solicitors, small businessmen and clerks. These *nouveaux riches* expressed their newly acquired wealth and rising social standing by becoming involved with the cricket clubs in the towns and rubbing shoulders with the leaders of local society and business. Some even formed their own teams, as Thomas Davis, the postmaster of Garndiffaith, in 1865 established an eleven in the small town. He clearly had high aspirations for his team given the content of a letter to a local newspaper. Davis wrote that 'I cannot see why the members might not, if they pulled together and practised regularly, obtain the honour of being the Eleven of All Wales, and become as competent at the game as the Eleven of All England.'[23] Grand aims and bold words, which illustrate the rising confidence among the middle classes. By the end of their first month, the Garndiffaith club had 30 members, but their playing strength was not sufficient for them to play the crack sides.

Even so, through the actions of people like Thomas Davis, as well as Samuel Copestake and Capel Hanbury-Leigh, the game spread to people of more humble and modest means. Educational reforms also meant that

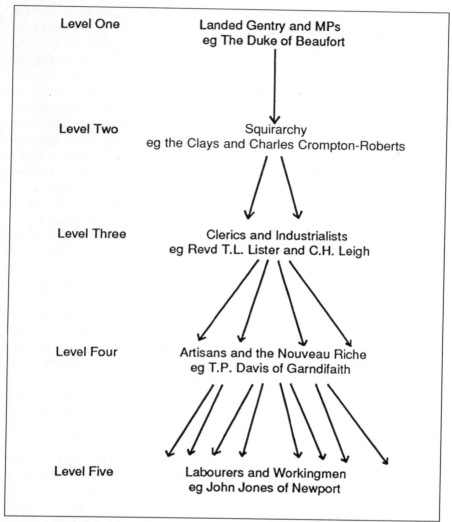

Figure 15 Hierarchical diffusion in nineteenth-century Monmouthshire

Source: Hignell, *A 'Favourit' Game*, p. 207.

many had learnt the rudiments of the game while at school, and now they were being given opportunities by their employers and religious leaders. The Early Closing Movement and the introduction of half-days on Saturdays helped to overcome some of the time constraints imposed by shift work. A few barriers still existed in the form of high subscriptions or restrictive membership clauses by some of the town clubs, but many of the labourers preferred to play and socialise with people of a similar background rather than the 'town toffs'. Consequently, a number of working men's or tradesmen's clubs were formed, together with 'crack o'dawn' or Morning Clubs which were ingenious ways of overcoming the constraints of shifts by staging games soon after sunrise on summer mornings, allowing people to play before they went off to work.

Therefore, the spread of cricket in Monmouthshire during the nineteenth century was a clear example of hierarchical diffusion. Figure 15 shows its spread down the social ladder, and the spider's web of diffusion channels, which began in the 1830s with the landed gentry copying patterns of action and recreation across the English border. Over the next 50 years the game had clearly spread down to the average working man, such as John Jones of Newport, who in 1880 could have joined any one of a number of working men's sides in the town, such as the Commercial, United, Athenaeum, Engineers or Tradesmen.

A Locational Analysis of the County Grounds of England and Wales

Central place theory and the rank–size rule

Cricket clearly did not evolve in a haphazard or random way. Rather, its diffusion during the eighteenth and nineteenth centuries, at all levels, from the regional to the local, bears clear similarities with Hagerstrand's diffusion theory. It is the purpose of this chapter to see if there was a similarly well structured and logical arrangement to the location of county games in England. The choice of location, both for playing venues and club headquarters, can be analysed by referring to two geographical theories which attempt to explain the arrangement, size and spacing of settlements, namely Central Place Theory and the Rank–Size Rule.

Central Place Theory was devised by Walther Christaller, who argued that a fixed hierarchy of settlements exists within each area, region or country.[1] He believed that this was a reflection of the service provision, with larger central places, such as large towns and cities, having more services and attracting larger numbers of people. Smaller settlements, such as small towns and villages, had fewer services and attracted a smaller number of people. In addition to this hierarchical arrangement, Christaller proposed that there was an ordered, hexagonal pattern to the location of settlements, as shown in Figure 16.

The Rank–Size Rule was produced by George Zipf, who showed that there was a proportional relationship between the size of a settlement and its position in the urban hierarchy.[2] He suggested that the ideal arrangement conformed to the Rank–Size Rule, whereby the population of settlement ranked n in the hierarchy was 1 nth of the population of the largest settlement in the region. This geometric order meant that the settlements could be arranged in descending rank as follows: 1, 1/2, 1/3, 1/4, 1/5, 1/6 ... n. When plotted as a logarithmic graph, an inverse linear relationship exists between rank and population size, as shown in Figure 17.

Both theories assume rational economic behaviour, with the providers of services aiming to maximise profits, and the consumers visiting their nearest central place. In the pre-industrial era, they would have travelled

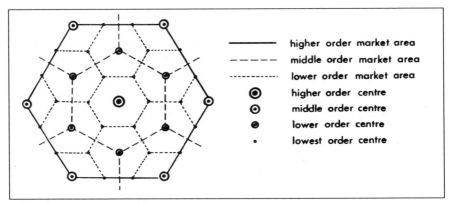

Figure 16   Christaller's central place theory

Source: Bradford and Kent, *Human Geography*.[1]

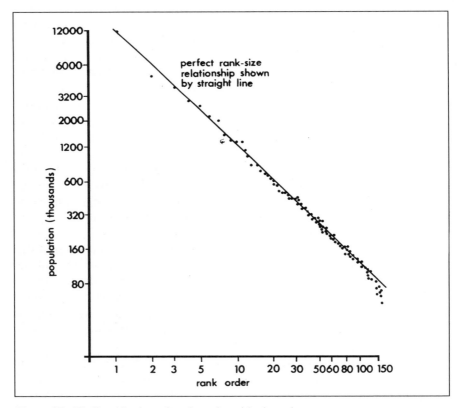

Figure 17   Zipf's rank–size rule using a logarithmic scale

Source: Bradford and Kent, *Human Geography*.[2]

to the village market, and competition between traders would have been minimal. Everything changed following the Industrial Revolution with major transformations in the settlement geography of England and Wales. Booming towns and sprawling cities replaced the previous patchwork of self-sufficient hamlets, villages and market towns. Central Place Theory and the Rank–Size Rule suggest that by the end of the nineteenth century there would have been an ordered arrangement of small hamlets and villages, plus larger towns and market centres, with the county town or city at the top of the hierarchy. Subsequent urban growth and industrialisation during the twentieth century will have modified this neat hierarchy, as the size and relative importance of each settlement will have changed. Even so, these concepts allow us to see if the establishment of the first county grounds took place at the centres of gravity within the county and the largest centres of population.

Locational patterns of the earliest Championship games

The first question to be asked is where did these county games take place. An interesting picture of the late Victorian pattern of county venues can be painted using the locations of the games played by each county in 1895, the year of the first 'proper' County Championship. Table 5, based on the 1896 *Wisden*, shows the diverse locations of the home games played by each county. Clearly many were played in quite sizeable settlements, so the next question to be asked is whether there was a distinctive relationship between settlement size and the number of fixtures, as one would expect if a perfect rank–size relationship existed. The scattergraph in Figure 18 plots these two variables and reveals that only a weak correlation existed in 1895 between settlement size and the number of fixtures.[3]

County cricket at the end of the nineteenth century clearly did not conform to the logical, hierarchical theories of Christaller and Zipf. Instead there were three separate types of locational patterns within the counties taking part in the Championship:

1. Group A – those with centralised fixtures: Derbyshire, Essex, Leicestershire, Middlesex, Nottinghamshire, Somerset, Surrey, Warwickshire.
2. Group B – those with most games at central headquarters, and a single outground for one or two 'festival' fixtures: Lancashire, Sussex, Hampshire.
3. Group C – those which took games to many venues throughout the county: Gloucestershire, Kent, Yorkshire.

TABLE 5
LOCATION OF HOME COUNTY CHAMPIONSHIP GAMES IN 1895

Derbyshire	all 8 games at Derby
Essex	all 8 at Leyton
Gloucestershire	5 at Bristol
	2 at Cheltenham
	2 at Clifton College
Hampshire	7 at Southampton
	1 at Portsmouth
Kent	2 at Tonbridge
	2 at Maidstone
	2 at Catford
	2 at Canterbury
	1 at Gravesend
	1 at Blackheath
Lancashire	11 at Manchester
	1 at Liverpool
Leicestershire	all 9 at Leicester
Middlesex	all 9 at Lord's
Nottinghamshire	all 9 at Trent Bridge
Somerset	all 9 in Taunton
Surrey	all 15 at The Oval
Sussex	10 at Hove
	1 at Hastings
Warwickshire	all 10 at Edgbaston, Birmingham
Yorkshire	4 at Sheffield
	3 at Bradford
	3 at Headingley
	2 at Scarborough
	1 at Dewsbury
	1 at Huddersfield
	1 at Harrogate

Source: John Wisden's Cricketers' Almanack for 1899.

Clubs in Group A clearly opted to stage games in one of the largest settlements in the county. But it is interesting to note that many others opted for a different route, so our next question is why did six counties opt against centralising fixtures in the largest settlement? This variation in the locational behaviour can be partly explained by the fact that there was no standard form of county club. Indeed, Eric Midwinter[4] has classified the late nineteenth-century counties in three categories, based on their composition and ethos:

1. highly professional, built around men born in the county, e.g. Yorkshire, Nottinghamshire;
2. predominantly amateur with each club having a social function. A small number of professionals was hired, chiefly for bowling, e.g. Middlesex, Sussex, Gloucestershire;
3. counties whose aim was to be a successful club with members watching the play, rather than undertaking a playing role. Such counties had a very catholic composition, e.g. Lancashire.

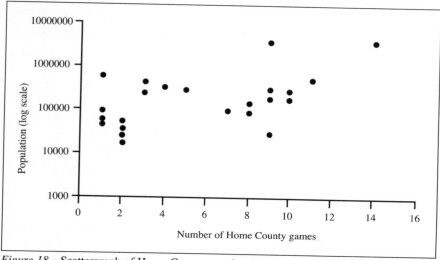

Figure 18   Scattergraph of Home County matches in 1895 against settlement size

However, this only provides a partial answer and does not explain why certain locations, such as Leyton in Essex, were chosen, rather than other towns higher up the settlement hierarchy, such as Colchester or Chelmsford. Moreover, clubs with a social function, such as Middlesex, opted for the same locational pattern as Nottinghamshire, one of the more professional county clubs, relying on home blood. For a more detailed answer we have to consider a number of other factors, and look at the specific factors which influenced the location of games.

Drawing up the fixture list

The creation of a county calendar and a national cricketing framework came at a time of major demographic, socio-economic and industrial change. During the Victorian era, the population of England and Wales rose from around 14 million in 1837 to almost 29 million by 1901. A new geography evolved as an industrial landscape replaced the agricultural one, whilst per capita incomes rose – the average wage in 1901 being 80 per cent higher than 50 years before. Both white and blue-collar workers could now afford to support a county team, in person via gate money, or through an annual subscription. Industrialisation also fuelled feelings of regional pride, of belonging and the desire to succeed, so the county clubs were keen to tap into this new support by playing at the largest and most accessible settlements in the county.

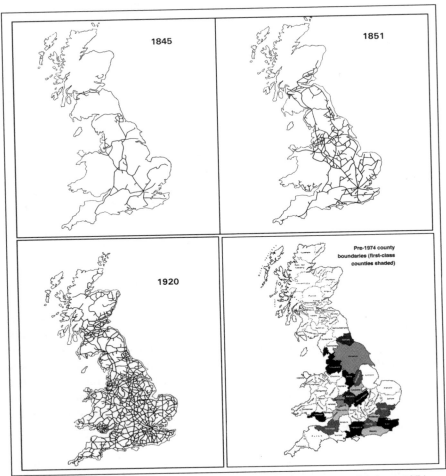

Figure 19   Development of the national railway system, and (bottom right) pre-1974 county boundaries (see Appendix 2, p. 220)

As mentioned in Chapter 3, improvements to public transport played a major role with the evolution of a national transport network, allowing people and products to be moved the length and breadth of the country. Indeed, Midwinter considers the railways to be the '*sine qua non* of first-class cricket. If a county was not accessible by rail, it could whistle in vain for first-class status.' The developing network of lines helps to explain why some county teams were elevated to first-class status in the 1880s, whilst others remained second or third-class, at a time when every county was playing cricket. The densely populated counties which could support, and finance, a good county side, were also those demanding and warranting an efficient railway service. Figure 19 shows the development of the national railway system, and how the original eight first-class counties were all on integral parts of the emerging network.

In respect of the specific choice of where to play within a county, the key factor, or positive externality, was the presence of a trunk railway line or mainline terminus. As Midwinter observed 'it was partly a matter of getting the audience to the venue, but what was essential was that competing teams could compete in an ever more complicated fixture list. They had to arrive in time for an early morning start and they had to be sure of meeting their next opponents often the morning after the previous match ended. Only the railways could provide that precision of service.'[5] Little surprise therefore that six of the seven counties to be admitted to the Championship during the 1890s had headquarters in nodal locations on the emerging network, at Taunton, Derby, Birmingham, Leicester, Southampton and Leyton.

The creation of county headquarters

The next question to answer is why some counties opted for a central base, whilst others opted for a more nomadic existence at a time when cricket emerged as the national spectator sport during the summer months. Legislation for a shorter working week and the introduction of four Bank Holidays all helped to provide greater opportunities for watching cricket. Clubs needed public arenas that were accessible and on level, well drained land where a decent wicket could be laid out, together with a pavilion, seating areas and possibly a practice area. As public interest grew there was also need for turnstiles, terraces, scoreboards, a print room and a basic catering area.

Locations that could meet all of these criteria were by definition likely to be found in urban areas, as there was little benefit in creating a county base in a remote rural area. Yet there was an interplay between the rural and the urban, as the people who gave the funds to help finance a county side and acquire a plot in a metropolitan area, were often country gentlemen or well-to-do businessmen who, having made money in the cities, had migrated to the rural hinterland.

Many county headquarters therefore developed in the large urban centres, as these settlements had large catchment areas and were highly accessible. The choice of where to locate the headquarters in some cases led to internal rivalry within counties, especially when there was more than one centre of gravity. This was the case with Somerset, where the two main centres of population, Bath and Taunton, lay at opposite ends of a county whose character was predominantly agricultural. Scattered throughout the county were many small market towns, plus a number of coastal resorts, but there was no major urban centre to act as a ready, reliable and exclusive source of income.

In October 1864 an attempt to form a county club took place in the east of the county at Yeovil, as the town club rather pretentiously attempted to turn itself into 'The Yeovil and County of Somerset Cricket Club'. The club failed to take off, and the formation of a proper club representing the whole of the county took place in August 1875 after an eleven called the Gentlemen of Somerset had challenged the Gentlemen of Devon at Sidmouth. While sipping their post-match drinks, the Somerset gentlemen passed a number of resolutions including 'there shall be no county ground' and 'county matches shall be played on any ground in the county that may be selected by the committee'.[6] Therefore, the founding members of Somerset CCC wanted the club to have a nomadic existence, and to visit as many of the centres as possible, reflecting the diverse geography of the county.

Even so, personal choices led to Somerset CCC subsequently centralising on Taunton, the county town. This was the result of the actions of Edward Western, the club's acting secretary. Western lived at Fullands House, Taunton and it was in the grounds of his house that the county's earliest games were staged. As David Foot wrote, Western believed 'if Somerset were to have county cricket, Taunton, the county town, was the logical base. He didn't really approve of outposts like Yeovil pre-empting them. Taunton had a healthy sporting instinct... organised rugby had started in the town and athletics had an increasing appeal. Mr Western foresaw no geographical problems now that Taunton was well served by the railway.'[7] For a while, games continued to be staged at other venues such as Bath and Wellington, but in 1886 the club took a long-term lease on the Athletic Ground in Taunton, and developed it into their headquarters.

Personal choices in other counties led to the location of headquarters in settlements that were not at the top of the county hierarchy. This was the case in Lancashire where the Manchester Cricket Club's ground at Old Trafford became the county's base, rather than Liverpool which, with a population of 684,958 in 1901, was larger than Manchester with 543,872. Liverpool had also been home to a successful club, and in 1859 the Edge Hill ground had staged a contest between the amateur teams representing the North and the South. Yet by 1895, Old Trafford was being used for 12 of Lancashire's fixtures, whilst the Aigburth ground in Liverpool was allocated only two.[8]

Lancashire CCC had been formed at a meeting in a Manchester hotel on 12 January 1864, where it was agreed that matches would be staged alternatively in Manchester, Liverpool, Preston, Blackburn and 'other places where interest was manifest'.[9] Whilst the committee were keen to take cricket around the county, they also wanted a grand headquarters, and one which lost nothing in comparison with those in southern England, such as The Oval. It was therefore agreed that Old Trafford would act as the county's base, but games were still played at a number of outgrounds.

During the 1870s, Manchester CC became increasingly influential in the affairs of Lancashire CCC, chiefly through the actions of S.H. Swire, the Lancashire secretary. He did not approve of the decision to take county games to other grounds, and in 1880 oversaw a merger between Lancashire CCC and Manchester CC, with the club's new official title being the 'Lancashire County and Manchester Cricket Club'.[10] As John Kay observed 'what was good for one was also good for the other, although as the years rolled by the growing public who watched and played cricket began to look upon the club as purely and simply Lancashire. Officially, it was never so, and it was almost a century later before the Manchester club officially ceased to be linked with the Lancashire one. And even today, there are old-timers who still insist that Lancashire cricket was essentially Manchester cricket in the very beginning.'[11]

Edgbaston – a high-class suburb and cricket centre

In some counties, the creation of a county cricket ground was encouraged by astute landowners as a way of maximising income from their land and to create the right sort of atmosphere and image to attract high-class housing. This was the case with the headquarters for Warwickshire CCC, which were developed during the late nineteenth century at the same time as Edgbaston emerged as a genteel and prosperous suburb. During the 1880s, Warwickshire were considering where to locate their headquarters. Rugby and Leamington Spa were on an initial short-list, but William Ansell, the secretary, considered that Birmingham would be a better bet. He showed how the city was well served by railway routes, and its large population was the potential audience to generate sufficient cash to employ professionals. Ansell also felt that a ground in Birmingham could also provide a constant source of revenue by being hired out for winter sports, such as football.[12] Ansell was an ambitious man, and he harboured three ambitions – a Birmingham headquarters for Warwickshire, first-class status for the club and staging Test matches on the ground. Through his hard efforts, and the support of the Calthorpe Estate, all Ansell's dreams were eventually realised.

During the mid-1880s, the Warwickshire committee started to look at suitable sites within the expanding city. Ansell favoured the Wycliffe ground on the Pershore Road, but the Calthorpe Estate believed that the land was attractive for high-class housing, so instead they offered Warwickshire an alternative 12 acres of rough grazing meadow along the banks of the River Rea. This plot was less attractive as a building plot, but the Calthorpe Estate realised that if it were leased for a cricket ground, it would create a positive externality which would enhance the whole area, and further the creation of a high-class suburb in Edgbaston. This was not an isolated action; the agents working for the estate had carefully controlled its use and lease for housing development following Lord Calthorpe's decision to move from Edgbaston Hall to live in Norfolk. Indeed, Figure 20 shows how the Calthorpes were successful in housing the aristocratic and upper middle class members of Birmingham's society by the start of the twentieth century.[13]

From the 1820s the estate imposed restrictive clauses in the covenants for leasing land, controlling the quality of what was built on it. As well as low-class housing, the estate did not want 'any workshops or other kinds of shop, nor any place or places for carrying on any trade or manufacture, nor any brewshop, ale house or tea garden'. Assisting Warwickshire was in keeping with their desire to create a high social tone for Edgbaston. Warwickshire also liked the potential of the Edgbaston plot. It was only 20 minutes walk from New Street station, a quarter of an hour from Moseley station and close to several tram routes. They therefore agreed in 1885 to let the land for £5 an acre over a 21-year period, and the first game on the ground took pace on 7 June 1886.

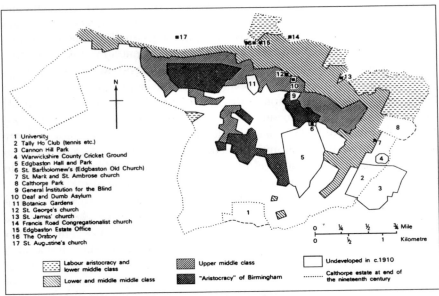

Figure 20   Residential zones in Edgbaston, Birmingham

Source: Cannadine, *Lords and Landlords*.[13]

All parties therefore benefited in the development of Edgbaston as a county headquarters. The wicket soon earned a fine reputation and Ansell's dream came about in 1902 as the ground staged its first Test match. For their part, the Calthorpe Estate benefited as Edgbaston became a thriving and up-market residential suburb, and as Figure 20 shows, an artery of high-class housing developed to the west of the ground along the Edgbaston Road.

Taking cricket around the county

Other counties opted for a more nomadic existence, taking cricket around the county, playing in more rural locations, in what John Bale has described as a form of periodic marketing.[14] Whilst there was a similarity with the way market-based activities had taken place in the pre-industrial era, there were other reasons for this nomadism. In some cases, it was a continuation of country house cricket, which had become the perfect vehicle for respectable recreation by well-heeled gentlemen, as well as giving them a chance to socialise in dignified surroundings with the elite of local and national society.

As David Frith described, 'it was at these games that the gentlemen members of such clubs at I Zingari, Free Foresters, the Grasshoppers and Eton Ramblers played their cricket, exercised impeccable table manners (if they desired a return invitation) and danced the evening away. Through a colourful splash of blazers and hat ribbons, the umpires – butlers, gamekeepers or gardeners of his Lordship – would commence proceedings which comprised an exhibition of all that was attractive and honourable in the summer pastime.'[15] Among those taking part in these games was a Mr Cornwallis-West, a debonair gentleman and member of the highest echelons of society. In his memoirs, he recalled how 'many large country houses had private cricket grounds, and cricket weeks in August after the London Season were most amusing. Invitations to them were eagerly accepted by those with any pretensions to playing the game.'[16]

While being in part a form of escapism for some of the amateurs, these games at country retreats or fixtures staged by wandering elevens were a fertile hunting ground for county scouts, looking to find decent amateur talent and thereby save expenditure on expensive professionals. It was also a very pleasurable way to recruit a wealthy patron, and secure a financial lifeline for the county's coffers. In the case of Kent, there was a very close connection between the country house games and the first-class game, largely through the efforts of the wandering club, and pseudo-county, The Band of Brothers, whose membership was restricted to players from within the county boundaries. The Band of Brothers were regular participants at the country house games, and as the standard of play was high, it meant that there were always good amateurs, in form and available for Kent. Indeed, many gentlemen flitted from appearances for the county eleven to games for the Band of Brothers.

For Kent, their choice of where to locate their headquarters was also related to the success, or otherwise, of various festival weeks. The club had been formed in 1859 at Maidstone, and like Lancashire, they initially resolved 'that the matches to be played shall not be confined to any particular locality'.[17] By 1870 there was a need for a central base, and the county committee resolved 'that if a permanent cricket ground be obtained in a suitable locality, the migratory principle should be abandoned, and all matches, except Canterbury Week, be played on the county ground'.[18] There were flirtations with Catford, Maidstone, Dover, Beckenham and Blackheath, before the club acquired in 1896 the St Lawrence ground in Canterbury following the death of the fifth Earl Sondes.

Kent CCC was delighted to locate its headquarters at Canterbury in 1896, where a successful festival had been staged since 1847. In these early years, the festival consisted of a game in the first half of the week between Kent and England, followed in the second by a match between the Gentlemen of England and the Gentlemen of Kent. From 1882, the festival was held during the first week of August and involved Kent playing another first-class side, a touring team or an MCC side. Attendance at Canterbury week was certainly the 'thing to do' in social and cricketing circles in south-east England, and a row of gaily coloured marquees spread around the ground, occupied by The Band of Brothers, I Zingari, the Buffs, the East Kent Yeomanry and all leading clubs from the Canterbury area as well as the Mayor of the city and various wealthy individuals. Canterbury week therefore had an air of country house cricket, as the county players performed in front of the rich and famous of Kent. The festival also had a certain rural charm, and this must have reinforced its popularity around the turn of the century as other clubs opted instead to develop their urban centres.

As county memberships swelled during the late nineteenth century, and attendances rose, several counties realised that they had to improve their grounds and a number of grand new pavilions were constructed – at Lord's in 1890, Old Trafford in 1895, The Oval in 1896, Chesterfield in 1898, Worcester in 1899 and Canterbury in 1900. Other clubs enlarged their buildings in order to take advantage of the income from non-cricketing functions, such as at Trent Bridge where, at the turn of the century, lucrative dancing classes were regularly held in the pavilion. Such grand edifices were not only architectural assertions of the growing confidence in cricket, but symbolised the nascent power of the county club and its place in the Championship.

1. An early home for cricket – a pencil and watercolour sketch by J.M.W. Turner circa 1795 shows cricket being played by the west front of Wells Cathedral in Somerset. (The Lady Lever Collection, Port Sunlight)

2. A painting of the grand challenge match in 1868 at Neath between the United South of England XI and a XXII representing Cadoxton and District. (Neath Borough Council)

3. An early county headquarters – The County Ground, Bristol in 1890. (Gloucestershire CCC)

4. The delightful New Road ground in Worcester – one of the most picturesque of all county bases as seen in the 1930s. (Worcestershire CCC)

5. The headquarters for Somerset CCC at Taunton, as depicted on a postcard around the turn of the century.

6. Leyton – the early base for Essex CCC to the east of London.

7. Lord's – the home of Middlesex CCC and the all-powerful Marylebone Cricket Club.

8. The players of Sussex CCC, in action at their seaside base in Hove.

9. Was there a breathless hush in the close that night? Cricket at Clifton College in Bristol.

10. A view of the College ground during one of Gloucestershire's Championship matches which formed part of the famous Festival at the College ground.

11. The picturesque Crabble Athletic Ground at Dover, used by Kent CCC for 106 matches between 1907 and 1976.

12. The Angel Ground in Tonbridge, which played host to Kent's county games from 1869 until 1939.

13. Leicestershire play Worcestershire in 1947 in the rural surroundings at the Kirkby Road ground, Barwell. The small Leicestershire town hosted three of Leicestershire's games in 1946 and 1947.

Locational Changes to County Cricket, 1901–1951

Introduction

By the start of the twentieth century, the game at the national level, had seen the staging of Test cricket against Australia and the creation of a countrywide Championship, based, almost by default, around the bounds of a county. But there was a rather diverse pattern to the actual location of county games, and various locations were chosen for county games. Logical, hierarchical models such as Central Place Theory and the Rank–Size Rule therefore offer little help when analysing these late nineteenth-century patterns. Both of these theories assume maximiser behaviour, i.e. that profit maximisation was a key factor, and that rational economic behaviour took place. As Eric Midwinter's classification showed, many county clubs operated in more of a philanthropic and social way during the Victorian era, so the lack of an ordered and rational pattern may not be surprising.

Indeed, Keith Sandiford and Wray Vamplew in their review of the economics of the county game before the Great War concluded that county cricket was not wholly profit-orientated, and attempts to maximise revenue was low on their list of priorities. The county treasurers relied on annual subscriptions and donations from a wealthy patron or cricket-loving grandee as the main form of income. Few clubs hired out their facilities or fixed assets during the winter months, whilst as far as gate money was concerned, sixpence was the norm, whether the visitors were county champions or wooden spoonists. Therefore, Sandiford and Vamplew concluded that 'basically cricket was so much an integral element of English ritual, mores and tradition that it was not viewed simply, or even primarily, as a business proposition'.[1]

However, the twentieth century saw dramatic changes to county cricket, with the rise in commercial interests, as it became a lucrative business. County clubs grew increasingly eager to hire decent professionals and do well in the Championship, as the game became firmly established as a spectator sport. Consequently, market forces and the chance to secure economies of scale became far more prevalent in the next phase in the game's development.

Over time, the location of games therefore started to assume a far greater importance than in the Victorian era, and it is the purpose of this chapter to analyse these subsequent developments in the County structure up to the 1950s. In particular, attention will be paid to the locational patterns that each county side adopted and how they changed during this time period. From *Wisden's Cricketers' Almanack*, surveys of three seasons – 1901, 1921 and 1951 – have provided a definitive listing of the locations used by each county for their first-class games.[2]

The pattern in 1901

It is possible to subdivide the locational behaviour in 1901 using the same three-fold classification as in Chapter 4:

1. Group A – those with centralised fixtures: Middlesex, at Lord's; Warwickshire, at Edgbaston; Surrey, at The Oval; Essex, at Leyton; Worcester, at Worcester; Leicester, at Leicester.
2. Group B – those who played most of their games at a central headquarters with one or two games at outgrounds: Lancashire, Nottinghamshire, Somerset.
3. Group C – those who took cricket to many venues throughout the county: Yorkshire, Sussex, Kent, Hampshire, Gloucestershire, Derbyshire.

When compared with the patterns in 1895, there had been a slight decrease in the number of counties in Group A from eight to six, as several counties with a central base also opted to take games around the county, and to stage fixtures in smaller places. There were still some bizarre choices, such as Welbeck, a tiny hamlet with just 15 houses, hosting Nottinghamshire's Championship fixture with Derbyshire. It was chosen again in 1904 for the same fixture. With a resident population of just 97, Welbeck must surely be one of the smallest settlements ever to host a first-class game, and it achieved this honour because Welbeck Abbey was the home of the Duke of Portland, a leading patron of Nottinghamshire cricket. During the 1880s the sixth Duke had overseen the laying of a wicket for country house games, and by the turn of the century, the influential Duke persuaded the county to play in the rarefied atmosphere of his private ground.[3] The number of counties in Group C had risen from four in 1895 to six in 1901, with Derbyshire having previously focused all their activities at Derby, now staging matches at Glossop and Chesterfield. Figure 21 shows that a clear rank–size relationship existed for Derbyshire with seven fixtures at Derby (pop. 105,912), and two apiece at Chesterfield (pop. 27,185) and Glossop

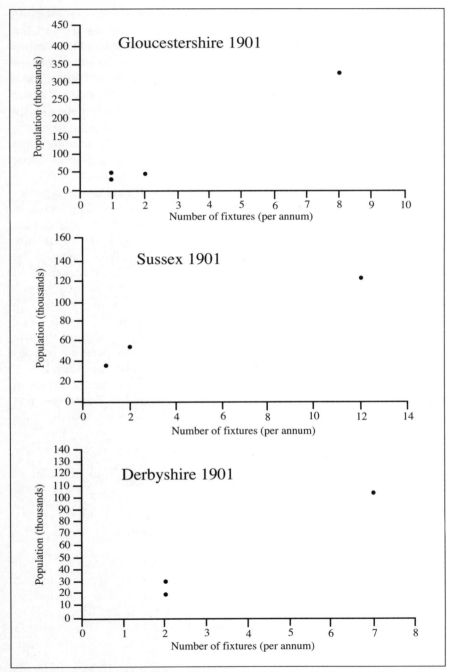

Figure 21　Rank–size relationships for Derbyshire, Sussex and Gloucestershire, 1901

(pop. 21,526). Figure 21 also shows that a clear rank–size relationship existed for two other counties in Group C, Sussex and Gloucestershire, but this was not so for Yorkshire. Indeed, continued industrial and urban expansion meant that some counties such as Yorkshire had no centre of gravity, and as a result, Yorkshire CCC used eight venues in 1901 without any sign of rank–size arrangement. As Steven Draper stated, 'where Yorkshire differed from many of their rivals was that the county did not have a natural centre whose supremacy over cricket would never be seriously be challenged, unlike Nottinghamshire or Lancashire, and Sheffield, which aspired to this role, suffered the disadvantage of being geographically remote from much of the rest of the county'.[4]

However, Group C was not solely occupied by the industrial counties of northern England, as Kent in the greener south-east used six grounds in 1901, and visited even smaller places within their county boundaries than did their industrial counterparts. Whilst the smallest settlement Yorkshire chose was Dewsbury, with 28,060 people, Kent staged three games at the Angel Ground in Tonbridge, a small town with only 12,736 residents. At face value this seems a strange decision when only a single match each was allocated to Maidstone, with 33,516 people, Tunbridge Wells with 33,373 and Gravesend with 27,196. However, the Angel Ground could boast an excellent wicket, having staged several major games in the late nineteenth century and, as in the Victorian era, there were personal reasons rather than economic ones, for Kent choosing the Tonbridge ground.

The prime mover behind the decision to play three games a year at Tonbridge was Tom Pawley, the Kent manager and a Tonbridge man through and through. His duties as manager involved liaison with the clubs on whose grounds the county were playing. It was not surprising therefore that Pawley helped to guide more county cricket in the direction of the Angel Ground, and in 1897 it was chosen as the location for the club's nursery. Financial problems before and after the Great War, and some internal wrangling, saw a subsequent decline in the Tonbridge influence, but in 1901 Tonbridge Week was second only to Canterbury on the county club's social calendar, with dances on the castle lawns, fireworks and a Venetian fete on the Medway.[5]

Whilst personal choice still affected some of the locational behaviour of counties in Group C, other nomadic counties opted for locations that offered financial benefits. This explains why Gloucestershire continued to play first-class cricket at the College ground in Clifton, an affluent suburb to the west of Bristol, with a population in 1901 of 44,428. This compared with the 49,439 residents of Cheltenham, and 47,955 of Gloucester, where the county also staged games, but was small fry compared with the 328,945 inhabitants of Bristol itself. But the county owed a debt of gratitude to the College for hosting their early county games, and allowing the club to boost its finances. The county club was established in 1870, and initially played on Durdham Down, a public common, but this prevented the county from charging admission, so in 1871 they secured the use of the College's facilities. This swelled the club's coffers and also allowed the club's batsmen to perform on the excellent College wicket, rather than the rougher surfaces on the Downs.[6] It also meant that the club could easily secure the services of many of the College's fine young players, and it was at Clifton in 1899 that a 13-year-old called Arthur Collins batted for over six hours to score a world record 628 in a Junior House match. Indeed, the school has a wonderful reputation as a cricketing academy, with its Close being immortalised in Newbolt's *Breathless Hush*. Moreover, Clifton was second only to Eton during the late Victorian and early Edwardian period in terms of the number of boys it sent on to play county cricket as amateurs. This was not surprising given the fact that one of the school's rules was that spectating at major matches was compulsory for the rest of the school. No doubt, for many boys the chance of watching Dr W.G. Grace was in any case far more preferable than being engrossed in their Latin primers!

The performances of the Grace family with bat and ball also helped to establish Gloucestershire as a leading county side, and crowds flocked to Clifton and Cheltenham to see the Graces perform. The Doctor was also the club's leading personality off the field, and ever mindful of the growing popularity of county games, realised that Gloucestershire badly needed a permanent base in Bristol, ideally near a railway line, so that spectators could easily reach the ground and further swell the club's finances.[7] By 1888 the Gloucestershire club had enough cash to acquire a plot of land at Ashley Down, near the Great Western Railway line to South Wales and Gloucester. It was here that a new ground was laid out, under W.G.'s specifications, and in 1899 the county moved to their new headquarters. Even so, they did not forget the part Clifton College had played in the club's history, and with many of the College's former scholars playing for the county side, Gloucestershire maintained their links with the College by staging county fixtures at Clifton until 1932.

Seaside festivals

By 1901 some of the fashionable seaside resorts had become successful county venues, adding extra diversity to an already varied calendar. The most successful of the seaside resorts to host county cricket was undoubtedly Scarborough, which from 1894 was used by Yorkshire on an annual basis. By the end of the nineteenth century, the county had established a pattern of fixtures with Sheffield, Bradford and Leeds being used for the lion's share of fixtures, whilst other locations staged annual games. Such a peripatetic existence involved considerable expenditure, so when considering the allocation of games away from these 'Big Three', the club had to ensure that venues had the potential of being financially rewarding. Therefore, at first glance it seems a little curious that Yorkshire should stage four matches in Scarborough, a town with a resident population of only 38,161 in 1901.

But Scarborough had established a reputation as being a fashionable and healthy resort during the late Victorian and Edwardian era, with an air of upper-class sophistication at the town's spa. Leading members of society, as well as royalty, visited the town from far and wide, and by the 1890s, the gentry of northern England were visiting Scarborough for summer relaxation and socialisation. The coastal resort had also become more accessible following the opening in 1845 of the York to Scarborough railway line, and as Hall and Found showed, 'visitors were brought to Scarborough from far afield, and from a broader social background. Industrial workers from Bradford, Leeds, Sheffield and the West Riding gained welcome relief from the factory and the pit in a trip on the train to the seaside'. Therefore, the town's population was swelled during the summer months by holidaymakers and influential members of Yorkshire society, creating a pool of potential supporters and benefactors.[8]

Cricket in Scarborough dates back to 1828, and by the middle of the nineteenth century the town's club was staging games on land opposite the Queen's Hotel on North Marine Road. A measure of its economic attractiveness can be gauged from the fact that in 1862 the All England Eleven paid a visit to the town. But the most influential fixture took place in 1871 when Lord Londesborough, a Yorkshire landowner and MCC president, organised a game in the town between his own eleven and C.I. Thornton's XI. The contest was a huge success from both a cricketing and social point of view, encouraging Lord Londesborough, to stage an annual game, thereby satisfying the demand for entertainment of the very highest quality amongst the higher echelons of Scarborough folk.

Londesborough was a shrewd and a very willing entrepreneur, and by 1876, these games had developed into an annual festival, with special exhibition games between Yorkshire and the MCC or I Zingari. Such games with illustrious opponents added considerably to the attractions of Scarborough as a fashionable holiday resort. As Hall and Found added, 'the later Victorians were always anxious to promote town identity, none more so than the aldermen of Scarborough. A sport like cricket, with its favourable moral connotations fitted extremely well with Scarborough's perceived image of gentility. At the same time, cricket would contribute by taking commercial advantage of the new wave of tourism.'[9]

The festival games that Lord Londesborough organised at Scarborough therefore quickly grew in popularity, and the sign that the resort had taken its place on the national cricket map came in 1885 when W.G. Grace appeared at the festival. The Doctor made 174, to the delight of the many people sitting in the gaily coloured marquees, erected specially for the festival along one side of the North Marine ground, and row upon row of holidaying Yorkshiremen, who took a keen interest in the performance of their county side.

Touring sides and elevens representing the Gentlemen of England were also invited to play in what some critics have described as 'His Lordship's Festival'. Indeed, some feel that his motives were not entirely altruistic, and instead were a vehicle for promoting his own social position. This might explain why Lord Londesborough never became president of Scarborough CC, a curious situation for someone whose contribution to cricket in the town appeared so immense. Whether one agrees or disagrees with this view, the actions of Lord Londesborough meant that the resort town became a highly lucrative venue for county cricket, and it explains why Yorkshire, having added Scarborough to their Championship fixture list in 1894, staged four games in the town each year from 1901.

The pattern in 1921

Several important changes affected the geography of county cricket by 1921. On the one hand, some counties still opted to focus their activities in the larger settlements, following further urban expansion in these central places.[10] But as the listing below shows, there had been a decrease in the number of counties in Group A from six to four, and by 1921 the most popular category was Group C:

1. Group A – those with centralised fixtures: Middlesex, at Lord's; Warwickshire, at Edgbaston; Surrey, at The Oval; Northamptonshire, at Northampton.
2. Group B – those who played most of their games at a central headquarters with one or two games at outgrounds: Lancashire, Nottinghamshire, Derbyshire, Glamorgan.
3. Group C – those who took cricket to many venues throughout the county: Yorkshire, Sussex, Kent, Hampshire, Gloucestershire, Somerset, Leicestershire, Worcestershire, Essex (see Figure 22).

More and more counties opted to stage games at popular outgrounds, with Essex, Leicestershire and Worcestershire all deciding to forsake centrality and to play fixtures at a number of outgrounds. Their decisions were the result of two related factors – the success of festivals such as Scarborough

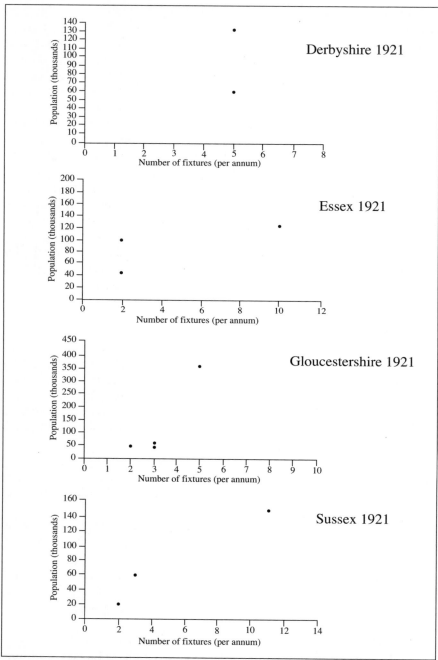

Figure 22 Rank–size relationships for Gloucestershire, Derbyshire, Sussex and Essex, 1921

and Canterbury, and secondly, financial considerations as the county's coffers were swelled by flying the county flag in as many places as possible. These economic factors therefore merit detailed consideration when attempting to understand the geography of county cricket in 1921.

From the smoke to the sea – the case of Essex CCC

Many county officials had shrewdly monitored how festival cricket, as at Scarborough and Canterbury, had become very lucrative. Moreover, the games had gained an air of respectability and dignity, previously associated with the leading matches at Lord's such as Gents and Players, the Varsity match and Eton v Harrow. As George Plumptre noted, 'these fixtures had become major events in Edwardian society's annual calendar, a part of the 'season' rivalled only by Royal Ascot. For men, morning dress with top hats was *de rigueur*, while the ladies vied with each other in their display of enormous hats and rustling full-length frocks. Later in the summer, the atmosphere was more relaxed but equally elegant at the festivals such as Scarborough or the week at Canterbury where the atmosphere was comparable to the late summer race meeting at Goodwood. Such ritualisation, the elevation of a sporting event into a social occasion, was something at which the Edwardians were unsurpassed.'[11]

Taking games to festival venues and other places around the county became an easier proposition, following further improvements in public transport, and the clubs with decent memberships could cover the greater travelling expenses for both their officials and professionals. Travelling to games was also much easier for spectators following the spread of railways into a national network of routes, linking the main centres of population, and running out from the central areas of main cities, like the tentacles of a huge octopus, into the leafy suburbs and rural–urban fringe. Fares were also more affordable in the early twentieth century, and working men could now readily consider spending money on a third-class fare, plus sixpence for gatemoney, and a few pennies on food and beer, to go and watch their county heroes on their treasured days off in the summer.

Therefore staging festival matches would be both financially rewarding and socially satisfying and correct, so in the years before and after the Great War, many counties opted to hold money-spinning festivals rather than have all their cricket played at one ground. This was the case with Essex CCC who were founded in 1876 and had spent their formative years playing on a rented field on the outskirts of Brentwood. It was some distance from a railway station, and doubts were raised about the viability of this venue. The club harboured higher aspirations, and given the success of their metropolitan neighbours, the Essex committee realised that if they were going to compete with Middlesex and Surrey, and achieve first-class status, they needed a headquarters in a more densely populated area than the sleepy county town.[12]

An approach was made to Lord Lyttleton and in 1886 they purchased his ground at Leyton, a developing suburb near the East End of London. At the time, the ground was a mile away from a railway station, had no bus or tram service and had cost Essex CCC £12,000. But it was a shrewd move, and a good example of property speculation, as Leyton became an expanding suburb, and within a few years, the London, Tilbury and Southend Railway opened a station a couple of minutes walk from the Leyton ground, followed by new tram and omnibus services.

Essex CCC were elevated to first-class status in 1894, but the purchase of the Leyton ground increasingly became a millstone around the neck of the club. In the early years of the twentieth century they were indebted to C.E. Green, their chairman and subsequent president, who personally guaranteed their bank and met mortgage payments out of his own pocket. The club badly needed to raise funds, and one way was to attract both more members and people through the gate. With so much competition from Middlesex and Surrey, Essex had to look at alternative venues, and in the early 1900s they considered other venues, further away from the London conurbation. With many popular resorts to the east of the county, it was not long before the Essex committee opted for a festival at a seaside ground, and in 1906 Southchurch Park in Southend-on-Sea was allocated the fixture with Leicestershire. A large crowd of holidaymakers attended the game, and the pretty tree-lined ground subsequently became the venue of an annual festival.

The lure of money – the case of Leicestershire and Worcestershire

Essex was not the only county to be facing economic hardship and substantial debts; in the years before the Great War, Somerset, Worcestershire, Derbyshire and Northamptonshire recorded sizeable deficits. The press had even called for a two-divisional Championship to help those counties in financial difficulties, and a reduced fixture list was certainly one way of saving money. However, after fighting for first-class status, the clubs were desperate not to be demoted, by name, to a second division, and in spirit, a second-class status. Deciding the venue for games therefore became a thorny issue in the committee rooms of some counties, with officials undecided on whether they should save money by playing at a single venue, or gamble by taking games to a new location in the hope of drumming up support.

There were strong economic arguments in favour of centralising activities in a large urban centre, but there were diseconomies of scale as well. By centralising their games at one ground, people in more distant parts of a county were deprived of seeing first-class cricket, and the activities of the county club were perceived as being synonymous with that city or town, rather than with the county as a whole. This may have persuaded some people not to join the county, so a more mobile existence could be financially rewarding and, in the case of Leicestershire, taking cricket around the county certainly helped to alleviate the financial worries.

In 1901 all Leicestershire's games were staged in Leicester at their new ground in Aylestone Road, but by 1921 matches were held at Hinckley and at the delightful Bath Grounds in the market town of Ashby-de-la-Zouch. The Ashby club had hosted many social forms of cricket during the late nineteenth century, and many of the Leicestershire amateurs mixed with members of the leading families of the county in the splendid Bath Grounds at the rear of the town's elegant Royal Hotel.[13]

These tranquil surroundings were in stark contrast to the sombre mood of the Leicestershire committee room in the early 1900s as dark financial clouds hung over the club. The situation had become so severe that in July 1909 the whole of the financial sub-committee resigned after an argument over expenses, and in 1910 a recommendation was put forward to save money by reducing the fixture list. By the start of 1912, Leicestershire had debts totalling £1,500 and a special general meeting was held to discuss what should be done to keep the club in business. Amongst the solutions were the opening of a 'Shilling Fund', agreements to start as many games as possible on Saturdays and to take cricket away from Leicester to outgrounds where there was a well established tradition of cricket and known support for the county.

Consequently, Ashby-de-la-Zouch was allocated the fixture with Derbyshire in 1912 – a shrewd move, given that the ground was close to the border with Derbyshire, and as a result, many supporters from over the border travelled to Ashby to see the game. Over the next few years, the Bath Grounds were the venue for this local derby and a cricket festival. The games continued to be well attended, reducing the club's financial worries, and as a result, the Leicestershire committee explored the possibilities of taking more cricket around the county, and by the 1920s Coalville, Loughborough and Hinckley were staging Championship fixtures.

Worcestershire was another county whose locational decisions were affected by financial worries during the first part of the twentieth century. The club had been elevated to first-class status in 1899, and were eager to develop their ground at New Road, Worcester into a decent headquarters. But the county's membership base was very small, with just 798 subscribers in 1899. This had risen to 1,153 by 1902, but even so, the club had debts of £780 and the situation was precarious enough for special fund-raising events to be held.[14] In an attempt to boost membership in the east of the county, the club allocated the 1905 fixture with Leicestershire to the Amblecote ground in Stourbridge. However, the debts continued to rise and membership started to drop, as the club had several modest seasons, playing as few professionals as possible in order to save money.

The Worcester club had entered a vicious cycle, and unless more money could be raised, their playing fortunes were unlikely to improve. With the club's whole future at stake, they held a special general meeting in 1908, and amongst the solutions proposed was staging all their games on the Earl of Dudley's ground in Tipton Road, Dudley. The Earl had been a kindly benefactor to the county club, and in the late nineteenth century, he had promoted cricket in Worcestershire by staging matches in Dudley against wandering England elevens, as well as fund-raising matches for the benefit of men who had been blinded in his limestone mines. The Earl had also spent an estimated £5,000 on the Tipton Road ground, although his motives were not entirely philanthropic, and like Lord Londesborough in Scarborough, he was aware of the money to be made from staging top-class cricket. Indeed, the Earl also held grander ambitions than just providing a home for Worcestershire CCC. This was shown in a report in the *Daily Herald* which commented that 'on completion of the pavilion, the whole area will be fully equipped and fit for even a Test match in due time'.[15]

To leave New Road and move lock, stock and barrel to Dudley would have been a very radical step, and a switch to the east of the county was one that the Worcester-based gentlemen successfully fought against. In 1908 a group of wealthy patrons from the area, plus Lord Cobham and Lord Plymouth donated sizeable sums to the county's funds in order to keep New Road as the club's base. Even so, the club's financial worries did not go away and by the middle of 1913, its liabilities stood at around £4,000. Lord Cobham, ably supported by the Earl of Dudley and Lord Plymouth, acted again to save the county by launching an appeal. Cash was also obtained from other counties, and this together with the appeal funds, saw the club survive into the 1920s.

The influence of the Earl continued after the Great War as the club steadily became financially stronger, but even so, they were hardly in a position to turn down the offer of further financial support from the industrial centres elsewhere in the county, and they took games to outgrounds at Stourbridge and Bourneville, as well as the grounds at Kidderminster and Dudley owned by the Earl.[16]

The 1951 pattern

The trend for taking cricket around the county continued apace during the inter-war period and by 1951, 72 locations were used for county fixtures. As the following shows, 13 of the 17 counties were now in Group C; only two counties were in Group A, as during the inter-war period, Surrey, Warwickshire and Northamptonshire had opted to stage games away from their county bases:

1. Group A – those with centralised fixtures: Middlesex, at Lord's; Nottinghamshire, at Trent Bridge.
2. Group B – those who played most of their games at a central headquarters with one or two games at outgrounds: Lancashire; Surrey.
3. Group C – those who took cricket to many venues throughout the county: Yorkshire, Sussex, Kent, Hampshire, Gloucestershire, Derbyshire, Somerset, Leicestershire, Worcestershire, Essex, Glamorgan, Northamptonshire, Warwickshire.

The number of outgrounds used by the counties in Group C had also increased – Somerset were now using six venues, Yorkshire, Essex and Glamorgan were all using seven, whilst Kent were staging games on ten grounds. Amongst the club grounds to be added to the cricket calendar during the late 1920s and 1930s were Blackburn, Buxton, Folkestone, Gillingham, Ilkeston, Kettering, Preston, and Yeovil, whilst the school wickets at Oakham and Downside Abbey hosted games for Leicestershire and Somerset respectively.

Despite these changes, the rank–size relationships from the inter-war period still remained as many of the counties still played the majority of their fixtures at their headquarters grounds. So the relationships (shown in Figure 22) for Gloucestershire, Derbyshire and Sussex remained (Figure 23). But in the case of Essex, the hierarchical pattern which had been established back in 1921, had completely disappeared by 1951, now that the club had fragmented their fixture list by taking games to many settlements.

Most of the rank–size relationships were still in existence as the majority of the counties played a large chunk of their fixtures at a metropolitan base or high order centre, with a number of annual games at smaller towns and outgrounds. An element of centrality, with a hierarchical arrangement of fixtures, therefore existed in many counties despite the dispersal of fixtures.[17]

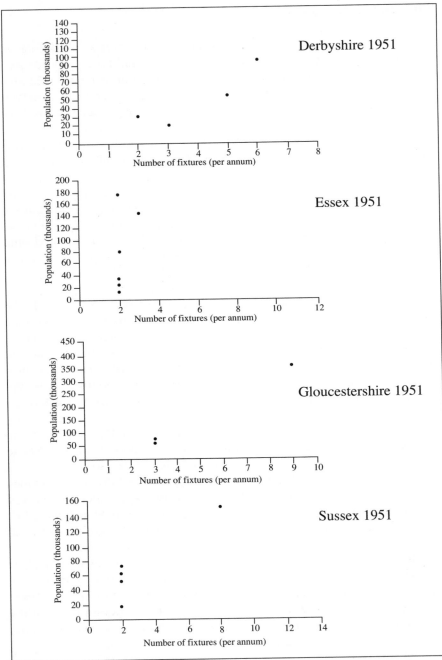

Figure 23 Rank–size relationships for Gloucestershire, Derbyshire, Sussex and Essex, 1951

The cricketing caravan

There were a host of economic reasons to explain the popularity of dispersing games to a number of settlements. Even so, there were also fundamental cricketing ones with the move away from a central base being related to the increase in fixtures during the inter-war period, as it was virtually impossible to maintain a good standard of wicket at some headquarters where the square was quite small. As shown by the example of Leicestershire and Essex, taking cricket to a number of grounds was also the result of clubs actively seeking more support, new members and probably a few favours from people both inside and outside their county boundaries. It was also a case of supply meeting demand as the inter-war, and immediate post-war period saw record crowds at many county grounds. When Warwickshire won the Championship in 1951 an aggregate of 43,000 people attended the three days of the match with Yorkshire – a record for county cricket, which broke the previous best of 32,091 set in Warwickshire's previous match at Edgbaston against Lancashire! As Charles Bray, the former Essex captain wrote in 1950, 'the public has shown amazing interest and a desire to watch the game. Those with money to spend have been limited in how they can spend it. Watching county cricket has been an easy and pleasant way of spending a free day.'[18]

This almost insatiable desire to watch county cricket after the Second World War was also in part a reaction to having had no proper cricket since 1939. As Rowland Bowen stated, 'for the first few years, there were the late afternoons and evenings of the young pre-war players whom everyone wanted to see in their prime or something near it. Another was the reaction from being in uniform and absent for long periods abroad – to sit in the sun and watch placidly the run-stealers flickering to and fro was pleasure enough.'[19]

Warwickshire, Surrey and Northamptonshire were the three counties during the inter-war period to adopt a more nomadic approach to their allocation of fixtures and to play fewer games at their large headquarters. In the case of Warwickshire and Surrey, who were hosting Test cricket, there were diseconomies of scale for the county to centralise their activities, and it was not in the club's interest to overuse their best wickets by focusing their activities at Edgbaston or The Oval. Warwickshire had taken the occasional match to club grounds used by Leamington, Nuneaton Town or Coventry and North Warwicks CC where many of the county's players had learnt their cricket before joining Warwickshire. Between 1925 and 1932 they experimented with annual games in Coventry at both the Butts ground and the Morris Motors ground, as well as at Nuneaton's Griff and Coton ground in the extreme north-east of the county. This cost the club around £100 more than they spent when staging matches at Edgbaston, but it kept the Warwickshire flag flying around the county, and at clubs where future players were being groomed.[20]

For Surrey CCC, centralising activities at The Oval had been a contractual necessity as they had agreed with the landowners, the Duchy of Cornwall, that 50 days of cricket would be staged each year at the Kennington ground. This did not leave much room for manoeuvre, but with the financial security of being a Test match venue, and the presence of many small grounds in the South London suburbs, the Surrey officials began to consider taking games away from The Oval. In the 1930s, the committee became aware of the demand for a festival to be staged in the south of the county. These areas in the rural–urban fringe were the homes of many members who commuted on a daily basis into the City and the dockland areas, and would actively support the county coming to play literally in their backyard.

There were many well established clubs and decent wickets to choose from outside the metropolitan areas and in 1938 the Surrey committee allocated the game with neighbours Hampshire to the prosperous county town and cathedral city of Guildford.[21] The first two days of the match saw an attendance of 10,000, and it was not surprising that *Wisden's* correspondent commented how 'the introduction of first-class cricket to the county town proved extremely popular and was a financial success'.[22] A festival air was provided by the Band of the Second Battalion of the Queen's Royal Regiment, who played during the intervals, and the success of this game prompted Surrey to play an annual match at the Woodbridge Road ground, which has subsequently become a well established feature of the county's fixture list.

For Northamptonshire, taking some cricket away from their Northampton base became of prime importance as the club lurched from one financial crisis to another during the inter-war period. The county had the smallest population of any of the first-class clubs, so following their elevation to the Championship in 1905, it was not surprising that their coffers were emptying. The club heavily relied on frequent public appeals and on several occasions there were grave doubts about whether the club could continue. However, the main factor behind their survival was the support and goodwill of Alfred Cockerill, who in 1923 handed over the Wantage Road ground to the county at a peppercorn rent for 1,000 years.[23]

Even so, the Northamptonshire club still struggled on the field, and a string of modest results, plus falling membership, led to a crisis meeting being held in 1929 to discuss the long term viability of the club. Like the other counties, one of the solutions to drum up more interest was a suggestion to use the home fixtures in a more imaginative way and to consider staging special festivals elsewhere in the county where support for cricket was known to exist. Consequently, Peterborough, Kettering, Rushden and Wellingborough were added to the county's fixture list.

Other counties became even more nomadic during the inter-war period. In the case of Somerset, this was still a function of their widely distributed population. For many years, annual games had been played in Bath and in the southern suburbs of Bristol,[24] but in the inter-war period the club expanded their number of grounds, firstly by adding the popular seaside resort of Weston-super-Mare. Somerset had first visited the Clarence Park ground in 1914, and the large attendances at games in the 1920s, meant that Weston became a regular feature in the county's calendar. Even so, the ground had a few critics, especially as the wicket, sited in a public park and with a thin veneer of soil on top of sand, had a tendency to crumble and frequently assisted the Somerset spinners. However, the sizeable crowds encouraged the committee to turn a deaf ear to the protests about the 'sporty' wicket.

Somerset also boosted their gate receipts by regular visits to Yeovil, Frome and Wells, where the lack of sightscreens and a decent scoreboard added a rustic charm and novelty, with bowling changes and other details announced at regular intervals over loudspeakers from the scorer's box. The intimacy was boosted by the small boundaries of the Wells ground, and Arthur Wellard, Somerset's big hitting batsman, often found them just to his liking. In 1936, he hit a rapid 86 against Derbyshire, hitting 8 fours and 7 sixes – five of which were in succession off Tom Armstrong.[25] This record still remains today, and it is one of cricket's most enduring characteristics that small places such as Wells and Weston-super-Mare still appear prominently in the record books alongside larger and more established centres such as Lord's and Old Trafford.

The players and supporters of Essex also enjoyed their travels around the county during the inter-war period. This had initially consisted of visits to Southend, Colchester and Leyton, but during the 1920s attendances at Leyton started to fall away. In 1933 the ground was sold to the Metropolitan Police, and a new base was established at Chelmsford. But the club's membership remained small, and in order to boost interest, the Essex committee decided to have a series of weekly festivals in the London suburbs at Ilford, Romford, and Brentwood, as well as at the seaside venues of Southend and Clacton. This meant that together with the Colchester week and games at their new base in Chelmsford, Essex were using no fewer than seven grounds in 1951, and their officials were spending countless hours overseeing the conversion of club grounds and public parks into first-class venues. As J.M. Kilburn and Norman de Mesquita wrote, 'by ingenious improvisation and organisation, they transported not only players but also the trappings of presentation – scoreboard, printing press, seating, secretarial offices and boundary boards. From seaside to inland centre, from public park to private club, the cavalcade of cricket moved down the lanes to the financial benefit of the county club and the far wider spread of public interest in the game.'[26]

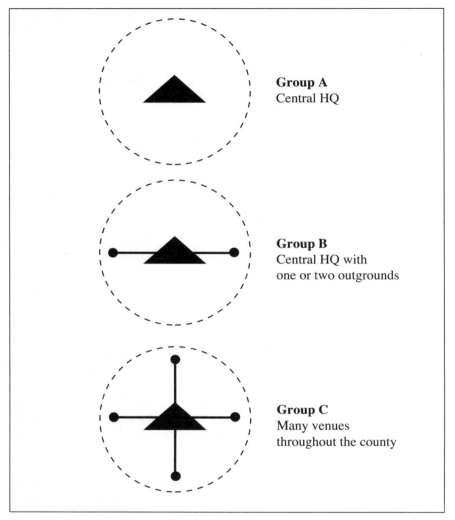

Figure 24 Locational models of County Championship venues

A summative model of county locations up to 1951

Figure 24 summarises the locational trends of the counties during the first half of the twentieth century. At the turn of the century, most of the counties were in either Group A or B, but new patterns were established in response to economic and social trends, and to the greater mobility of both players and the general public alike during the inter-war period. The clubs

TABLE 6
NUMBER OF PAYING SPECTATORS ATTENDING THE HOME FIRST ELEVEN MATCHES
PLAYED BY THE FIRST-CLASS COUNTIES, 1934–36

County	1934	1935	1936
Derbyshire	82,279	89,585	76,077
Essex	n.a.	75,948	73,801
Glamorgan	68,972	92,038	53,111
Gloucestershire	78,440	52,842	62,230
Hampshire	77,749	57,325	79,251
Kent	113,922	97,410	74,505
Lancashire	107,999	87,650	93,094
Leicestershire	44,980	47,175	31,795
Middlesex	120,536	67,226	110,532
Northamptonshire	37,230	30,429	25,540
Nottinghamshire	65,145	72,749	73,882
Somerset	49,447	55,931	64,170
Surrey	162,923	128,914	129,940
Sussex	102,067	78,759	68,447
Warwickshire	80,762	86,853	38,670
Worcestershire	50,722	34,067	33,932
Yorkshire	177,155	175,790	153,383

Source: Findlay Commission, 1937.

still retained their headquarters in large centres, but more counties entered the 1950s with a pattern of fixtures in Group C, with popular festivals and cricket weeks at outgrounds in smaller settlements.

Finding a lucrative venue must have been quite satisfying for the county treasurers especially as all county gates fluctuated during the 1930s[27] (see Table 6). Even so, making a maximum profit was not of prime importance and clubs revealed their sporting motives, by endeavouring to cover costs, rather than maximise profits.

Therefore, it is possible to agree with Jack Williams that 'first-class cricket was not highly commercialised between the wars. Neither the MCC nor any county club was a limited liability company with even a nominal obligation to make profits for shareholders. It is likely that many felt that cricket, and especially county cricket, offered few opportunities for risk-taking or profiteering, but the importance extended to a sport which was barely economically viable is further evidence that English culture was far from being governed by values sympathetic to the remorseless accumulation of profit.'[28]

Taking cricket to the people was therefore of paramount importance, and this was clearly evident in an article in *The Cricketer* magazine in 1954. In explaining how the counties drew up the fixture list, the article stressed how 'amongst typical considerations which affect the issue are county weeks and festivals, Lancashire "wakes" and Bradford holidays, availability of grounds and the encroachment of football in the summer at both ends of the season. Important fixtures are between bordering counties, and it is of consequence that Kent and Sussex should play their games against each other at Tunbridge Wells and Hastings, respectively. Surrey like to play Sussex and Hampshire at Guildford in alternate years, while Somerset emphasise the importance of Glamorgan playing at Weston-super-Mare during that Festival. Colliery holidays anywhere and similar occasions at Kettering and Coventry are matters of great consequence to the counties concerned.'[29]

People clearly came first, and it was on this geographical framework that the county game evolved further as it entered the age of real commercialisation and one-day cricket during the second half of the twentieth century.

The Location of County Cricket in the Commercial Age, 1951–1991

The bubble bursts

The inter-war period saw a rise in the importance of economic factors for the location of county fixtures, but the game was still chiefly being run along Victorian lines as a sport dependent on its patrons and its fans. During the 1950s and 1960s, there were further changes to these geographical patterns, especially as public interest started to wane, and the British public found new ways of spending their leisure time during the summer months. Table 7 shows how most counties suffered a sharp decline in gross gates between 1951 and 1961, with 12 of the counties grossing smaller gates in 1961 than in 1951.[1] Some of the decline was quite sizeable, with the gates recorded by nine counties – Derbyshire, Glamorgan, Gloucestershire, Lancashire, Middlesex, Northamptonshire, Warwickshire, Worcestershire and Yorkshire – all falling by over £500 during this period.

TABLE 7
GROSS GATES (£) OF EACH COUNTY, 1951–61

Year	1951	1952	1953	1954	1955	1956	1957	1958	1959	1960	1961
Derby	1,018	1,671	1,071	1,458	1,105	991	1,565	725	1,679	1,134	452
Essex	1,410	1,260	978	670	690	942	1,381	888	1,448	1,042	1,120
Glam	1,397	1,394	N/a	1,043	627	909	666	871	918	663	533
Glos	1,821	1,264	1,722	1,064	1,396	1,101	1,461	682	1,406	1,079	951
Hants	681	772	1,052	1,483	1,756	1,030	1,284	1,128	1,713	849	2,224
Kent	1,370	1,183	1,903	1,678	2,013	1,392	2,017	2,800	1,998	1,679	1,926
Lancs	4,548	4,903	4,629	2,826	4,435	3,673	3,652	1,696	3,986	7,917	3,360
Leics	536	1130	1,186	578	1,150	994	413	816	606	371	398
Middx	3,039	2,416	5,848	3,267	3,307	2,409	2,714	3,342	2,640	3,291	2,440
N'hants	840	970	719	963	931	783	686	714	550	692	438
Notts	862	1,220	1,743	991	2,452	1,809	927	1,096	1,278	1,203	822
Somst	1,096	939	1,069	900	910	972	1,552	1,599	1,031	1,478	1,490
Surrey	2,695	3,624	3,178	2,439	5,253	2,015	3,321	3,061	3,233	2,487	2,330
Warw	3,381	1,741	1,415	1,460	1,728	829	1,223	718	1,842	896	726
Worcs	1,276	906	863	553	745	669	822	897	1,071	593	623
Yorks	1,690	4,306	4,171	3,516	4,317	4,484	2,423	2,630	2,885	3,367	2,161

Note: No data were available for Sussex CCC during this period or Glamorgan CCC in 1953.
Source: *Cricket Quarterly*, (1963), 49.

It had been a very different story in 1950 when 58,530 spectators paid £4,326 to watch the contest between Middlesex and Surrey. This was in excess of the cumulative gross gate receipts of all the counties in 1961. Indeed, the years in the immediate aftermath of the Second World War saw vast crowds at county grounds, The programme of 30 days cricket at Lord's in 1945 had drawn over 400,000 people, and in 1947 2,200,910 paying customers watched County Championship games.[2] But the honeymoon period was soon over as the wheels started to fall off the county caravan as it meandered to a host of places, both large and small.

As the economy grew, so did inflation, and the costs of running a county club steadily rose in the post-war period. No longer could county treasurers turn to Sir Home Gordon's adage that the annual cost of running a county club would be around £10,000. By the 1950s a figure nearer £60,000, and rising, was closer to the mark. The rise in per capita incomes, especially those of manual workers, also had an impact on county clubs. Previously, a professional cricketer could earn twice as much as a blue-collar worker, but this was no longer the case as the latter saw their salaries and terms of employment improve. Clubs therefore had to pay more to professionals in order to make a cricketer's job an attractive proposition. The economic recovery also meant a drop in the unemployment figures and a rise in the economically active population meant that fewer people had time on their hands that they could while away at a county ground.

Social factors also played a role in addition to these economic ones, as the 1950s saw important changes in leisure and holiday activity, with families looking for a United Kingdom holiday being attracted to the new caravan parks or Butlin-style holiday camps. There was also the start of a trend to overseas holidays, and as a result, those people who might have gone to Scarborough or Blackpool with their family during the inter-war period were now venturing *en famille* to somewhat more exotic locations nearer the shores of the Mediterranean. This may have improved the children's grasp of the French language, but it meant many young boys learnt new leisure patterns during the summer months, rather than watching and idolising Hobbs, Hammond or Woolley as their fathers had done at an early age. And when these young boys subsequently became fathers themselves, they continued the trend in the 1970s and 1980s for a summer exodus abroad to the package holiday capitals on the Costa del Sol, the Algarve, the Greek Islands or in Florida.

In short, fewer people were catching the cricket bug, despite a steady rise in the population and the post-war baby boom. Sports such as tennis, golf, badminton and squash came within the reach of more people, and where once there was the prospect of football in the winter, cricket in the summer, and an evening at the dance hall or cinema, there was now a greater choice. New leisure habits and pastimes were introduced, fuelled by the images now seen daily on the television set, and with greater personal mobility, cars opened up new avenues for people to follow. The negative and unadventerous play which some captains advocated was hardly the sort of carrot to attract people in their droves to watch county cricket, and the number of spectators attending Championship games fell away during the 1950s and 1960s as games frequently meandered slowly to a draw. By 1961 less than 4,000 people on average were paying to watch a county game.

As Jim Laker observed, 'the pace of life had begun to increase. No longer were people content to sit in the sun and while away an entire Saturday. They looked for new avenues to explore and many thousands found a new way of spending leisure time. Possibly the single biggest factor was the motor car, a luxury even in post-war years, but a necessity as life and time moved on. Of all the major sports, cricket, which demanded so much time, was the principal sufferer. Crowds dwindled to a hard core of real enthusiasts; officials and players became desperate and this appeared to reflect in their performances. Cricket went on the defensive, and the game as a whole reached its lowest ebb. Something had to be done to give the game a shot in the arm; to fill the grounds again; to increase the tempo of cricket in line with the modern way of living. The demand was for all-action entertainment.'[3] It was clearly time for the structure and pattern of county cricket to change.

Calls for reform

There had been calls for a reform prior to the post-war slump, especially as many other sports had already changed or adapted their previous structure. In 1937 the Findlay Commission estimated that county cricket was being run at an annual loss of £27,000, and suggested a reduction in the number of counties and standardisation in the number of fixtures.[4] It was thrown out by cricket's introspective and conservative leaders, who adopted a safety first approach as cricket provided a cosy reminder of the golden era, and the counties continued to play an unequal number of fixtures, often carefully selecting. attractive or slightly weaker opponents.

A more revolutionary suggestion was made by a working party in 1944,[5] who advocated a regional split for the counties into the following sub-groups:

| North: | Derbyshire, Lancashire, Yorkshire and Nottinghamshire |
| Midlands: | Leicestershire, Northamptonshire, Warwickshire and Worcestershire |

South-West: Glamorgan, Gloucestershire, Hampshire and
                Somerset
South-East: Middlesex, Essex, Sussex, Surrey and Kent

But when the county game restarted in 1946, the MCC threw out the working party's suggestions, and opted for the status quo pattern, as a tangible sign that things were getting back to normal, with the county game continuing in its outmoded form. But it also proved to be a missed opportunity as the county game entered the next stage in its maturation still with vestiges of youth, like a boy entering senior school still wearing short trousers!

The rapid fall in the number of spectators was clear evidence that society was changing, and the rows of empty seats eventually stirred the MCC into action. In 1956 they set up a committee under the chairmanship of H.S. Altham to investigate the decline in gate money recorded by the county clubs. A further committee was set up in 1960, and like the Altham group, amongst its many recommendations was the introduction of a knockout competition based on limited overs matches.[6] There were a few doubts raised about a knockout competition, chiefly the additional expense of transporting cricketers around the country for just a one-day game. Others were concerned about the problems of bad weather interfering with games, and no guarantee of large gates. A few critics also pointed to how the knockout cricket cup promoted 90 years earlier by the MCC had been an abysmal failure, but many people felt that the time was right to introduce limited overs games.

One of the strongest advocates for a limited overs competition was Mike Turner, the secretary of Leicestershire. He fervently believed in the value of one-day cricket, and in 1962 he arranged an experimental competition in the Midlands between his county, Derbyshire, Nottinghamshire and Northamptonshire. The final between Leicestershire and Derbyshire produced a closely fought contest, with 493 runs being scored without ever making a mockery of the game.[7] This helped to allay many fears and in November 1962 Gillette agreed to sponsor the knockout competition, starting in 1963, initially with each team batting for a maximum of 65 overs. It was subsequently reduced to 60 overs and now 50 overs, with sponsorship taken over by National Westminster Bank PLC and subsequently the Cheltenham and Gloucester Building Society, this remains the premier one-day competition.

Nineteen sixty-three was also the first season when there were no distinctions between the amateur and the paid players, as everyone became professional cricketers. This was another of the recommendations to stem from the investigations by the MCC's sub-committees. On the one hand, it made cricket more professional in substance and attitude, and the prospect of a county contract helped to attract more people into the county game. But with higher wage bills, and no more amateurs who could pay their own hotel bills, some cash-strapped counties had to reduce even further their playing staffs. This caused some players to become even more introspective, as a series of low scores could mean a spell in the 2nd XI, and the threat of the end-of-season axe, as clubs strove to save money.

The mid-1960s also saw another change, with the addition of a series of exhibition games to the cricketing calendar, with county sides playing a star-studded International Cavaliers XI. These limited overs matches were usually held on Sundays, which had been the traditional day of rest for county cricketers. A programme was drawn up by the sponsors Rothmans, with games staged, whenever possible, in aid of the county beneficiary, or alternatively a local or national charity. The players who represented the Cavaliers were household names, including Denis Compton, Godfrey Evans, Fred Trueman or Ted Dexter, plus Graham Pollock of South Africa and West Indians Gary Sobers, Clive Lloyd and Lance Gibbs. With such a star-studded eleven turning out, these games drew large crowds, much to the delight of the county beneficiary and sums in the region of £3,000 were handed to Warwickshire's Tom Cartwright and Yorkshire's Ken Taylor after games at Edgbaston and Huddersfield.[8]

Rothmans also arranged television coverage, and the entertainment produced by these friendly games, generated decent viewing figures. In addition, the Cavaliers over a three-year period were able to hand over to the MCC a sum of just under £10,000. As Jim Laker observed 'it was patently obvious that if the MCC were to sit down and organise a Sunday competition on a national scale, involving every county playing each Sunday, plus substantial sponsorship and television coverage, they were sure to be on a winner. They were also bound to have the support of the counties, for whereas the Cavaliers were attracting an average gate of say 10,000 per Sunday with their solitary fixture, this weekly estimate could be multiplied eightfold if all the counties were involved each week and the financial benefits would obviously be much greater.'[9] Consequently, the MCC started to plan a national competition, and accepted a generous offer of sponsorship from another tobacco company, John Player and Son, and in 1969 the John Player Sunday League was introduced, with each county taking part in a 40 overs competition.

County cricket had therefore fully entered the new age of commercialisation, with county clubs gaining additional sources of income through corporate sponsorship. Right from the earliest days, they had looked to extraneous finance, and in the past had supplemented gate returns with cash from private patronage, philanthropists, public appeals and a share of Test match takings. In the 1950s new sources of income were introduced, initially with a shilling-a-week football pool and other lotteries.

Leicestershire, Worcestershire, Glamorgan and Warwickshire all introduced lotteries in the early 1950s, and by 1964, when Yorkshire finally succumbed, all the county treasurers were accepting donations from supporters organisations and football pools. The fact that the actual playing of cricket was no longer the sole source of income had important consequences for the geographic allocation of the games, both first-class and limited overs

The pattern in 1971

On the face of it, the pattern for first-class games in 1971 appeared very similar to that in 1951:

1. Group A – those with centralised fixtures: Middlesex, at Lord's; Leicestershire, at Leicester; Warwickshire, at Edgbaston.
2. Group B – those who played most of their games at a central headquarters with one or two games at outgrounds: Surrey.
3. Group C – those who took cricket to many venues throughout the county: Yorkshire, Sussex, Kent, Hampshire, Gloucestershire, Derbyshire, Somerset, Worcestershire, Essex, Glamorgan, Northamptonshire, Lancashire, Nottinghamshire.

The most popular category was still Group C, but by 1971, the number of outgrounds had declined. Most counties now had one main centre for Championship games, with two or three outgrounds. The headquarters was in the largest centre, with the exception of Essex, Kent, and Somerset, where an anachronistic pattern still existed with higher order settlements getting fewer games than their smaller counterparts.[10]

The rank–size graphs give a clear indication of the trend for playing more Championship games at higher order centres, as shown in Figure 25 for Hampshire, Gloucestershire, Northamptonshire, Nottinghamshire and Sussex. Even Yorkshire, who had been one of the traditionally nomadic counties had opted for more games in larger centres.

The commercial age therefore saw a clear trend for a more sharply defined hierarchical arrangement, focusing Championship activity at the county headquarters. As far as the limited overs games were concerned, the only major change to the groupings above was that Lancashire moved to Group A by staging all their one-day games at Old Trafford. All the other counties opted for greater dispersal, and a number of smaller settlements staged county games, including Harlow, Purfleet, Lydney, Brackley and Yeovil.

Therefore two contrasting trends operated in 1971 on the geography of county cricket – one for the centralisation of Championship fixtures at a headquarters ground, and the other, the dispersal of other games, especially one-day games, to a small number of outgrounds.

Creation of modern headquarters for first-class cricket

The most tangible indicators of the rise in commercial interests were the county headquarters themselves, and from the 1950s a number of counties have developed their headquarters as money-making ventures with cricket being a form of corporate entertainment. Before the 1950s, county grounds had rows of deckchairs, nestling close to the boundary ropes, or 'free' seats in covered enclosures. The modern ground now included hospitality boxes, sited behind advertising boards and executive suites where the cheap seats had once been. Under health and safety legislation, there were also special areas for the disabled, to say nothing of adequate press facilities and car parking spaces. The stadiums also included indoor schools, club shops and various fast-food outlets, all of which brought in cash for the county club during summer and winter, with hospitality facilities being used for conferences, weddings and other off-season functions.

The move towards centralisation was therefore an example of an economy of scale, in an attempt to gain maximum income. This maximiser behaviour is best exemplified by looking at Warwickshire and Leicestershire, which had both previously been in Group C. Even in the early 1960s, Leicestershire were still visiting Ashby-de-la-Zouch, Loughborough and Hinckley, but this was becoming increasingly expensive and in 1963 after a deficit of £12,874, the committee decided that they could no longer afford the expensive weeks at these outgrounds, and a decision was made to focus activity at the Grace Road ground.

The prime mover behind this decision was Leicestershire secretary Mike Turner, who subsequently became recognised as the prototype cricket administrator of the modern age – someone who realised that running a county would become increasingly expensive, and someone who appreciated that the crowds would not always be there. He argued that Leicestershire needed a sound financial base, and a ground whose infrastructure was sufficient to attract members, casual spectators, sponsors and commercial hosts. Some piecemeal improvements took place in the early 1960s, but since the ground was owned by Leicester Education Department, little headway was made. Consequently, Turner oversaw the purchase of the ground in 1966 from the education authorities for £24,500, and in the following years an £80,000 building improvement scheme was undertaken, comprising a new pavilion, office complex and a covered seating enclosure. The money to pay for all of this came from the Leicestershire football pool, which over a ten-year period raised around £100,000.[11]

Cash from football pools was also the source of funding behind the extensive ground improvements at Edgbaston. In 1953 the Warwickshire

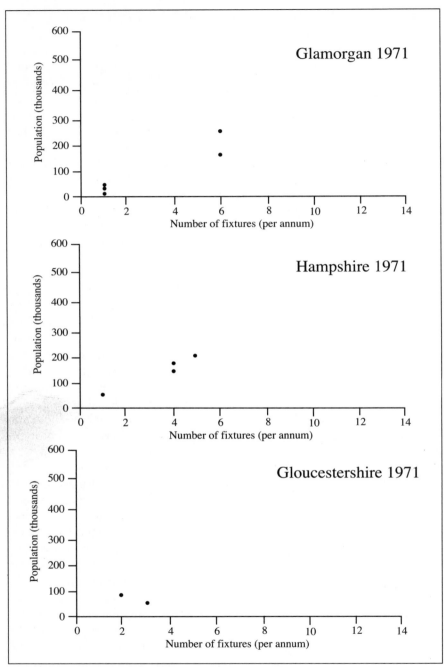

Figure 25   Rank–size relationships for Glamorgan, Hampshire and Gloucestershire, 1971

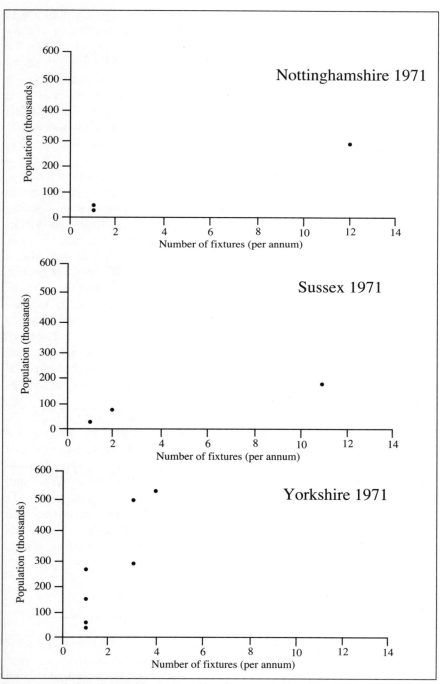

Rank–size relationships for Nottinghamshire, Sussex and Yorkshire, 1971

County Cricket Club Supporters Association ('The Warwick Pool') was formed and under the leadership of Ray Hitchcock, the former county player, the Association during the next 20 years raised over £1 million for the Warwickshire club towards ground development and building projects. Even so, the Warwickshire officials had a few reservations at first, 'that it was an undignified method of raising funds and that the officials of a supporters club would undoubtedly in time wish to influence County Club policy'. Assurances were subsequently given that the Association would be an independent organisation, and after much head-scratching, the club became involved with commercial fund-raising.[12]

Their scepticism proved unfounded, as by the end of the first winter the Association had raised £46,000. Work began with new wings to the pavilion and an indoor school, followed by a new Pavilion suite, dressing room area and members' room. All was finished by the time Test cricket returned to Edgbaston in 1957 after a break of 27 years. Further improvements saw other covered areas of seating, restaurants and a modern press facility, in addition to a Social Club with snooker rooms, dance floor and two bars. The Edgbaston complex became the envy of other county clubs, who tried to emulate the Midlands county. As Jack Bannister commented, 'many clubs, in and outside cricket, vainly tried to copy the most successful post-war fund-raising scheme in sport, but there was never a magical formula to adopt. It was the case of the right person, Hitchcock, having the right ideas at the right time in the right industrial climate to launch a scheme which, like most successful concepts, was simple and yet appealing to the public.'[13]

By 1972 the Warwick Pools had raised over £2 million for cricket as a whole, including nearly £400,000 for other county clubs looking for capital to spend on ground improvements. The Association owed its success to good organisation and a sphere of influence that spread out to Wolverhampton, Burton-on-Trent, Coventry, Stratford-upon-Avon and Stourbridge, as well as supporters in Oxfordshire and Leicestershire. In turn, this economy of scale allowed Edgbaston to become one of the main Test grounds in the country, and helped Warwickshire display its commitment to maximising the improved facilities by staging all its Championship games at Edgbaston.

Conquests and colonisation

Whilst concentrating activity at one centre could lead to economies of scale, there were disadvantages as well, and the post-war period saw a new type of locational behaviour as counties increasingly staged games in adjoining districts outside their geographical boundaries. This policy of conquest and colonisation applied to Glamorgan CCC, who in the words of Jack Morgan 'started to serve a county and grew to represent a nation'.[14] The Welsh county had initially staged their Championship matches at Cardiff and Swansea, but over time they took first-class and limited overs games to many parts of the Principality, including venues in the old counties of Monmouthshire, Caernarvonshire and Cardiganshire, latterly named Gwent, Gwynedd and Dyfed, respectively.

Such a wandering existence began as a necessity on several counts – firstly, the club did not own any ground of its own, and instead operated from 1921 as tenants at a number of locations, including Cardiff Arms Park and the St Helens ground in Swansea. Secondly, the club initially had representations from the west and the east of the county, and it was felt that the number of games should be split between these two areas.

During the club's first few seasons, the novelty of first-class cricket attracted decent crowds to Arms Park and St Helens, but the club's modest membership meant that the finances were never healthy. Like some of the other counties, this meant that a smaller number of professionals could be employed, and consequently, results suffered. The financial situation was grave enough in 1932 for calls to wind up the club, but club captain Maurice Turnbull and his close friend Johnnie Clay thought otherwise, and began a fund-raising campaign. They also suggested that the club should fly the flag around South Wales in order to drum up more support. The club had already tried to boost membership by staging fixtures from 1926 at Ynysangharad Park in Pontypridd, and briefly at Cowbridge, where the standard of the wickets was poor.[15]

In the mid-1930s other venues were considered, including Stradey Park in Llanelli, where the county staged the 1933 fixture with Worcestershire. *Wisden* commented how the match 'proved a very successful venture, for apart from the win by an innings, Carmarthenshire folk showed so much appreciation of being given the chance to see first-class cricket that on the first day the attendance exceeded 4,000, whilst gate receipts amounted to exactly £200'.[16] The success of this experiment meant that the county allocated regular fixtures to Llanelli, and also went to other grounds including The Gnoll in Neath, where in 1948 a crowd of 12,000 saw the match with Warwickshire.

A third reason for Glamorgan becoming a nomadic county was that they amalgamated in July 1934 with Monmouthshire, whose troubled existence as a Minor County led them to approach their neighbours for a merger.[17] There were many reasons why Glamorgan agreed to the proposal – firstly, it allowed all the very promising players in Monmouthshire to qualify for Glamorgan, thereby opening up a new nursery of talent. Secondly, it further enhanced Glamorgan's identity as representing all of South Wales, and thirdly, it allowed them to enter a second eleven in the

Minor County Championship, thereby grooming their raw talent. The fourth advantage was that Glamorgan agreed to stage first-class cricket in Monmouthshire, and this allowed them access to new grounds in Newport and Ebbw Vale where there were both decent wickets and a pool of support to tap into. This was the case when visiting Rodney Parade, Newport, where a large crowd watched the 1939 match with Gloucestershire, seeing the visitors amass 557–4, Wally Hammond making 302 before Glamorgan replied with 505–5 and Emrys Davies unbeaten on 287.

Therefore, Glamorgan had a long tradition of taking cricket to the people of South Wales, and in the mid-1960s they looked for other areas to conquest and colonise. The leading figure in the affairs of the club was Wilf Wooller, the former Welsh rugby international, and county captain from 1947 until 1960. He had been brought up in North Wales in Rhos-on-sea, and had learnt his cricket at both Rydal School and the Colwyn Bay club.[18] The ground had staged many fund-raising and benefit matches after the Second World War, and given the success of other seaside festivals, Wooller suggested to the county that they venture to the North Wales coast. In 1966 Colwyn Bay hosted the match with Derbyshire, and with a crowd of over 4,000 attending both of the first two days play, the Rhos ground was allocated an annual fixture. On occasions this has meant that the Glamorgan players have had to travel further from their homes in South Wales to Colwyn Bay, than their opponents based in northern England!

However, their conquests of new areas did not always meet with success. In the early 1950s, the Steel Company of Wales approached the county about using its new ground alongside the Margam works. The prospect of financial support from the company resulted in their 1953 friendly with The Gentlemen of Ireland being held at the Margam ground, followed in the early 1960s, by four other first-class games. However, the ground lacked covered seating, and with smoke drifting over from the adjoining strip mill, it was a very unreal location for county cricket. As Jack Morgan wrote in 1963, 'perhaps the strangest thing of all was that on Tuesday a first-class match was played on a ground completely deserted. Glamorgan must seriously consider whether it is worthwhile giving Margam another fixture. The ground is not only exposed to the weather but is inconveniently situated.'[19] The gate receipts bore out his point – £70 was taken on the first day, £35 on the second and nothing at all on the final day. Glamorgan could simply not risk taking another game to Margam, not even a limited overs game, especially when the games at St Helens, overlooking Swansea Bay and Mumbles Head, were well attended and popular with tourists to South Wales.

Just for a day

The inauguration of the Sunday League in 1969 opened up greater opportunities for dispersal and to fly the county flag at outgrounds. This was particularly the case with the 40 overs competition on Sundays, when there was less corporate hospitality, and the one-day package, with a definite result at the end of the game, likely to appeal to new and occasional spectators. Some of the International Cavaliers games had also been staged at club grounds where the county had rarely played before. The inauguration of the Sunday League, and the prospect of hosting a televised game, therefore became attractive for local clubs and their pool of sponsors. It was far easier for them to stage and support a one-day game, than try to host a three-day game, with the consequent difficulties of arranging car parking or catering over three days, to say nothing of preparing a wicket which would last for the full duration of a Championship match.

This potentially lucrative source of new income was tapped into in the early years of the Sunday League by several counties who opted to take games away from their county headquarters to new or underused venues. Essex took games to Harlow and Purfleet, Surrey visited Sutton, Byfleet and Leatherhead, while Kent played at the Midland Bank ground in New Beckenham. Northamptonshire went to Kettering, and Nottinghamshire played at Newark as well as the John Player Ground a mile and a half from the centre of Nottingham, to the delight of the competition's sponsors.

Several counties also took the opportunity to colonise new areas by staging Sunday games outside their county boundaries. In 1970 Gloucestershire ventured into Wiltshire by staging a game at Swindon. Somerset was another county to take Sunday games around and outside the county. In the first couple of seasons of the John Player League, they staged games at Yeovil, Glastonbury, Frome and the Brislington ground in Bristol, besides going outside their traditional boundaries, in search of new members and fresh support. On 24 August 1969 Somerset took on Sussex at the Recreation Ground in Torquay. The ground, only a six hit away from the sandy beaches of Torbay, had staged festival matches in the 1950s and 1960s, with county players taking part in special two-day games. Like the Minor County fixtures staged by Devon at the seaside ground, the games had attracted a large number of holidaymakers, and locals who would have occasionally visited Taunton to see Somerset play. The county officials deliberately chose late August as a suitable date for venturing into South Devon, and they were rewarded with a sizeable crowd. The game was played on what *Wisden* described as 'a green pitch with varied bounce and pace',[20] and to the delight of the locals, Sussex, having been put in, were dismissed for 114, before Somerset passed their total for the loss of six wickets. The Somerset treasurer also had a smile on his face, as the game produced gate receipts of £500.

One-day cricket also colonised the traditional programmes of three-day games at other festival venues such as Scarborough. Even this most popular of seaside resorts was not immune to the changing social trends, and the long established guest houses and small hotels began to be converted into self-catering flats. The motor car and day tripper replaced the train and the weekly lodger as a main contributor to the town's tourist industry, while the elegant Grand Hotel, so popular with the Victorian holidaymakers, was sold to Butlins, and amusement arcades, fish and chip shops, and ice-cream parlours opened up in the old seaside buildings. Crowds started to dwindle at the three-day games, such as MCC against Yorkshire, and in an attempt to woo back the spectators, a one-day game was organised in 1965 between an England XI and the Rothmans Rest of the World XI. Other special exhibition games and single wicket competitions were staged, alongside the three-day fixtures, but as Ian Hall noted 'the traditional three-day matches could no longer sustain the Festival against the advances of the new limited overs cricket which was attracting a younger, more vibrant audience. The old had to be married to the new.'[21]

As a result, a limited over knockout competition was organised from 1970 by Fenner, the Hull-based power transmission company, who had been loyal supporters of Yorkshire cricket for many years, and had provided winter employment for their professionals. The concept was that Yorkshire would be joined for a knockout competition of 60 overs per side by the three major trophy winners from the previous season – the County Champions, Gillette Cup holders and the winners of the Sunday League. The new event replaced the MCC–Yorkshire fixture, and it proved to be a sound financial move, as the Fenner Trophy in 1970, watched by crowds in excess of 25,000 produced receipts of £5,045 compared with only £901 for the previous year's three-day fixture.

Further changes to the county system

County cricket underwent further changes during the 1970s – with the arrival of even more overseas stars, new fund-raising initiatives and further corporate sponsorship, plus the introduction of one-day internationals and a third limited overs competition between the counties following the creation in 1972 of the Benson and Hedges Cup. In order not to clash with the Gillette Cup, it was suggested that the new competition should be held in the first three months of the season. Gallagher Ltd, the parent company of Benson and Hedges, liked this idea as the twelve-week period would yield more public exposure than the three minutes or so it took to run a horse race, or the four days of a golf tournament. But doubts were expressed in the corridors of power at Lord's as to whether it should be a knockout competition. Instead, they opted for more variety by introducing zonal groupings, similar to football's World Cup, and teams batting for a maximum of 55 overs. In order to produce four groupings of five teams, University and Minor County teams joined the first-class counties, followed by the addition of Scotland and Ireland.[22]

The Championship programme also saw changes following the introduction of a third limited overs competition at a time when first-class games would otherwise have taken place. It led to an extension of the playing season further into September as well as a reduction in the number of games. The Championship had already seen a cut in the number of fixtures from 28 to 24 in 1969 following the introduction of the Sunday League, and in 1972 there was a further reduction to 20 games to accommodate the Benson and Hedges Cup. Several counties and their supporters protested about this reduction, and following claims that too much one-day cricket was being played, the timing of some of the one-day games was rearranged to make room for 22 Championship fixtures from 1977 and then 24 from 1983.

However, this led in turn to calls that the county calendar was too congested, that the counties were playing too much cricket, and that there had been increased pressure to win the limited overs games, to the detriment of the run-of-the-mill Championship games. Various working parties were set up, and in the wake of poor Test results, 1988 saw a reduction in the number of Championship games to 22 and the introduction of a number of four-day games in an attempt to raise the standard of play. The top four sides in the Sunday League (now sponsored by Refuge Assurance) also took part in an end-of-season knockout competition called the Refuge Assurance Cup, adding an extra competition, but more crunch games for the toiling county professionals, who opted for rest in games against the tourists or the Universities. As Trevor Bailey commented, 'the Championship itself was once the honour available; it was regarded as the cricketing grail. In Essex, our largest gate was normally for the tourist match. Nobody would have considered fielding a substandard side, as has sadly become common practice, but then the counties were not chasing four honours, or five if one includes the quite unnecessary Refuge Assurance Cup ... The dichotomy is that while the one-day game at county level has its faults and weaknesses, without it many counties would have gone out of business.'[23]

Another development in the early 1980s saw the introduction of floodlit cricket at various grounds, following the example of Australia, who since the Packer Revolution in 1977 had successfully staged floodlit games.

Nineteen eighty saw night cricket being played on football grounds, such as Chelsea FC's pitch at Stamford Bridge. Despite being an important innovation, the Editor of *Wisden* was rather disparaging about these games. 'There are in cricket administration today, marketing men whose desire to bring money into the game causes them to trifle with its origins and gamble with its charm. Night cricket in Sydney, being on a genuine cricket ground, indeed a great one, can be a dazzling spectacle, not far removed from the real thing; at Stamford Bridge it smacks of gimmickry.'[24]

Even so, 1981 saw the first floodlit competition involving all 17 first-class counties, sponsored by another cigarette manufacturer, Lambert and Butler. The ten overs a side competition on September 17th and 18th took place at the homes of Bristol City FC, Chelsea, Crystal Palace, Manchester United and West Bromwich Albion. Each county fielded a seven-a-side team, and Lancashire eventually defeated Leicestershire in the final. Whilst adding new locational variety, many of the playing areas were too small or lacked a proper wicket for a meaningful game to take place. The fact that there were only seven players, and a very reduced innings, meant these games lacked the feel of a real cricket match.

Despite these teething problems and an artificial feel to the floodlit matches in the 1980s, the 1990s have seen the successful introduction of this form of cricket into the domestic calendar. Their inclusion in the AXA League was a positive spin-off from the success of floodlit games in the World Cup competitions, as well as the sale of replica clothing. Ever anxious to exploit a new commercial avenue, the TCCB agreed to the introduction of coloured clothing in the 1993 Sunday League, followed in 1997 by floodlit matches.

There have also been important changes to the personnel in charge of county clubs. Whereas the offices used to be inhabited by retired servicemen or players, they are now the domains of sharp, young graduates and administrators with a background in industry and commerce. This has been a necessary change, for as Phil Carling observed, 'the counties have been forced to use their facilities and their grounds to the full. Investment has been made in executive boxes, entertaining suites and, in some counties, the building of squash courts. Local firms have responded to this encouragement, and the partnerships at county level between business and cricket have increased considerably the game's income.'[25]

The modern era of cheque book cricket has seen every facet of the game become sponsored, with companies paying for their logo on the players' clothes, the scorecards and on other buildings on the grounds, whilst the boundary, which had evolved almost by accident in the nineteenth century, has now become the most marketable asset of the twentieth-century county game, with every county ground boasting perimeter advertising. Some companies, such as Fosters at The Oval, even sponsored the ground itself, giving an even higher profile to their corporate association with county cricket. The prize money on offer in the one-day competitions has also dramatically risen, and by 1987 £53,500 was on offer in the NatWest Trophy, with £84,900 on offer in the Benson and Hedges Cup. The total amount of sponsorship in each competition exceeded £400,000, and in 1987 when Refuge Assurance took over the Sunday League, they committed themselves to an expenditure of £2.5 million over a period of five years.[26]

With such corporate support, there has also been a dramatic change to the finances of many county clubs, including Lancashire, who in 1962 had an annual turnover of £67,000, with £39,000 from gate receipts and subscriptions, plus £8,000 in Test and broadcasting receipts. By 1990 Lancashire's income was in excess of £2 million with £500,000 from subscriptions and match receipts, plus £1.5 million from Test matches, one-day internationals, broadcasting, sponsorship, perimeter advertising, corporate hospitality and catering facilities which operate all year round. Even the non-Test match counties have seen a dramatic change in their finances. Take the case of Sussex, who in 1992 had gate receipts of £53,000, including £10,000 in car parking fees. Sponsorship and marketing brought in £315,000 with £110,000 from perimeter advertising.

As Eric Midwinter observed, 'spectators, and their income, are scarcely part of the formula any more: in 1990 only 8 per cent of county income was from gate money and 17 per cent from subscriptions, with 70 per cent from commercial and TCCB sources',[27] By 1997 and 1998, the figure for match receipts was down to 5 per cent, as shown in Table 8. In short, it was a case of attracting businesses and business people to the games, and rather than Joe Public, it was now NatWest or Benson and Hedges who held sway. In some cases, success in attracting sponsors was far more important than winning games. Indeed, a survey of the finances of the county sides in 1998 showed no causal link between a healthy income stream and success in the County Championship. The 1998 Champions, Leicestershire, had a total income of £2 million, plus an expenditure of £1.2 million on wages, playing costs and ground expenses. In contrast, Essex finished bottom of the Championship table after a series of dreadful defeats, yet they generated a total income of £2.4 million, over £400,000 higher than the County champions![28]

In 1992 some 40 companies were playing a leading role at county level in sponsoring the county game. Half of these were in finance or insurance, with a quarter being brewers, distillers or food and drink retailers. The financial and retailing sectors now dominate English cricket, and these trends mirror the growth of services as a whole in the British economy, where de-industrialisation has resulted in the decline of the manufacturing sector and a 'tertiarisation' process has seen the rise of the services since the 1970s.

TABLE 8
INCOME OF THE FIRST-CLASS COUNTIES IN 1997 AND 1998

| | 1997 | | 1998 | |
	£000s	%	£000s	%
ECB income	18,905	40	21,379	42
Commercial*	9,792	21	10,570	21
Membership	5,428	12	5,728	11
Match receipts	2,253	5	2,313	5
Other +	10,229	22	10,746	21
Total	46,607		50,736	

* sponsorship, plus advertising
+ net income from catering, bars and retail, investment income, indoor schools, use of nets etc.

Source: 'Financial Survey of Cricket, 1999', Ambition Management.

These recent changes in county cricket are therefore a microcosm of the changes in the British economy. For the counties, these changes have allowed them to survive, and the annual 'gravy train' from Lord's has meant that many counties have retained a decent-sized playing staff, rather than downsizing. To a Marxist, such as Mike Marqusee, these changes have been far less palatable – 'modern cricket sponsorship has inherited from traditional cricket patronage an ancient function: the binding together of an elite. The insignificance of gate money has stripped spectators of what little power they ever had. Sponsors now take priority even over county members, who are asked to pay more for less.[29]

The patterns in 1991

With fewer first-class fixtures and a need to maximise income, most counties might have opted for centralising all their nine home Championship fixtures at their headquarters, to the detriment of the outgrounds. But as the following list shows, every county opted to keep playing at their outgrounds, and for the first time, none centralised all of their games at one place.

1.   Group A – those with centralised fixtures: none.
2.   Group B – those who played most of their games at a central headquarters with one or two games at outgrounds: Derbyshire, Middlesex, Leicestershire, Nottinghamshire, Surrey, Warwickshire.
3.   Group C – those who took cricket to many venues throughout the county: Yorkshire, Sussex, Kent, Hampshire, Gloucestershire, Somerset, Worcestershire, Essex, Glamorgan, Northamptonshire, Lancashire.

Leicestershire, Middlesex and Warwickshire who had opted for centralisation in 1971 now opted for games as well at Hinckley, Uxbridge and Coventry, respectively. Essex, Kent, Worcestershire and Somerset also opted to focus the majority of their games at centres smaller than some of their outgrounds. Derbyshire and Nottinghamshire moved from group C to B by contracting their fixture list, and playing Championship games at just one outground each – Chesterfield and Worksop.

Every other county opted for at least two outgrounds, but generally there was a smaller number, which reflected the fewer Championship fixtures, as well as maximiser behaviour. Indeed, there were risks when playing at outgrounds, as wickets could be of an inferior standard to those at the headquarters ground. The TCCB had introduced a 25 point penalty for counties 'preparing' poor wickets and in 1989, Essex had their council-prepared wicket at Southchurch Park, Southend reported in the games against Kent and Yorkshire. They duly became the first county to be docked bonus points, and in the eyes of many, the loss of 25 points was one reason why they failed to win the Championship.

Kent and Essex, two of the more nomadic counties, used just four venues, whilst Yorkshire opted to play most games at Headingley, with a couple of games at Sheffield and Scarborough, plus one each at Harrogate and Middlesbrough. Figure 26 shows that Yorkshire still had a hierarchical arrangement by staging most games at larger settlements, although their rank–size pattern was not as clear as that for Glamorgan, Gloucestershire and Sussex.

As far as the limited overs games were concerned, the counties also split into two groups, but interestingly they were not the same as for the first-class fixtures. Some opted for complete centrality of all one-day games, whilst others chose dispersal to several outgrounds. Even so, those opting for dispersal still staged their major one-day games, quarter and semi-final matches at their headquarters, given the massive potential support from spectators and businessmen alike as well as media interest from radio and television.

1. Group A – those with centralised fixtures: Lancashire, at Old Trafford; Leicestershire, at Leicester; Nottinghamshire, at Trent Bridge; Surrey, at The Oval; Warwickshire, at Edgbaston; Worcestershire, at Worcester.
2. Group B – those who played most of their games at a central headquarters with one or two games at outgrounds: none.
3. Group C – those who took cricket to many venues throughout the county: Yorkshire, Sussex, Kent, Hampshire, Gloucestershire, Derbyshire, Somerset, Middlesex, Essex, Glamorgan, Northampton-shire.

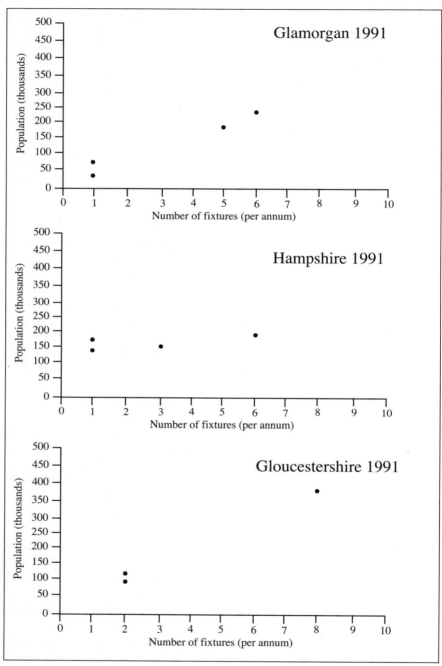

Figure 26 Rank–size relationships for Glamorgan, Hampshire, Sussex, Yorkshire and Gloucestershire, 1991

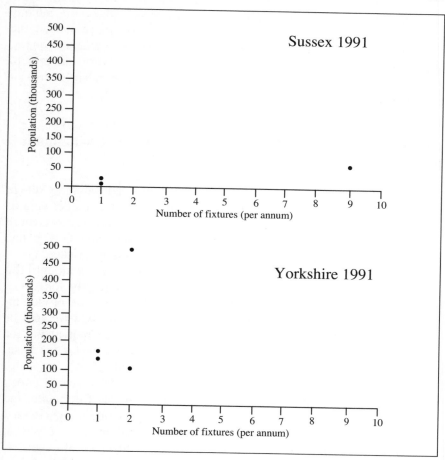

Of the six counties opting for centralisation of limited overs games, four selected Test venues – Old Trafford, Trent Bridge, The Oval and Edgbaston – where substantial investment had taken place in corporate hospitality and these counties, together with Leicestershire and Worcestershire clearly wanted to maximise their returns.

Some of the counties showed their desire to maximise revenue with Championship fixtures by continuing a nomadic approach with Sunday fixtures, when there were fewer businessmen wishing to use hospitality facilities. Even so, there was less colonisation than in 1971, with only Glamorgan playing at Ebbw Vale, the old county ground of Monmouthshire, Gloucestershire crossing the border into Wiltshire by visiting Swindon, and Derbyshire flying the flag in Checkley at Staffordshire. The other nomadic counties tended to opt for 'safe' outgrounds, such as Chesterfield, Colchester, Basingstoke, Bath and

Eastbourne, where they had traditionally played and where the Sunday
League fixture was part of the annual festival or Cricket Week. Indeed, the
counties spending a fair amount of time and cash arranging marquees,
hospitality, car parking and catering at these venues were unlikely to
contemplate shifting the staff, players, catering vans, boundary boards or
mobile toilets to another venue in the middle of a festival.

Anachronism or money-spinner – the case of the Cheltenham Festival

The survivial of one-off festivals, such as the one held at the College
Ground in Cheltenham, seems to be an anachronism in this modern era of
cheque book cricket and the quest for maximum profits. Indeed, as George
Plumptre observed, 'one could be forgiven for wondering how it has
survived into the world of late twentieth-century county cricket. For a
start, it is a school ground, and as a result, the county has to wait until the
end of the summer term. It is also a festival, and at 11 days, the longest in
county cricket. Most festivals have given up the effort of producing
anything festive, but Cheltenham, by contrast, is vigorously alive and for
the first week and a half in August, it is the main event in Cheltenham; for
many Gloucestershire folk, it is an annual social occasion, for the hosts
Cheltenham College, it is a source of considerable pride.'[30]

The inaugural county fixture at Cheltenham was the match between
Gloucestershire and Surrey in 1872, and in 1878 James Lillywhite, the
former Sussex player and cricket coach at the College, persuaded
Gloucestershire to play two games a year at Cheltenham. In return,
Lillywhite was paid £120 to run the games and cover all local expenses.
He more than recouped his expenditure through imaginative and prudent
promotion, instigating reduced admission for spectators who attended
more than one day's play. He also guaranteed entertainment if the county
fixture finished early, with the prospect of a contest between the county
side using broomsticks and the town side using normal bats.[31]

Lillywhite died in 1882 and never survived to witness the huge success
of the Cheltenham festival, both from a cricketing point of view and as a
social event. In 1906 a third game was added to extend the festival into a
second week, and on several occasions, the festival included a match with
a touring team. The prospect of watching entertaining cricket drew many
people into the delightful spa town, and the many hotels, public houses
and guest houses did a roaring trade, as many Gloucestershire exiles year
after year returned to Cheltenham to see the cricket and catch up with old
friends. The festival also attracted many cricket followers from the
neighbouring counties of Worcestershire and Warwickshire, and

Cheltenham's strategic position on the Great Western Railway also helped many visitors to reach the town for the festival.

By the inter-war period, the highlight of the cricket season for Gloucestershire diehards was the annual visit to Cheltenham. The attractive tree-lined setting, surrounded by the imposing Gothic architecture of the school buildings and gaily decorated marquees, to say nothing of the Cotswold Hills as a backdrop, made a most welcome break from the monotonous brick and mortar of suburban Bristol plus the gaunt and imposing façade of Mullers Orphanage that overlooked the Nevil Road ground.

In 1947 the fixture with Middlesex drew a record crowd of 15,000, and during the 1950s the games managed to attract significant crowds of some 8–9,000. Even during the 1960s, when attendances in general were severely declining on a national basis, the delights of the festival guaranteed a sizeable return for Gloucestershire. As Table 9 shows, in both 1968 and 1969 the gate receipts and number of paying spectators for the week and a half of cricket at Cheltenham exceeded that of nearly a month's cricket at Bristol. In 1968 the nine days of cricket at the College contributed 46 per cent of total gate receipts, whilst in 1969 the ten days accounted for almost 40 per cent of annual takings.

TABLE 9
ATTENDANCES AND GATE RECEIPTS AT THE CHELTENHAM
CRICKET FESTIVAL – 1968, 1969

| Venue | Days | 1968 | | Days | 1969 | |
		Paying spectators	Receipts £		Paying spectators	Receipts £
Bristol	30	16,938	3,746	26	13,266	3,076
Lydney	3	1,717	344	4	4,725	1,069
Gloucester	6	2,369	493	7	11,212	2,474
Cheltenham	9	17,841	3,930	10	17,595	4,352

Source: Gloucestershire CCC, Yearbook for 1970, p.52.

There have been several recent changes to the format of the festival, starting in 1969 with the addition of a Sunday League game to the itinerary, and in the past few seasons, the festival has been reduced to two Championship games. But as Table 10 shows, it is still a most valuable money-spinner for Gloucestershire, and the festival is an ideal venue in the modern era of corporate hospitality, with marquees hosting many of the companies who have relocated to the town from London and the south-east. On average, corporate guests total around 4,000 per festival, with gate receipts bringing in around £45,000 per annum.[32] So while appearing on the surface to be a quaint reminder of the relaxed atmosphere and cosy informality of county cricket in the inter-war years, the Cheltenham festival is a most lucrative location for Gloucestershire CCC, and in the modern era of profit maximisation, a location they would not want to lose.

TABLE 10
GATE RECEIPTS AND ATTENDANCES AT CHELTENHAM, 1996–98

	Gate receipts £	Paid attendances	Members
1996	45,346	8,199	3,509
1997	45,057	8,024	6,391
1998	45,533	7,576	7,524

Source: Gloucestershire CCC.

A summative model of county cricket in the 1990s

Despite the survival of festival venues such as Cheltenham, the modern era of cheque book cricket has seen many changes in the locational patterns of county cricket. Keith Sandiford believes that the spirit of professionalisation has dominated English cricket since 1963, and since that time economic factors have definitely replaced the social and demographic ones in the locational equation.[33]

The introduction of one-day cricket has been a lifeline for many clubs, and without the injection of sponsorship, some clubs could have folded. But the introduction of three limited overs competitions has necessitated a fundamental change to the structure of the county calendar. The cricket played at Scarborough has been a microcosm of these changes, with a clear shift in emphasis towards the more lucrative limited overs games, and the festival is now a mix of one-day and four-day games.

On a national scale, the county programme of first-class and limited overs games has evolved into a mix of traditional festivals such as at Cheltenham, cricket weeks at Tunbridge Wells and Ilford, and regular matches at county headquarters such as Trent Bridge, The Oval or Leicester. There is a combination of both centralisation and dispersal, for focusing games at one point has not been a direct route to success. The building of large stadiums has brought with it increased overheads and higher running costs, but these have to a large extent been offset by the money to be made from sources outside cricket, and the all year round use of luxurious amenities has been one way to keep money coming in. But the nomadic counties have also found that taking games to popular outgrounds, festivals or seaside resorts remains a lucrative proposition.

Moreover, the games at Cheltenham, Southend, Weston-super-Mare, Blackpool or Scarborough gain special significance, or added value, over the routine fixtures at headquarters such as Bristol, Chelmsford, Taunton, Old Trafford or Headingley.

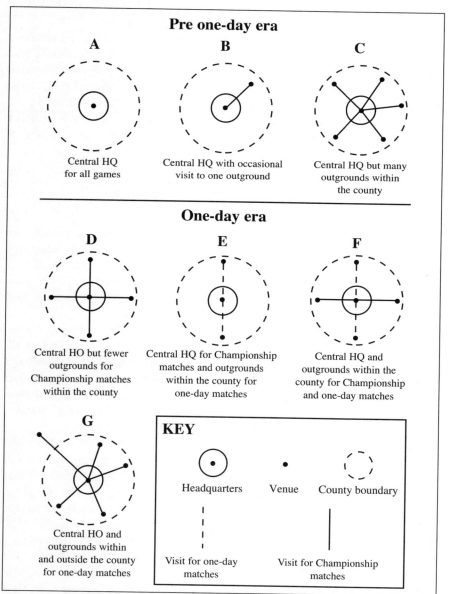

Figure 27   Models of county match locations

Some critics would argue that the counties were betwixt and between centrality and dispersal, and the 1991 calendar represented a geographical halfway house. But, like many things in life, the secret of success has been a balance, and today the modern counties have a secure base, plus a select number of accessible or lucrative outgrounds which they use for Sunday fixtures and an annual or bi-annual Championship fixture.

These patterns are shown in Figure 27 which updates the summation proposed in Figure 24 to take account of these modern additions and changes. Categories D, E, F and G have been introduced to make allowance for this modern variety, although it is worth noting that B, E and F now seem to be the most common form of locational behaviour. In the future, perhaps B and E will become more common, following further changes to the county programme and a reduction in the number of Championship fixtures.

Rain Stops Play: A Meteorological Analysis

The weather and cricket

So far, the focus of attention has been on the human geography of cricket, and the role of socio-economic factors on the game's development. It is now time to look at the geography of county cricket from a physical point of view, especially as cricket is one of the summer sports where rain can prevent play from actually taking place. Some jovially believe that the phrase 'rain stopped play' actually heralds the arrival of the English sporting summer, and depending on the state of the game and allegiance to the participants, it can lead to frustration if it prevents a win or conversely bring salvation if it stops a county from losing! Even at Test level, the weather is one of the factors determining the financial success and enjoyment by the general public, as well as possibly the actual outcome of the contest.

There have been occasions, most notably in 1975 at Buxton, when solid forms of precipitation, in this case snow, stopped play, but our main concern here is with liquid precipitation, whether it be rain or drizzle. However, cricket is also influenced by other weather-related factors. For example, a heavy cloud cover or humid conditions can assist swing bowling and make batting more difficult. This chapter considers all of these meteorological factors, especially as distinctive regional patterns can be identified in the pattern of precipitation.

As far as England and Wales is concerned, the average seasonal precipitation largely depends on the frequency, intensity and tracks taken by the frontal systems as they move in an easterly direction across the country. The highest precipitation totals are often produced by depressions involving maritime air masses – polar maritime, or more usually tropical maritime.[1] As these depressions move east, the moist air masses rise over the hills and upland areas of the United Kingdom, so that large quantities of cloud and relief rain is produced. A föhn effect (or rain shadow) occurs in Eastern England when these air masses descend on the leeward side of these topographic barriers. Consequently, seasonal precipitation totals in winter over the highest parts of Wales are around 600 mm, compared with a more modest 150 mm in East Anglia.

During the summer months, the south and east of England are affected by another air mass – tropical continental. Its source area is in North Africa and as the warm air moves north across the European landmass, it can trigger convectional rain, often in the form of thunderstorms as a deep and moist layer of unstable air allows the formation of towering, cumulonimbus clouds.

The wettest season on record – the national picture

A small number of surveys have been undertaken identifying which cricket season has been the wettest ever recorded. Ross Reynolds has used notes from players' recollections to piece together a picture of the seasons between 1868 and 1895. By its very nature, this is a rather subjective analysis, rather than an accurate analysis of the precise amounts of play lost. Even so, some of the comments give a good indication of the scale of disruption, such as the following for 1879 – 'very wet. Many unfinished matches. Eleven days rained off at Lord's.'[2]

The most extensive analysis so far has been undertaken by David Jeater, who used data from the Climatic Research Unit at the University of East Anglia for the period between 1890 and 1993. Whilst appreciating the regional variations mentioned above, Jeater produced a mean precipitation value, using summer aggregates from the weather stations at Cardiff, Kew, Manchester and Weston-under-Lizard, 25km north-west of Birmingham.[3] The ten wettest and driest seasons are listed in Table 11 below.

TABLE 11
THE TEN WETTEST SUMMERS ON RECORD, 1890–1993

Year	Total precipitation mm
1931	441
1912	418
1924	414
1958	404
1920	363
1954	362
1903	356
1891	353
1946	349
1927	347

Source: D. Jeater, 'Cricket Season Weather 1890–1993', *The Cricket Statistician*, 89 (1995), 26–9.

John Kitchin has undertaken a survey of wet summers using Meteorological Office data for Hampstead,[4] and Table 12 shows what he believes were the nine wettest summers during the twentieth century. Kitchin declared that 1903 was 'the wettest summer of them all', but as he used records from a weather station in the drier east, there are bound to be discrepancies with Jeater's survey, where 1903 was in seventh place. Kitchin used contemporary witnesses to confirm the amount of damage caused by the heavy rain, and cited the Editor of the 1903 *Wisden* who claimed that 'never has county cricket been so much affected by rain as in 1903. The summer was the wettest within the experience of anyone now playing first-class cricket, worse even than 1879 and in nearly all parts of the country, the game had to contend with overwhelming disadvantages. As was inevitable under such conditions, the various county clubs suffered severely in pocket.'[5]

TABLE 12
MOST SUMMER RAINFALL AT HAMPSTEAD

Year	Total precipitation in
1903	17.89
1924	16.85
1958	14.00
1946	13.41
1956	13.33
1931	12.63
1954	12.00
1985	11.37
1912	11.26

Source: J. Kitchin, *Wisden Cricketers' Almanack 1986*, pp.77–80.

The next wet summer, 1912, had a severe financial impact on county champions Yorkshire who lost £1,000, whilst in 1924 H.S. Altham commented how 'the county clubs saw match after match make inroads into their funds or pile a balance even greater against them'.[6] Even worse happened when there was a succession of damp summers in 1930, 1931 and 1932. During 1931 there was a total of 111 days on which not a ball was bowled in first-class cricket, then in May 1932, 63 whole days of first-class cricket were lost in the second wettest May this century, with more than twice the average rainfall. The cumulative effect of three poor seasons hit several counties very hard, with Glamorgan recording a deficit of £2,015 in 1931 followed by £1,530 in 1932, but only after making stringent economies and releasing several professionals in order to cut expenditure by £2,000. The county launched a Special Appeal in the winter of 1932/33, and like the other counties, they were mightily grateful that 1933 and 1934 were fine summers, allowing Glamorgan to record a profit in 1934 of £1,401.[7]

In the post-war era, rain interfered with the 1946 season, and again in 1954 when the counties between them made a loss totalling £75,000. Nineteen fifty-eight was another poor summer with attendances falling by more than 500,000 compared with 1957. Test receipts were also severely affected, and the sum for distribution among the first-class counties was just £51,000 – half of the 1957 figure. The New Zealand tourists lost 174 playing hours, equivalent to a month's cricket, whilst Lancashire lost 159 hours. Moreover, the game at Hull between Yorkshire and Nottinghamshire, scheduled to last three days, was abandoned on the second morning as the ground was so waterlogged.[8]

In 1959 the Editor of *Wisden* lamented the weather and the inadequate way the counties combated the English climate. 'In order to re-start games as soon as possible after rain, experiments in drying the pitch have been tried with the aid of blankets, absorbent rubber mats, rollers of various textures and suction machines which quickly pick up surface water. Yet with all these aids, irritating delays continue and the public becomes less inclined to risk hanging about in the hope of seeing some cricket.'[9]

In an attempt to prevent further financial damage, an experiment took place in 1959 to increase the covering of pitches, when in the opinion of the captains and the umpires, the pitch had reached saturation point, then it may be wholly covered. With great irony, 1959 proved to be one of the best summers on record, and the experimental covering of wickets was discontinued. The 1960s saw several damp summers, especially 1965 and 1968, with the latter most famously remembered for the final day of the Fifth Test between England and Australia at The Oval. During the afternoon, a freak storm completely flooded the playing area, before a mopping up operation took place, and play restarted, with Derek Underwood exploiting the damp conditions to take 7 for 50 and secure a famous England victory by 226 runs, with just five minutes' playing time left.[10]

Nineteen eighty was the next damp summer with four matches abandoned without a single ball bowled. Three were in the round of matches starting on 14 June, and persistent heavy rain resulted in no play whatsoever at Swansea, Bristol and Bath. At the end of the season, the TCCB decided that all pitches from 1981 should be fully covered. It was a contentious decision, with the Editor of *Wisden* in 1981 'lamenting a loss of a part of the very heritage of English cricket – a drying pitch and a sizzling sun. Some of the great feats of batsmanship have been performed under these conditions. It is to try to make county cricket as much as possible like Test cricket, in which full covering is universally practised.'[11]

Despite the increase in the amount of pitch covering, the weather continued to affect county cricket during the 1980s. This was clearly evident in an analysis by Hosking of the number of completely blank days of both one-day and Championship cricket between 1983 and 1988. His data are shown in Table 13, from which he estimated that around 8 per cent of all days when cricket was scheduled resulted in no play whatsoever.[12]

TABLE 13
PROPORTION OF DAYS WHEN NO PLAY WAS POSSIBLE, 1983–88

Year	Possible Playing Days	Blank Days	% Blank
1983	1,001	111	11.09
1984	973	33	3.39
1985	1,011	89	8.80
1986	1,001	97	9.69
1987	982	99	10.08
1988	976	37	3.79

Source: K. Hosking, *The Cricketer*, 1989.

The general impact of the weather on English cricket during the 1980s and 1990s was also briefly analysed by Philip Eden in the 1999 issue of *Wisden*.[13] He utilised a 'summer index', or I, incorporating rainfall amounts and frequency, total sunshine and average maximum temperature between 1 May and 31 August, using the following formula:

$$I = \frac{20\,(\,Tx - 12) + (S - 400)}{3 + 2Rd + (250 - R/3)}$$

where Tx = average maximum temperature
S = total sunshine
Rd = number of dry days
R = total rainfall

Despite its complex appearance, this formula has been designed so that each weather factor contributes roughly 25 per cent of the total, giving an index which ranges from zero for the theoretical worst possible summer to 1,000 for the best. Table 14 shows the values between 1979 and 1998 with a value over 650 indicating a good summer, whilst one below 500 shows a poor summer. This index, derived from meteorological averages, confirms that 1987, 1988, 1991, 1992 and 1998 were damp summers for cricket.

TABLE 14
EDEN'S SUMMER INDEX, 1979–98

1979	546	1986	568	1993	573
1980	542	1987	444	1994	651
1981	541	1988	507	1995	777
1982	564	1989	770	1996	663
1983	634	1990	746	1997	601
1984	602	1991	538	1998	565
1985	568	1992	556		

Source: P. Eden, 'Cricket and the Weather, 1998', *Wisden Cricketers' Almanack 1999*, pp.1464–5.

Cricketing indicators of a wet summer

As well as using raw weather data to obtain a picture of weather disruption, there are also ways of using cricketing statistics. This was attempted by Philip Crofton, using Jeater's data for the period from 1946 until 1993, and involved a correlation analysis looking at the number of runs scored. Crofton's hypothesis was that there would be fewer runs scored in Championship games in bad summers than in good ones, and as he expected, an inverse relationship of -0.52 was found. He also undertook a regression analysis, predicting that in a summer without any rain whatsoever, an average of 1,025 runs would be scored in each Championship match, and that this would be reduced by just over one run per match for every millimetre of rain that fell in the season. In the wettest post-war summer, 404mm of rain fell and using his regression analysis, this gave a predicted value of 621 runs per match. In reality, the average was even less, at 588.[14]

Another analysis of poor summer weather using cricketing indicators was undertaken by Kitchin[15] who used:

(a) the number of batsmen averaging between 40 and 50 in a season,
(b) the number of batsmen averaging over 50 in a season,
(c) the number of bowlers averaging under 20 in a season,
(d) the number of first-class hundreds scored during a summer,

He used these when trying to assess which was the worst season on record, and as seen in Table 15, a different picture emerges compared with the meteorological data. Two trends are immediately apparent: 1958 emerges as one of the worst for batsmen, coming top in (a) and (d), and coming second in (b), whilst bowlers prospered on the damp wickets, with 1958 coming second in (c). Nineteen eighty-five, which was amongst the dampest, was far from being the worst for batsmen following the covering of wickets, and it came bottom of all the tables. Perhaps the most striking change is that just four bowlers averaged below 20, compared with 22 in 1931, the next wettest summer using (c) as the indicator. As far as (d) is concerned, the reduction in the number of fixtures in recent years makes it difficult to make comparisons between the rain affected summer of 1968 when 28 Championship games were played, and 1998 when they were just 17 fixtures. The loss of 11 Championship games will inevitably cause the absolute number of centuries to fall, but as (a) (b) and (c) are relative indicators, these can be used to compare earlier periods with the 1980s and 1990s.

TABLE 15
CRICKETING INDICATORS OF POOR SUMMERS, 1901–85

(a) Batsmen averaging between 40 & 50

1958	3
1954	5
1931	7
1912	8
1924	10
1956	10
1903	11
1946	11
1985	25

(b) Batsmen averaging over 50

1956	0
1958	1
1903	2
1924	3
1912	3
1954	6
1946	7
1931	9
1985	19

(c) Bowlers averaging below 20

1903	44
1958	43
1924	41
1912	41
1954	41
1946	30
1956	29
1931	22

(d) Number of first-class hundreds

1958	146
1903	148
1924	164
1912	164
1956	189
1954	231
1946	257
1931	266

Source: J. Kitchin '1903–The Wettest Summer of Them All?' *John Wisden's Cricketers' Almanack for 1986*, pp, 77–80.

Table 16 shows the pattern since 1986 using (a) (b) and (c), although care needs to be taken given the recent trends for heavier bats and smaller seams on the balls. Nineteen ninety-nine was certainly the year of the bat, seeing a match aggregate of over 1,000 runs in 108 out of the 241 first-class games. This beat the previous best of 72 out of 312 games in 1928. Nineteen ninety also saw 428 centuries during the summer, beating the 1928 record of 414, although the 1990 total of 32 double hundreds was two short of the record set in 1933. However, the damp summers of 1988, 1997 and 1998 all stand out, especially with indicators (b) and (c).

TABLE 16
CRICKETING INDICATORS OF POOR SUMMERS, 1986–98

Season	Summer rain mm	(a) Batsmen Av. 40–50	(b) Batsmen Av. +50	(c) Bowlers Av. below 20
1986	218	38	10	7
1987	251	32	7	8
1988	268	15	8	9
1989	156	25	10	11
1990	157	50	40	2
1991	202	31	21	2
1992	262	39	26	3
1993	212	28	21	4
1994	157	33	20	3
1995	67	50	25	6
1996	187	43	28	3
1997	234	42	19	7
1998	369	25	12	11

Source: First-class averages from *Wisden*, using the qualification of 8 innings and bowling in more than 10 innings. Rainfall figures from Hulme and Barrow.

The Raining County Champions

Assessing the impact of rain on each county

In addition to the national trends, it is important to consider the weather interruptions county by county. Few studies have been undertaken at a county level, with one of the earliest attempts to assess the impact of rain in each county being undertaken by Graham Llewellyn in 1969 using match reports from *Wisden*.[1] Llewellyn attempted to quantify the number of blank days between 1946 and 1968 in first-class matches, and from this he estimated the 'wettest county' and 'driest county' for each season, as shown in Table 17. He concluded that Lancashire was the wettest county overall, with Kent being the driest during this 23-year period.

The match reports in *Wisden* were used again by John Thornes in 1974. He classified games as rain-affected if *Wisden*'s correspondent mentioned 'green', 'sticky', 'wet' or 'drying' wickets, or if time was lost owing to rain or bad light. Table 18 shows the total amount of hours lost by each county, home and away, during the 1974 season. Glamorgan lost most time overall, yet it was not the result of being in the wet west, as the vast majority of time lost was when they were playing away from home, their matches at Scarborough, Maidstone, Burton-on-Trent and The Oval being badly affected. In contrast, Leicestershire lost much more time when playing at their Grace Road base and were fortunate enough to escape the rain when away from Leicester. Overall, Thornes found that exactly half of the 1974 Championship matches were affected by the weather.[2]

An even damper situation occurred in 1998 when 90 out of the 158 Championship matches saw play lost. This represented 57 per cent of the games, and the figure could have been even higher had not many of the games, scheduled to last for four days, been completed within three or even two days. Overall, Glamorgan and Northamptonshire were the worst affected counties with 13 out of their 17 games losing time to the weather. Lancashire had 12 affected fixtures, followed by Hampshire, Nottinghamshire, Surrey, Worcestershire and County Champions Leicestershire with 11 fixtures. This was based on my own quite detailed record of weather interruptions on each Championship fixture. This match-by-match analysis was based on an estimate of the number of overs lost on each day's play, either through bad light or rain (or even sleet as in the case of some early season fixtures), using the ECB regulation of one over lost for every three and three-quarters of a minute the players were off the field. On the first three days of each Championship fixture, a minimum of 104 overs must be bowled, with 96 on the final day. In addition, two overs were deducted for a change of innings. Hence, by comparing the number of overs at the close of play each day with the ones from the previous evening, it was possible to produce a viable estimate, in hours, of weather interference.

TABLE 17
RAIN INTERRUPTIONS IN FIRST-CLASS MATCHES, 1946–68

	Number of matches	Number of Blank Days	Wettest County	Driest County
1946	279	53	Glamorgan	Worcestershire
1947	285	24	Glamorgan	Kent
1948	288	43	Warwickshire	Gloucestershire
1949	292	12	Glamorgan	Sussex
1950	307	48	Glamorgan	Kent
1951	308	62	Yorkshire	Warwickshire
1952	304	32	Worcestershire	Hampshire
1953	310	58	Lancashire	Somerset
1954	305	90	Lancashire	Gloucestershire
1955	305	36	Worcestershire	Leicestershire
1956	311	83	Derbyshire	Hampshire
1957	312	39	Lancashire	Nottinghamshire
1958	309	102	Yorkshire	Somerset
1959	312	9	Glamorgan	Hampshire
1960	321	54	Surrey	Leicestershire
1961	334	23	Derbyshire	Worcestershire
1962	319	26	Gloucestershire	Sussex
1963	322	63	Leicestershire	Northamptonshire
1964	319	56	Middlesex	Gloucestershire
1965	319	63	Gloucestershire	Worcestershire
1966	318	66	Lancashire	Nottinghamshire
1967	325	83	Lancashire	Surrey
1968	318	95	Warwickshire	Derbyshire

Source: G.J. Llewellyn, 'The Weather and Post-War English Cricket', *The Cricketer* (Winter Annual, 1969/70), pp. 32–3.

Table 19 shows the amount of time lost by each county, both home and away, during the 1998 season. Overall, Northamptonshire lost most time, with almost 100 hours or around 1,600 overs being lost to rain or poor light. However, much of this was during the away matches, especially in late April with Surrey at The Oval, and Hampshire at Southampton, as well as their match in mid-June with Durham at Chester-le-Street. Lancashire and Glamorgan were the other counties in the top three for play lost, and in each case a sizeable proportion of time was lost at Old Trafford and Cardiff, especially as rain-bearing fronts from the Atlantic passed over these grounds.

TABLE 18
NUMBER OF HOURS LOST BY EACH COUNTY IN 1974

County	Home	Away	Total
Derbyshire	45	31	76
Essex	41	32	73
Glamorgan	1.5	76	77.5
Gloucestershire	61	12	73
Hampshire	36	22	58
Kent	24	52	76
Lancashire	30	39	69
Leicestershire	42	5	47
Middlesex	34	8	42
Northamptonshire	23	21	44
Nottinghamshire	12	22	34
Somerset	11	44	55
Surrey	26	27	53
Sussex	32	5	37
Warwickshire	19	28	47
Worcestershire	19	35	54
Yorkshire	29	26	55

Source: J.E. Thornes, 'Rain Starts Play', *Area*, 8 (1976), 108.

The impact of frontal rain can also be seen on the amount of play lost at home by Worcestershire and Somerset, although Gloucestershire lost less. Perhaps they were lucky enough not to be playing at home when these deep depressions swept across the south-west, or maybe the Bristol ground had better underground drainage or ground-covering systems than their western neighbours? Overall, Gloucestershire lost just 48 hours of play, with only Essex losing less. It was little surprise that Essex was one of the counties least affected by the frontal rain from the Atlantic Ocean. Sussex also escaped a lot of weather interference, as did Yorkshire on their away trips. They were less lucky at home when their matches at Headingley and Scarborough saw the loss of 47 hours' play.

Similar trends are apparent when comparing the time lost at home by each county with Eden's Summer Index for 1998, based on the actual meteorological conditions (Table 20). It is clear that Durham, and to a lesser extent Derbyshire, were both fortunate to play so much at home given the poor summer in the north. This may well have been the result of the timing of the fixtures – a factor which explains the discrepancy in Gloucestershire's position in this table, as they were playing most of their home games when the weather in the Bristol area was fine. Their neighbours, Somerset, were not so fortunate, neither were Hampshire, and both counties lost more playing time than Eden's Index would have otherwise suggested.

TABLE 19
NUMBER OF HOURS LOST BY EACH COUNTY IN 1998

County	Home	Away	Total
Derbyshire	21.25	55.25	76.50
Durham	35.50	29.25	64.75
Essex	20.75	24.25	45.00
Glamorgan	58.00	37.50	95.50
Gloucestershire	18.50	30.00	48.00
Hampshire	42.75	35.25	78.00
Kent	28.75	46.75	75.50
Lancashire	70.50	28.25	98.75
Leicestershire	53.00	39.50	92.50
Middlesex	11.25	55.25	66.50
Northamptonshire	28.25	71.25	99.50
Nottinghamshire	31.00	39.00	70.00
Somerset	58.00	16.00	74.00
Surrey	36.00	47.50	83.50
Sussex	21.00	31.50	52.50
Warwickshire	38.75	30.00	68.75
Worcestershire	42.25	38.00	80.25
Yorkshire	47.00	15.50	62.50

TABLE 20
HOURS LOST BY EACH COUNTY AT HOME IN 1998,
COMPARED WITH EDEN'S SUMMER INDEX

	Hours lost		Eden's 1998 Summer Index
Lancashire	70.50	Lancashire	441
Glamorgan	58.00	Durham	461
Somerset	58.00	Glamorgan	489
Leicestershire	53.00	Yorkshire	498
Yorkshire	47.00	Warwickshire	527
Hampshire	44.75	Gloucestershire	560
Worcestershire	42.25	Derbyshire	568
Warwickshire	38.75	Leicestershire	570
Surrey	36.00	Nottinghamshire	579
Durham	35.50	Northamptonshire	584
Nottinghamshire	31.00	Somerset	599
Kent	28.75	Worcestershire	586
Northamptonshire	28.25	Essex	648
Derbyshire	21.25	Middlesex	664
Sussex	21.00	Surrey	668
Essex	20.75	Kent	686
Gloucestershire	18.50	Hampshire	695
Middlesex	11.25	Susssex	719

Sources: Author's survey of the 1998 season and Eden's data in *Wisden Cricketer's Almanack 1999*.

It is also possible to identify some other interesting trends when comparing these results from 1998 with Thornes' survey for 1974. Table 21 shows the county-by-county comparison, in terms of the home fixtures staged by the 17 counties. The largest increases in weather interference were in the west, most notably Glamorgan, Lancashire and Somerset, whilst a smaller increase can be seen in Worcestershire and Warwickshire, despite the advent of the 'Brumbella' at Edgbaston. There is also a marked east–west split during these two time periods with Essex, Kent, Middlesex and Sussex all losing less than their western counterparts, with the notable exception of Gloucestershire. Once again, comparisons with data from other seasons could show whether these are becoming more obvious trends.

TABLE 21
HOURS LOST BY EACH COUNTY AT HOME, 1974 AND 1998

County	1974	1998
Derbyshire	45.00	21.25
Essex	41.00	20.75
Glamorgan	1.50	58.00
Gloucestershire	61.00	18.50
Hampshire	36.00	42.75
Kent	24.00	28.75
Lancashire	30.00	70.50
Leicestershire	42.00	53.00
Middlesex	4.00	11.25
Northamptonshire	23.00	28.25
Nottinghamshire	12.00	31.00
Somerset	11.00	58.00
Surrey	26.00	36.00
Sussex	32.00	21.00
Warwickshire	19.00	38.75
Worcestershire	19.00	42.25
Yorkshire	29.00	47.00

Sources: Author's survey and Thornes' 'Rain Starts Play', *Area*, 8 (1976), 108.

Complete washouts

Another yardstick of weather interference is to look at Championship matches where no play has been possible on any of the scheduled days. This was undertaken by Duncan McLeish, using the rain affected Championship matches between 1886 and 1991.[3] Table 22 shows his calculations showing the number of home and away games which were abandoned as a percentage of the total number of Championship games each county was scheduled to play. Once again, the western counties and those close to the Pennines had the worst record for abandoned home games, and although McLeish offered no meteorological reasons to explain these trends, it is clear that relief and frontal precipitation played a significant role.

TABLE 22
ABANDONED CHAMPIONSHIP MATCHES BY COUNTY, 1886–1991 (%)

County	Home	Away
Derbyshire	1.48	0.65
Essex	0.57	0.85
Glamorgan	0.85	0.85
Gloucestershire	1.42	0.67
Hampshire	0.36	0.90
Kent	0.16	0.96
Lancashire	1.31	0.69
Leicestershire	0.58	0.77
Middlesex	1.22	0.35
Northamptonshire	0.43	0.76
Nottinghamshire	0.17	1.07
Somerset	0.47	0.47
Surrey	0.82	0.67
Sussex	0.31	0.94
Warwickshire	0.76	0.57
Worcestershire	0.30	0.59
Yorkshire	1.11	0.67

Source: D. McLeish, 'Abandoned County Championship Matches', *The Cricket Statistician*, 80 (1992), 33–5.

Nottinghamshire seemed to be amongst the unluckiest counties, losing very few games at home, but being at the top of the list of visiting teams in abandoned games! As expected, Kent in the drier east had the smallest number of home games abandoned, but it is also worth noting that their metropolitan neighbours – Middlesex and Surrey – had a much higher figure than expected.

The only drawback with McLeish's work is that his calculations are based on games where no play had taken place, and given the recent improvement in pitch covering this may not be a viable measure of rainfall interference. Moreover, games now take place over four days, and there are many instances of storms relenting in time for a double forfeiture or a one innings game on the final day.

Wet weather compensation

There have been few summers when rain has not interfered in some way to deprive the county members of a chance to see their heroes in action and in the case of 1974, rain in Hampshire's final match against Yorkshire cost them the Championship and around £1,000 in prize money. Similarly, in 1977

Kent, who shared the title with Middlesex, may well have been deprived of an outright win by the abandonment of their match in Essex, whilst in 1983 the abandonment of the game between Middlesex and Yorkshire possibly robbed the former of the victory they required to secure the title.

Our meteorological records in Britain are among the most comprehensive in Western Europe and at the present time there are over 8,000 rain gauges collecting data. If the British Isles are the most densely gauged region in the world, could we identify regional patterns and adjust the county calendar to reduce the number of matches spoilt by rain? If a distinctive pattern could be found, county officials might, in an ideal world, refer to these trends and stage more of their home games in the statistically drier months, and act as host to other clubs in their particular wet month.

John Thornes showed that 'in an average July, Worcestershire has fewer rain days than Northamptonshire, whereas in September the reverse is true. It would appear sensible for the two counties to play each other in Worcestershire in July, and in Northamptonshire in September. Unfortunately, such a marriage is rare, and the western counties are consistently wetter on average; also in any one season, the rainfall pattern may be very different from the average. In order to compensate for weather interference, it does not appear feasible to adapt the fixture list to average rainfall.'[4] It would also be impossible to base the calendar on the pattern from the recent past, in terms either of when the worst rain days were or which areas were affected given the variability of precipitation across the United Kingdom noted in the previous chapter.

TABLE 23
WET WEATHER COMPENSATION POINTS, BASED ON TIME LOST

Hours lost	Points awarded 1974 system	Points awarded Current system (including draw points)
+18	6	10
16–18	5	9
14–16	4	8
12–14	3	7
10–12	2	6
8–10	1	5

Source: Thornes, 'Rain Starts Play'.

As an alternative scheme, Thornes has suggested awarding compensation points to make up for lost bonus points in weather-affected Championship fixtures. He plotted a scattergraph showing the total number of bonus points accrued in each rain-affected match, plotted against the total number of hours of play lost. As expected, there was an inverse relationship in the 58 matches plotted, with a cluster of games that despite a little interference from the elements, still had a positive outcome. Yet none of the matches with over eight hours interference reached a definite outcome, and Thornes used this as the cut-off for his system, shown in Table 23, of wet weather compensation allocated if games are drawn.

These compensation points would be added to any bonus points already achieved, providing the game ends in a draw. Under the 1974 scoring system, ten points were awarded for a win, compared with 12 today. But another difference with 1974 is that there are now four points available for a draw, so the right hand column in the table makes a readjustment for counties who would pick up the four draw points, plus any batting or bowling points in whatever play took place.

Critics of these suggestions believe that this could take away the unpredictability of cricket, and that it adds an extra layer of complexity and paperwork to a game which in its one-day format has already become over-complicated by the introduction of the Duckworth–Lewis system of re-adjusting targets in rain affected games.[5] Another argument against such a system of compensation is that it might prevent unadventurous captains from actually playing, depriving the spectator of even more cricket. There are bound to be occasions, as in 1998, when the entire programme of county games is affected by rain, so that all the counties get a chance for compensation. Those teams who want a prompt start in damp conditions, would be spurning the chance of compensation points if they adopted a more cautious approach. Critics of the compensation system might also prefer introducing the regulation, successfully used in Test cricket, whereby lost time can be made up, simply by playing on, for up to an hour after the scheduled close of play.

But even if this were introduced the western countries could still be handicapped as this would only allow up to four hours to be made up in a match. The basic premise for compensation is that it is grossly unfair, given the maps of regional rainfall in the United Kingdom, that counties playing games in wet areas are deprived a large number of points that counties playing concurrently in dry areas could gain, simply because of geography and the precise location of the grounds. Indeed, John Mace has estimated that the complete abandonment of ten Championship fixtures at Bristol between 1971 and 1985 'provided a handicap over the 15 seasons, with the team's position being lower by three places. For example, had the team been able to obtain just average bonus points from abandoned Bristol games, we [Gloucestershire] would have been Champions in 1977, not third.'[6]

It is at times of rain interruption in one part of the country, that the link between geography and cricket is most clearly demonstrated, and if we know so much geographically about precipitation that we can analyse and model rainfall patterns across the country, then it seems logical from a cricketing point of view to introduce a system of compensation as suggested above. Even so, the Champion Counties of 1997 and 1998 both lost sizeable amounts of time through bad weather. In 1997 Glamorgan lost 121 hours of Championship play, whilst in 1998 Leicestershire lost 92.5 hours. One could argue that had a system of compensation been in place, they would have won more easily and not so much importance would have been placed on the end of season matches in 1997 at Taunton and Canterbury, and in 1998 at The Oval and Old Trafford. In both cases, the Championship, rain and all, went right down to the final match, and an argument could be put forward for not meddling any further by adding such a 'McCaskill–Fish' system of wet weather compensation, and for maintaining the status quo.

Patterns of humidity

So far we have been looking at the way the weather hinders play, but damp conditions can actually assist play, especially bowling. In the old days of uncovered wickets, many slow bowlers would gleefully exploit a wet or drying wicket, and it is argued that many great batsmen learnt their craft on such surfaces and against a wickedly turning or bouncing ball. Many bemoan the loss of these challenges on covered wickets, but even so, bowlers can prosper in damp conditions, especially when humidity levels are high, with the swing bowlers finding help from the atmosphere.

Humidity is a function of the air temperature, as the water-holding capacity of the atmosphere depends on the temperature. Warmer air can hold more water vapour, with saturated air at 20°C holding 3.6 times more water vapour than air at 0°C. Relative humidity is the standard measure used by the Meteorological Office, indicating in percentage terms the amount of water vapour in the air, compared with the maximum amount the air can hold at that particular temperature.

Mechanical engineers and aeronautical scientists have suggested several reasons for the ball to swing in humid conditions. The most widely accepted view is that of Lyttleton, in which humid conditions enhance the roughness effect on the surface of the ball, thereby reducing its 'critical speed' and increasing the amount of turbulence in the 'boundary layer'.[7] The latter is the thin veneer of air in contact with the cricket ball and the net result, according to Lyttleton, is that the greater turbulence and slower critical speed will make swing more readily obtainable.

An alternative suggestion by Daish was that the seam of the ball might be heightened in humid conditions, creating greater turbulence and the disturbance of the boundary layer needed for swing. This was, however, a subjective view, as Daish believed that 'there is no objective experimental evidence to confirm or deny this explanation of the possible effects of humidity'.[8] Whatever the precise mechanism, a practical demonstration of the enhanced effects of humidity came in the first Test of the 1999 series between England and New Zealand at Edgbaston. Batting had been very difficult on the first two days, when the Birmingham ground was subjected to a heavy cloud cover. The humid atmosphere caused the ball to move around lavishly, but conditions were completely different on the third morning. Under clear skies and a lower humidity, the English batsmen found batting far easier, and their night-watchman, Alex Tudor, made a remarkable 99* as England comfortably reached their target to win the Test by seven wickets.

In the same way that there are subtle variations at regional level in terms of rainfall patterns, there are important differences in humidity. Overall the warmer south and south-east have increased levels of humidity as they are affected by tropical continental air masses. There are also subtle mesoscale variations, with coastal sites having a smaller range over the year, chiefly because of the constant supply of moisture in maritime areas and differences in specific heat. This causes the sea to retain its heat, whilst land areas warm up and cool down more quickly, so that sea breezes are generated early in the morning and at night, bringing moisture-laden air.

From a cricketing point of view, this means that swing bowlers are more likely to find conditions in their favour at coastal grounds such as Hove, Swansea or Weston-super-Mare. Indeed, the higher humidity in the morning and late afternoon has been one of the features assisting swing bowlers at Hove. As Robertson-Glasgow once described at the Sussex ground, 'was it the sea-fret that sharpened the turf there, and in a never-to-be-explained manner, helped the often derided swerver'.[9]

One of the greatest exploiters of these conditions was Maurice Tate, who in the 1920s bowled from the northern end of the ground, down the slope towards the sea, making the most of the morning sea breeze. It was in the words of Ian Peebles 'to see the glory of Tate, in his opening overs at Hove on a green wicket, freshened by a slight sea haze. Uneasy was the captain who had won the toss and decided to bat.'[10] John Arlott has also heaped praise on the marvellous efforts of Maurice Tate at the Eaton Road ground in Hove. 'Before him and after him, the ground at Eaton Road was regarded as an absolute batsman's paradise, and many are the big and quickly made totals recorded there. Only Maurice Tate ever made batsmen feel that Hove was not a good ground for them; even those bowling from the other end gave no hint of it. It was said that it was the sea-fret in the air or on the pitch; that it was because the tide was in – or because the tide was out – but no one ever truly argued away the fact that, with almost monotonous frequency, Maurice Tate was next door to unplayable at Hove.'[11]

In 1923, Tate took 219 wickets, followed by 205 in 1924 and 228 in 1925. However, even he found that during the afternoon bowling could be arduous on the fast and true pitches in unhelpful meteorological conditions. A classic example came in the match between Sussex and the Australians in August 1930. The tourists put out their full Test batting side, with the exception of the legendary Don Bradman, who had scored 254 in the second Test at Lord's, as the tourists amassed a mammoth 729 for six declared. But it was a different matter at Hove as they struggled in the dank, maritime conditions, facing the magnificent bowling of Maurice Tate. At lunch on the first day, they were 69 for six wickets, with Tate having taken all six wickets for just 18 runs. However, they received during the afternoon, thanks to a century from Alan Kippax as the atmosphere cleared and Tate's bowling became more manageable.

Another venue with a quirky maritime character is St Helen's, Swansea. The ground was laid out in the nineteenth century on a reclaimed sandbank and in places the soil is reputed to be barely 18 inches deep, before sand is reached. As well as moist sea breezes, the rise and fall of the tide can affect the humidity levels at the micro-scale, and assist the seam bowlers. So much so, that Glamorgan legend has it that Wilf Wooller, Glamorgan's great post-war captain would sometimes check the tide tables before going out to toss, knowing full well that if the tide was in, it could be an advantage to bowl first in the moist conditions.[12] *Wisden* sadly does not record the tide conditions or the humidity levels, so we cannot assess how effective Wooller's strategy was, except to say, that even when Mike Selvey briefly captained the Welsh side in 1983 and 1984, he too would cast an eye on the tide tables.

But knowing about local idiosyncrasies was one thing, actually getting the chance to exploit them, was another, and this was entirely dependent on winning the toss. In June 1974 luck deserted Glamorgan in their Gillette Cup tie with Lincolnshire. As *Wisden* recorded, 'Moore, their captain, made an astute move when on winning the toss, he put Glamorgan in to bat. In the humid atmosphere and on a damp wicket, conditions were just right for the Lincolnshire attack, and before lunch, Glamorgan lost eight wickets for 62.'[13] A ninth wicket partnership of 87 by Malcolm Nash and Tony Cordle saw Glamorgan to 155, but by mid-afternoon, the wicket had dried out into a fine batting surface, and Lincolnshire strolled to a six-wicket victory. At the time, it was only the second time in the history of the 60-overs competition that a minor county had defeated a first-class one, but it also highlights the importance of meteorological conditions and the unique micro-climate of certain county grounds, which gives English cricket its unique charm.

Sunspot Activity and Golden Summers

Golden summers

So far our attention has been focused on the interruptions by rain, or the moist conditions in which swing bowlers profit. We now switch to those long, hot days of summer when the sun shone, batsmen prospered and fast bowlers toiled for little reward. Perhaps the best example of such a golden summer was in 1947 when Denis Compton topped the first-class batting averages with 3,816 runs at an average of 90.85, closely followed by his Middlesex colleague Bill Edrich with 3,539 runs at 80.43. During that marvellous summer for batsmen, Compton hit 18 centuries and Edrich 12, whilst their team-mate Jack Robertson chipped in with 12. Many other batsmen had fine seasons during 1947, with 11 centuries being scored by Yorkshire's Len Hutton and Cyril Washbrook of Lancashire, for whom Winston Place also registered 10 hundreds.

Such golden summers with many weeks of fine weather can, from a meteorological point of view, be caused by a blocking anticyclone, or cell of high pressure, that establishes itself over north-west Europe. On such occasions, the westerly winds, both near the earth's surface and in the upper atmosphere, are not sufficiently strong enough to 'break down' or shift the blocking anticyclone.[1] During summers when the westerlies are strong, pressure is lower over north-west Europe so that Britain is affected by a sequence of depressions moving in from the Atlantic, bringing cloudier and cooler weather, as well as pulses of rain.

However, there is another and more intriguing explanation for the occurrence of golden summers – the solar sunspot cycle. King has shown that exceptional weather conditions have taken place during sunspot maxima and minima. He pointed to the fact abnormal rainfall totals have been recorded in minima years. Out of the driest winters between 1697 and 1970, four out of the 18 driest occurred in sunspot maxima. Whilst the driest springs tended to occur during sunspot maxima, the wettest springs also tended to occur around sunspot minima.[2]

Exceptional summers

If King is correct that exceptional weather events occur during the extremes of the solar cycle, is there evidence to support a link between outstanding cricketing feats and sunspot activity? King has already tentatively suggested a link, citing the fact that of the 28 occasions when cricketers have scored over 3,000 runs in an English season, 16 have been in sunspot maximum or minimum years. Similarly, 13 out of the 15 occasions when a batsman has scored 13 or more centuries in a season, took place in, or within a year, of a sunspot maxima or minima. He has also shown that out of the 59 occurrences of a bowler taking 200 wickets or more in a season, 37 have been in the year before, or the year after, maximum or minimum sunspot activity.[3]

Using absolute values such as the number of centuries or wickets, or even reaching a total of 3,000 runs in a season, is not the best comparative indicator for the modern Championship era, when batsmen rarely exceed 1,500 runs in a season and are said to have had an exceptional summer if they score more than half a dozen Championship centuries. Bowlers nowadays are also highly praised if they exceed 50 wickets, never mind the elusive and somewhat distant 100.

Therefore, to assess whether county cricketers have the opportunity to record exceptional performances during the extremes of the solar cycle, we have to use, once again, three of John Kitchin's indices,[4] and compare seasons with a similar number of Championship fixtures. Table 24 covers performances between 1947 and 1964, with the number of batsmen averaging between 40 and 50, over 50, and the number of bowlers averaging under 20 in the solar cycle from 1947 to 1954. There appears at first to be a pattern with batsmen prospering in the sunspot maxima of 1947, and bowlers doing very well in the sunspot minima of 1954. But 1957 disturbs this neat picture, as in this particular minima, there were more bowlers averaging below 20 than in the minima of 1954. By the next minima in 1964, it was the batsman's turn to prosper with a similar number averaging over 50 as in the previous minima.

TABLE 24
EXCEPTIONAL BATTING AND BOWLING PERFORMANCES DURING
THE SOLAR CYCLES 1947–64

Season	Solar Cycle	Number of Games	Batsmen av. 40 to 50	Batsmen av. over 50	Bowlers av. under 20
1947	Maxima	26	18	11	17
1950		28	17	8	22
1954	Minima	28	5	6	31
1957	Maxima	28	6	2	33
1960		28/32	10	2	24
1964	Minima	28	7	6	20

Source: Statistics from *Wisden* 1947–64, with the qualifications based on batting in more than 8 innings, and bowling in more than 10 innings.

Therefore, there is no distinctive pattern during this period from 1947 until 1964 with either batsman prospering in the maxima years, and the bowlers doing well in the minima years. Even so, the years with the greatest number of batsmen averaging over 50, and the season with the most successful bowlers were in maxima years. To see whether this was a coincidence or not, a similar comparison was made with the solar cycles between 1986 and 1996. The results in Table 25 show that the summer when the greatest number of bowlers averaging under 20 was in the solar maxima of 1989, and the summer when most batsmen averaged between 40 and 50 was in the minima of 1995. The picture was disturbed by 1990, but this was the season of low seamed balls, and the number of batsmen averaging over 50 was a freak. By ignoring this season, the summer when most batsmen averaged over 50 was 1995 – a solar minima.

TABLE 25
EXCEPTIONAL BATTING AND BOWLING PERFORMANCES
DURING THE SOLAR CYCLES, 1986–96

Season	Solar Cycle	Batsmen av. 40 to 50	Batsmen av. over 50	Bowlers av. under 20
1986	Minima	38	10	7
1987		32	7	8
1988		15	8	9
1989	Maxima	25	10	11
1990		50	40	2
1991		31	21	2
1992		39	26	3
1993		28	21	4
1994		33	20	3
1995	Minima	50	25	6
1996		43	28	3

Source: Statistics from *Wisden* 1987–97, with the qualifications based on batting in more than 8 innings, and bowling in more than 10 innings.

Whilst the data in Tables 24 and 25 come from relatively small samples, the results suggest that King was, in fact, correct to spot the coincidence that county cricketers produce exceptional performances at the ends of the solar cycle, although there is no way of predicting if it is going to be with the bat or ball!

The sunniest summers

Given that doubt still exists over the impact of sunspots on meteorological processes, it is worthwhile also considering other weather phenomena as indicators of exceptionality, such as sunshine hours. Once again Jeater's analysis of 1890–1993 can be used to look at the performances in sunny and dull seasons.[5] He used the total amount of sunshine over the four summer months, measured in hours, taken from a standard series for England and Wales as a whole.

Table 26 shows the ten most sunniest and least sunniest seasons, and by using Kitchin's three indicators in each of these, it is possible to clearly show that the batsmen have profited in the sunniest summers, whilst bowlers have done better in the cloudiest. This is not unduly surprising, but as Table 27 shows it is possible to quantify the level of exceptionality in these fine and poor summers. The mean values in this table show that on average 25.3 batsmen average between 40 and 50 in sunny summers, compared with 5.2 in the cloudier ones, whilst there were almost five times as many batsmen averaging over 50 in sunny seasons compared with cloudy ones.

TABLE 26
THE MOST, AND LEAST, SUNNY SUMMERS, 1890–1993

TEN MOST SUNNY SUMMERS		TEN LEAST SUNNY SUMMERS	
Year	Hrs sunshine	Year	Hrs sunshine
1989	1024	1912	539
1976	944	1954	555
1911	943	1907	570
1975	910	1894	582
1959	904	1890	604
1949	895	1968	611
1990	866	1932	617
1921	850	1891	619
1935	844	1958	621
1984	831	1902	621

Sources: D. Jeater, 'Cricket Season Weather 1890–1993', *The Cricket Statistician*, 89 (1993), 26–9.

As far as bowling is concerned, three times as many bowlers averaged below 20 in cloudy summers compared with sunny ones. This confirms the belief that overcast conditions favour the seam bowlers, although there are disputes over exactly what it is that causes the ball to swing in cloudy conditions. For many years, it was believed that the increased humidity on cloudy days assisted swing, but a more recent and radical idea is that clouds interfere with the micro-thermals rising up from the grass, thereby assisting the swing bowlers.

The warmest summers

Other indicators of exceptionality are the temperature records and Table 28 shows the ten warmest and ten coolest summers between 1890 and 1993, as identified by Jeater, using the average daily temperatures for the

summer months based on the Meteorological Office's standard series for
Central England.[6]

TABLE 27
COMPARISON OF PERFORMANCES IN THE TEN SUNNIEST AND TEN LEAST
SUNNY SUMMERS

(a) Year	Sunniest summers Batsmen av. 40 to 50	Batsmen av. over 50	Bowlers av. under 20
1989	25	10	11
1976	24	9	8
1911	21	4	23
1975	31	7	12
1959	24	8	14
1949	27	11	8
1990	50	40	2
1921	12	5	21
1935	12	–	23
1984	27	12	4
Mean	25.3	10.6	12.6
(b) Year	Least sunny summers Batsmen av. 40 to 50	Batsmen av. over 50	Bowlers av. under 20
1912	8	3	41
1954	5	6	31
1907	6	–	42
1894	–	–	48
1890	2	–	38
1968	9	1	27
1932	13	12	20
1891	2	–	37
1958	3	1	43
1902	4	1	35
Mean	5.2	2.4	36.2

TABLE 28
TEN WARMEST AND TEN COOLEST SUMMERS, 1890–1993

Year	Av. Temp. Deg.C	Year	Av. Temp. Deg.C
1976	16.35	1907	12.83
1947	16.15	1902	12.95
1911	15.95	1909	13.20
1959	15.93	1894	13.20
1933	15.90	1979	13.25
1893	15.63	1963	13.25
1989	15.60	1956	13.28
1970	15.40	1954	13.35
1983	15.38	1891	13.35
1990	15.28	1972	13.38

Source: Adapted from data collected by David Jeater (1993).

Table 29 shows the performances in these warm and cool summers using three of Kitchin's indicators, and once again it is possible to quantify how much better batsmen or bowlers perform. In the warm seasons, 24.9 batsmen averaged between 40 and 50, whilst just 8.3 were in this category during the ten coolest summers. More than four times as many batsmen averaged over 50 in the warm summers, whilst there were twice the number of bowlers averaging under 20 in cool summers than in warm ones.

TABLE 29
COMPARISON OF PERFORMANCES IN THE TEN WARMEST AND TEN
COOLEST SUMMERS

(a) Warmest summers Year	Batsmen av. 40 to 50	Batsmen av. over 50	Bowlers av. under 20
1976	24	9	5
1947	18	11	17
1911	21	4	23
1959	24	8	14
1933	22	11	21
1893	4	–	28
1989	25	10	11
1970	22	7	5
1983	39	13	10
1990	50	40	2
Mean	24.9	11.3	13.6

(b) Coolest summers Year	Batsmen av. 40 to 50	Batsmen av. over 50	Bowlers av. under 20
1907	6	–	42
1902	4	1	35
1909	6	1	31
1894	–	–	48
1979	27	8	15
1963	6	–	30
1956	10	–	30
1954	5	6	31
1891	2	–	37
1972	17	10	13
Mean	8.3	2.6	31.2

Source: Adapted from data collected by David Jeater (1993).

So far we have been looking at climatic trends at the national and regional scale, but as the examples of Hove and Swansea showed, distinctive microclimates can cause localised differences in maritime areas. Similar small-scale anomalies also occur in urban areas, and since the 1960s geographers have appreciated that cities and towns tend to be warmer than the surrounding countryside. This has led to the concept of the 'urban heat island', and it is the purpose of the next chapter to explore the cricketing impact of this phenomenon, and the other aspects of an urban micro-climate.[7]

Cricket in the Cities: A Microclimatic View

Urban microclimates

The first person to suggest that temperatures were different in urban areas was Luke Howard in 1819, and during the 1930s geographers in central Europe undertook surveys which confirmed that urban areas experienced different weather patterns compared with the adjoining suburbs and rural areas.

One of the first British geographers to study the effect of built-up areas on air temperatures was T.J. Chandler in London.[1] He showed how under spring conditions of clear skies and light winds, temperatures in central London reached a minimum of 11°C, whilst in the rural–urban fringe they fell to 5°C. Overall, Chandler discovered that annual temperatures in central London were 0.9 degrees higher than in the suburbs. He concluded that these higher temperatures were caused by darker surfaces, such as tarmac as well as concrete, glass, and other bricks, which absorb heat during the day and conduct it slowly back into the atmosphere at night.

The buildings therefore act like a huge storage heater, releasing at night a reservoir of heat accumulated during the day. The main factors would appear to be the density of buildings, the materials used for construction and the geometry of the built-up area itself, with a combination of curved glass and concrete forms in a wide variety of shapes and dimensions. These buildings will all reflect the incoming solar radiation and allow it to bounce off many other surfaces. Recent research has also shown that artificial heat makes a contribution to the 'island effect' with heat emanating from artificial lights and vehicle exhausts. Therefore, the warming is not just taking place at ground level, as tall skyscrapers will release and re-radiate heat into higher parts of the atmosphere.

The local wind patterns also play a role, and it was no surprise that Chandler found a distinctive heat island under calm conditions. Strong winds, especially at night, can diminish or even destroy the heat island by blowing in cool air from rural areas. Interestingly, the island can generate its own breeze, blowing in from rural areas. This mechanism for a 'country breeze' is analogous to that for the coastal sea breeze, and is simply triggered by the city's warmth. During the late evening it can even set off showers as cool rural air meets and uplifts warmer urban air.

Another feature of an urban microclimate is that the city atmosphere is likely to have a higher level of pollutants than air in suburban or rural areas. Indeed, particulate matter can be between three to seven times greater over cities than in the rural areas, and urban air can hold up to 200 times more gaseous pollutants such as sulphur dioxide and carbon monoxide. These pollutants also act as hygroscopic particles and provide an abundance of condensation nuclei, thereby assisting the rain generation process. An example of this was in Rochdale in Lancashire where surveys showed less rain fell in the past on Sundays when mills and factories were not producing as much smoke as on weekdays.[2]

These particulates mean that together with the warmer air, the urban areas have a perfect recipe for intensifying convectional activity. Indeed, Bruce Atkinson has shown a clear link between convective cloud dynamics and thermal sources in the London area. In particular, Atkinson showed how London was more prone to thunderstorms between May and September. Using data for the period 1951–60, he found that rain associated with summer thunderstorms, which comprises 5 to 15 per cent of the total precipitation, was particularly concentrated in west, central and southern London. Indeed, during this time period, London's thunderstorm rain was 20 to 25cm greater than in the more rural parts of south-east England. Atkinson also suggested that the causal factors were an increase in warmer surfaces in the conurbation, producing strong thermal updraughts, as well as the mechanical effect of buildings on the air flows close to the ground. In particular, he believed that the urban areas created obstacles and increased rates of friction and turbulence, thereby inducing faster upward velocities and assisting the convectional activity. The turbulent eddies also caused urban dust, pollutants and other hygroscopic particles to rise up and assist the rain-forming processes.[3]

However, it is not the case that only the central parts of the urban area will receive significantly higher amounts of precipitation. As T.R. Oke pointed out, 'it will take some time for the hygroscopic materials to be carried up to cloud level and for the droplets to form and grow to a sufficient size to fall to the surface. Therefore, any effects are likely to occur downwind of, rather than within, the city itself.'[4] Consequently, this convectional activity in the City of London has meant that the Greater London area itself has witnessed some severe and localised summer storms.

Time lost in the cities

All of these studies into the urban micro-climate would therefore suggest that large built-up areas could host more rain-affected cricket matches during the summer months. To see if this is the case, we can first of all turn to a listing produced by Philip Bailey of all Championship matches abandoned without a ball bowled between 1886 and 1987.[5] Table 30 shows the grounds that lost most games during this period. Lord's comes out on top, with Old Trafford in second place, although if the matches at The Oval are added to those at Lord's a total of 25 matches in the capital city were lost, equivalent to 17 per cent of all abandoned Championship matches during this period. (If four abandoned games in suburban Leyton are added to this total, the percentage for metropolitan London rises to 19.86 per cent).

TABLE 30
GROUNDS WHERE COUNTY CHAMPIONSHIP MATCHES WERE ABANDONED
WITHOUT A BALL BOWLED, 1886–1987

Ground	Abandoned Matches
Lord's	14
Old Trafford	13
Bristol	11
The Oval	11
Chesterfield	9
Edgbaston	7

Source: P. Bailey in *The Cricket Statistician*, 78 (1990), 34–8.

The data for rainfall interruptions in 1998, already outlined in Chapter 8, was also disaggregated by ground to allow a survey of the amount of time lost at each venue in the County Championship. Table 31 shows the amount of time lost at those venues hosting five or more first-class fixtures in 1998. Old Trafford in Manchester and Cardiff's Sophia Gardens emerged as the two grounds where most play was lost through the weather, with Leicester, Taunton and Southampton also figuring highly as 'damp grounds'.

The unseasonal passage of moisture-laden fronts throughout the season across much of South Wales probably explains much of the time lost in Cardiff, where the figure for time lost was well above average. 52.25 hours of play were consequently lost at Sophia Gardens, a figure more than the amount of time in the three previous years combined. In 1995 ten hours were lost in Championship games at Cardiff, followed by 13.5 in 1996 and 23 in 1997. Glamorgan's penultimate Championship game of the 1998 season, against Derbyshire, was one of the worst affected matches, as rain-bearing fronts moved up the Bristol Channel. Had Gloucestershire been playing in Bristol, they might also have been severely affected, but they were fortunate to be playing away from home. Indeed, another consideration behind the major loss of play at Sophia Gardens was the timing of fixtures, either early in the season or in the final month, when cyclonic activity was taking place. When a ridge of high pressure built up over South Wales, and fine weather developed, Glamorgan were playing fixtures outside the Principality!

TABLE 31
TIME LOST AT GROUNDS STAGING FIVE OR MORE CHAMPIONSHIP GAMES IN 1998

	% total time
Old Trafford	37.82
Cardiff	34.15
Leicester	25.98
Taunton	22.43
Southampton	21.41
Leeds	20.87
Worcester	20.71
The Oval	20.17
Chester-le-Street	19.89
Edgbaston	19.00
Canterbury	16.11
Chelmsford	15.88
Northampton	13.84
Trent Bridge	12.75
Hove	11.76
Bristol	10.46
Derby	8.26
Lord's	6.30

Old Trafford, in Greater Manchester, once again emerged as the 'raining champion' of the 1998 season. High levels of precipitation are recorded in any case in north-west England as maritime air masses rise, cool and condense as they pass over the Pennines and Lake District.[6] But there are some peculiar seasonal divisions to these patterns, with Gregory and Crowe finding from data for Merseyside and Greater Manchester that February to June is drier than July to January.[7] Indeed, Table 32 shows how August is a particularly damp month in the region, based on the data between 1961 and 1990 for Manchester Airport, Bidston, Bolton and Macclesfield. In fact, August was the wettest month during the period for the weather station at Manchester Airport.

TABLE 32
MEAN MONTHLY AND ANNUAL PRECIPITATION TOTALS FOR SELECTED
STATIONS IN NORTH-WEST ENGLAND, 1961–90

Location	J	F	M	A	M	J	J	A	S	O	N	D	Tot
Manchester Airpt	69	50	61	51	61	66	65	79	74	77	77	78	808
Bidston	60	44	51	49	55	54	57	71	72	77	74	69	733
Bolton	115	74	93	70	77	89	83	109	109	127	120	120	1,186
Macclesfield	91	62	79	69	71	79	79	91	88	91	99	97	996

Source: L. Tufnell, 'North-West England and the Isle of Man', in D. Wheeler and J.C. Mayes (eds.), *Regional Climates of the British Isles* (London: Routledge, 1997), p.187, Table 8.4

In the past, an explanation for the Manchester area having damp summers might have been the high level of condensation nuclei and airborne pollutants from manufacturing industry, encouraging cloud formation and precipitation. But, between 1956 and 1988 the mean annual concentration of smoke declined by 90 per cent. It would appear more likely that the urban heat island, as outlined by Barratt was the causal mechanism behind the greater incidence of summer rain. Barratt undertook an extensive survey of precipitation patterns in the Manchester region, both in summer and winter, and he found marked intra-regional differences that could only be explained by the modifying influence of the conurbation.

In particular, he showed how the weather stations to receive an above average amount of rainfall were 'just east of the city centre, spreading laterally to include the ring of satellite towns from Salford to Bolton, Bury, Rochdale, Oldham and Stockport ... The axis of increased rainfall was aligned from north-west to south-east across the conurbation, and this may represent a critical line along which the prevailing southerly and westerly air masses can be expected to rise in anticipation of the Rossendale-Pennine Hills. Any extra instability resulting from urban heat island influence might, therefore, have a remarkable powerful and immediate effect upon precipitation along this "trigger axis".'[8]

Subsequent research has also shown how Manchester's heat island is also responsible for the city region having an above average number of days with thunderstorms, especially between May and August. On average, the weather station at Manchester Airport records 12 days of thunder each year compared with 8.5 days at Macclesfield and 2.8 days at Douglas on the Isle of Man. Webb highlighted how the area also has an above average number of summer hailstorms, as a result of the physical barrier of the Pennines, which forces air masses to rise, having previously passed over the overheated ground surface of the urban area. This mechanism resulted in severe hailstorms in May and June 1983, when hailstones, some with a diameter of 25mm, fell over the area.[9]

Another factor behind the greater number of rain days in the Manchester area might be a 're-fuelling' process, with south-westerly airflows having passed over the upland areas of south-west Ireland, warming up due to a föhn effect, allowing them to gain more moisture as they pass over the Irish Sea before reaching the Lancashire coastline.[10] Further research clearly needs to be undertaken to see if this föhn effect is adding to the amount of rainfall caused by the convectional activity generated by Manchester's heat island.

The argument for an urban enhancement of precipitation mechanisms therefore seems to be a very persuasive one in the Manchester area. But the Lancashire conurbation may not be alone in the United Kingdom in modifying the rainforming processes, leading to the question of whether the same modifications and enhancements are happening in other urban areas, such as London? Indeed, both Lord's and The Oval appeared prominently in Table 30. The south-east of England has fewer frontal and relief influences than other parts of the United Kingdom, so could the sizeable loss of play be the result of the distinctive urban climate?

Table 33 shows the temporal distribution of abandoned games at Lord's and it is not surprising to see games in 1903 and 1931 appearing on this list, as these were two notoriously wet summers. But in none of the wet summers after 1931 were matches at Lord's completely washed out without a single ball being bowled. This bucks the national trend, so perhaps other factors have contributed to their abandonment rather than the regular bouts of rainfall which were falling elsewhere over the country.

TABLE 33
ABANDONED CHAMPIONSHIP MATCHES AT LORD'S, 1889–1987

Year	Date	Match
1889	June 10–12	Middlesex v Kent
1902	August 18–20	Middlesex v Lancashire
1903	June 15–17	Middlesex v Essex
1903	August 24–26	Middlesex v Kent
1931	August 19–21	Middlesex v Derbyshire
1957	August 14–16	Middlesex v Leicestershire
1966	Aug. 31–Sep. 2	Middlesex v Hampshire
1967	May 24–26	Middlesex v Gloucestershire
1978	May 3–5	Middlesex v Hampshire
1979	May 26, 28, 29	Middlesex v Sussex
1979	June 13–15	Middlesex v Nottinghamshire
1981	May 23–26	Middlesex v Sussex
1983	May 11–13	Middlesex v Yorkshire
1987	July 18, 20, 21	Middlesex v Nottinghamshire

Source: P. Bailey, *The Cricket Statistician*, 78 (1990), 34–8.

An answer might well be the urban heat island, plus the influence of air pollution. In fact, only five of the games in Table 33 took place before the introduction of the Clean Air Act in 1956. This legislation was introduced to reduce the amount of particulate matter in the lower atmosphere over urban areas, yet of the 14 abandoned games at Lord's, nine have taken place since the passing of this legislation. Whilst some of these games were in damp seasons, it could well have been that human activity and the release of other types of particulate matter, in association with the urban heat island, triggered localised convectional activity over the London conurbation for several days, resulting in the complete abandonment of games.

As far as the other grounds are concerned, relief and frontal rainfall over the Pennines explains why Chesterfield hosted nine abandoned games in Table 30, whilst Sheffield had four and Buxton three. In contrast,

Essex in the drier east only completely lost one game at Chelmsford and one at Colchester, whilst Kent lost just one at Tonbridge, one at Tunbridge Wells, but none at Canterbury. At the other end of the scale, 11 of the abandoned games took place in Bristol in the wetter west. At first one could argue that the Nevil Road ground is in the wetter west, yet on the other side of Severnside just two games were washed out at Cardiff and only three in Swansea.

A survey by John Mace of the impact of rain at Bristol also showed an increase in complete abandonments since 1971.[11] Despite looking at uneven time periods, his findings in Table 34 show that the number of three-day Championship games at the County Ground which were abandoned without a ball bowled had risen from a fraction over 1 per cent between 1889 and 1970 to nearly a quarter between 1971 and 1985.

TABLE 34
ABANDONED COUNTY CHAMPIONSHIP MATCHES AT BRISTOL, 1889–1985

Period	Games at Bristol Held	Total abandonments Abandoned	National	% at Bristol
1889–1970	483	1	95	1.05
1971–1985	97	10	41	24.40

Other information relating to Gloucestershire's home games has shown the increased amount of time lost at Bristol during the 1980s.[12] These results, shown in Table 35, show that around the equivalent of 16 days of Championship cricket were lost in 1980, yet by 1985 this figure has risen to over 22 days.

TABLE 35
TIME LOST BY GLOUCESTERSHIRE DURING COUNTY CHAMPIONSHIP MATCHES, 1980, 1985

Season	Minutes lost Bristol	Away
1980	2,858	3,640
1985	4,728	3,251

This sizeable loss of playing time, and the long delays for play to restart after rain, led to Gloucestershire calling for surveys into the likely causes. These drew attention to the passage of rain-bearing fronts across the Bristol regions, but as Mace showed, enquiries were also made about the effectiveness of the drains and the location of the local water table.[13] The advisers subsequently confirmed that the answer lay in the soil, with the ground urgently needing 'aerating'.

W.J. Adams subsequently reported that 'the square on the Phoenix

County Ground has the distinction of being sited on a heavier clay soil than any other county square. The mean clay content of the topsoil of the county squares is a little over 30 per cent; the sub-soil of the Phoenix ground contains over 50 per cent. A clay content of this magnitude in our climate presents considerable difficulties because the soil is either very sticky or stiff when moist and dries out extremely slowly.'[14] Consequently, during the mid-1980s remedial work was undertaken on the Bristol square to improve the situation, and allow it to dry quicker after rain. A measure of the success of the work is that the Bristol ground lost just under three days play in 1998 and a shade over five in 1999.

This case study of the Bristol ground shows that other factors, apart from meteorological, have contributed to the significant loss of playing time, and these pedological aspects merit further detailed analysis at other urban grounds. Indeed, the authorities at Lord's have already authorised work from September 2002 on relaying the outfield on a new base of sandy soil, which will improve, and speed up, rates of drying. It may prompt others to follow suit, but although millions might be spent on remedial work at ground, or below ground, level, little can in fact be done, at present, to prevent the rain from actually falling over these urban areas.[15]

An urban paradise for bat or ball?

It is clear therefore that the climatic conditions in large urban areas are different to those in smaller towns and rural areas, and might contribute to the loss of time. It has to be asked whether these damp and warm microclimates in the largest urban centres were affecting individual performances, and were more exceptional performances recorded in smaller urban centres?

To answer these questions, an analysis was initially undertaken of the location of all of the Championship hundreds in 1951 and 1971. The results are shown in Table 36, and highlight the excellent batting wickets at Trent Bridge, Nottingham during this time period. Whilst Lord's and The Oval featured in the lists, it was the grounds lower down the settlements hierarchy, rather than the conurbations at the top, which saw more Championship hundreds. As far as 1951 was concerned, if the two London grounds are removed from the list, the grounds where batsmen excelled did not have more than 307,000 people. Interestingly, the larger settlements of Bristol (442,994), Leeds (500,000), Manchester (703,082), and Birmingham (1.1 million) were absent from this list. This was confirmed by a correlation analysis between the size of settlement and the number of centuries. It showed a weak positive relationship with a value of +0.40 in 1951 rising to +0.56 by 1971, suggesting that more Championship hundreds were being recorded in the large settlements, but not in the largest.

TABLE 36
LOCATION OF CHAMPIONSHIP HUNDREDS IN 1951 AND 1971

Year	Ground	No. of 100s	Population
1951	Trent Bridge, Nottingham	29	306,055
	Lord's, London	15	3,347,982
	New Road, Worcester	15	59,703
	The Oval, London	14	3,347,982
	Wantage Road, Northampton	13	104,432
	Grace Road, Leicester	12	285,181
1971	Grace Road, Leicester	19	276,775
	Trent Bridge, Nottingham	13	300,630
	Edgbaston, Birmingham	12	1,014,670
	Lord's, London	9	7,452,346
	Wantage Road, Northampton	9	126,642
	The Oval, London	9	7,452,346
	Old Trafford, Manchester	9	543,650
	St Helen's, Swansea	9	168,340

Source: Listing of first-class hundreds in *Wisden's Cricketers' Almanack* 1952 and 1972; Population Census totals for 1951 and 1971.

Another analysis was undertaken for the more recent period from 1987 until 1997 using double hundreds as an indicator of batting exceptionality. The results are shown in Table 37, with Northampton, Leicester, Edgbaston and Cardiff emerging as the grounds where batsmen excelled – once again, large settlements, but not at the top of the urban hierarchy, with the grounds in London lower in the list compared with other headquarters in smaller cities and towns. It was this category of settlement that witnessed an increased number of exceptional batting performances, yet as section (a) of Table 36 shows, back in 1951 Lord's was the venue for the second highest number of Championship hundreds. In addition, Old Trafford was conspicuous by its absence in 1951, but later appeared in the 1971 list. The sizeable interruption from rain and the damp outfields were two factors preventing a large number of double centuries from being recorded.

This leads to the inference that batting performances may have become less exceptional in the largest conurbations where a distinctive heat island has started to develop in the post-war era, assisting the swing and seam bowlers. To see if this was the case, an analysis was made of the venues where bowlers between 1987 and 1997 took more than ten wickets in an innings. A distinction was also made between the seam bowlers and the spinners, with the results shown in Table 38.

It is clear that faster bowlers perform significantly better in Championship games staged in larger urban areas, with over 150,000 people, rather than the largest. At Derby all 16 of the 10 wicket hauls were recorded by the seam bowlers, whilst at Leicester all 14 hauls were taken by the quicker bowlers. At Edgbaston, 15 five wicket hauls were recorded by the fast bowlers, with just two from spinners. Similarly at

Northampton, just one of the 14 hauls was recorded by a slow bowler. Table 38 also shows the grounds where the slower bowlers were most effective, but none of the top six were spinners' paradises. At Taunton, 11 hauls were taken by the seam bowlers, compared with 8 by spinners. At Old Trafford, the 16 hauls were split equally between spin and seam, whilst at Hove, the 10 hauls were similarly divided. At Trent Bridge, 10 out of the 16 hauls were recorded by seamers, whilst at Lord's, 7 out of the 12 hauls were recorded by quicker bowlers.

TABLE 37
LOCATION OF COUNTY CHAMPIONSHIP DOUBLE HUNDREDS, 1987–97

Ground	No. Double Hundreds	Population 1991
Northampton	11	178,570
Leicester	9	272,133
Edgbaston	9	937,763
Cardiff	8	279,055
Lord's	8	6,679,699
The Oval	8	6,679,699
Headingley	7	676,579
Canterbury	7	127,701
Southampton	6	195,906
Worcester	6	81,538
Chelmsford	6	123,026
Trent Bridge	6	262,235

Source: Listings in *Wisden's Cricketers' Almanack* 1988–1998; Population Census, 1991.

TABLE 38
LOCATION OF INSTANCES OF BOWLERS TAKING TEN WICKETS OR MORE
IN COUNTY CHAMPIONSHIP MATCHES, 1987–97

Ground	No. instances	Population
Seam Bowlers		
Derby	16	218,802
Edgbaston	15	937,763
Leicester	14	272,133
Northampton	13	178,570
Taunton	11	42,148
Trent Bridge	10	262,235
Spin Bowlers		
Taunton	8	42,148
Old Trafford	8	2,499,441
Chelmsford	7	123,026
Trent Bridge	6	262,235
Hove	5	143,356
Lord's	5	6,679,699

Source: Listings in *Wisden's Cricketers' Almanack* 1988–98; Population Census, 1991.

Only at Chelmsford have spinners performed exceptionally better than seam bowlers, with 5 hauls from the quicks and 7 from the spinners. The slower bowlers were especially successful at the festival venues or annual outgrounds, with 50 per cent of the grounds where 10 wicket hauls were recorded falling into this category. This was the case particularly with Essex where 3 hauls were taken at Ilford and 2 at Colchester. Only 37 per cent of the grounds where seam bowlers took ten wicket hauls were festival venues or outgrounds, but there were some notable exceptions, such as the Cheltenham College ground where 8 out of the 9 hauls were taken by the quicker bowlers.

Therefore, slow bowlers perform better at the occasional venues, and some would say that this is because the wickets at club grounds might not be so well prepared as at the headquarters venues. If one extends this argument, you would expect shirt front wickets at the headquarter grounds, so that the large urban centres were the venues for the exceptional batting performances. But as Table 37 showed, this is not the case, and despite the fact that many county games were regularly staged at The Oval and Lord's, the urban centres where most of the exceptional performances took place were not at the top of the urban hierarchy. Indeed, it was in the West and East Midlands where most of the exceptional performances were recorded, with county batsmen and bowlers prospering at Leicester, Derby, Trent Bridge and Edgbaston.

Our concern in this chapter has largely been with meteorological processes, but as the example of the Bristol ground showed, the answer could be pedological, and the quality of the wickets may well influence these patterns. Whilst there is a link between the atmosphere and the soil, the groundsmen at the Test venues and county headquarters in the West and East Midlands could be producing fine wickets for batting, as at Trent Bridge and Leicester, or hard, bouncy wickets for the quicker bowlers, as at Derby. Even so, the absence of the two London grounds from the top of any one of the lists of exceptional batting or bowling performances is intriguing, and an interesting trend in Table 37 is the decline in the number of County Championship hundreds at both Lord's and The Oval from 1951. Given the fact that these grounds lost more Championship games than any others, further research is needed to see if the urban heat island is affecting play at Lord's and The Oval, with the build up of hot and humid conditions favouring seam bowlers. With global warming taking place, this research might unearth some interesting results.

Global Warnings and Global Warming

Cane and rain

English cricket is not unique in having interference from the weather, as the game is played in other nations, where even more volatile climates exist in contrast to the temperate British climate. Indeed, it is another one of cricket's endearing features that the game is played in locations where temperatures regularly soar over 30°C or where there are torrents of rain.

Whilst the torrential downpours can hinder playing cricket, the warmer conditions in some nations, such as those in the Caribbean, are certainly a bonus. According to Michael Manley, the hot, tropical climate is one of the factors behind the success of cricket in the West Indies. The former Prime Minister of Jamaica believes that the long 'summer', relieved only by spring showers and autumnal storms, has greatly assisted cricket. 'No cold weather drives Caribbean people into huddles around a living-room fire. There are no generations of the young, impatiently awaiting the thaw that will melt the snow, and in due season, restore the meadows to running, jumping and the throwing of balls...those same climatic conditions encourage a freedom, almost a spontaneity of movement. These sons and daughters of the tropics are loose-limbed and athletic, relaxed and free-moving, because they spend so much of their time in the warm outdoors. Sprinting and fast bowling come easily.'[1]

However, it has not always been the case in the West Indies that cricket has been played in glorious sunshine. Indeed, B. Stoddart has shown how early matches in Barbados had to be played during the wetter months, as in the longer warm and dry period, the sugar cane was maturing and being harvested. Consequently, the 'crop' took precedent over cricket, and the ball games were staged during the rainy period. Hence, many of the games played by the Wanderers Club in the 1890s were disrupted by rain, and in 1896, the Pickwick Club made only 45, but still defeated Leeward by 4 runs after no less than five inches of rain had fallen![2]

But such storms are nothing compared to the amount of rain that annually falls over India, where Cherapunji receives no less than 1,079 cm of precipitation each year. This small settlement is in the north of India, and not surprisingly little first-class cricket takes place in these more rural areas. Cricket in India has, by and large, become an urban game, and as Mihir Bose suggests, 'it is an essential part of modern, industrial India.

Ruled by an elite, anxious to convince the world that it heads the tenth largest industrial power, one capable of producing atom bombs and exporting food grains and machinery, cricket is an essential status symbol. In the social set up of modern urban India, cricket is one sure way of obtaining acceptance for the urban poor and lower income groups, it forms a valuable distraction from their appalling poverty and struggle to survive.'[3]

Yet despite the involvement of the industrial and urban bourgeoisie, the game is still at the whim of the weather during the monsoon season between May and October, when parts of the Indian sub-continent receive 80 per cent of their annual rainfall. No amount of money can be spent to allow a host of games to be played at the height of the rainy season, so like many other aspects of Indian life, cricket has been adapted to the climate.

It never rains, it pours

The causes of the Indian monsoon are very complex, but put simply, it is caused by the uplift of air masses, which have picked up significant amounts of water vapour by evaporation over the Indian Ocean and the Arabian Sea. These moist parcels are then blown inland by southerly winds and the air is forced to rise over the Indian landmass and funnelled up the Ganges Valley. The monsoon usually arrives, or 'bursts', in Southern India and Sri Lanka, around 20 May, before reaching Nagpur in Central India by 1 June and Peshawar in Northern Pakistan by 1 July. A reversal of pressure then takes place as a high pressure cell steadily builds up over Eurasia, and the rains withdraw, leaving Peshawar on 1 September, Nagpur in mid October, and usually clearing Sri Lanka during December.

Meteorologists therefore identify four distinctive climatic periods over the Indian sub-continent:[4]

1. a cooler 'winter' period between January and February, when average daily temperatures range from 15°C in the north-west to 25°C in the south;
2. a hot period from March until May when temperatures are between 27°C and 33°C over most of the sub-continent;
3. the monsoon period between June and September when heavy rains sweep across the sub-continent; and
4. the post-monsoon period from October to December, as the monsoonal systems retreat in a south-easterly direction.

In India, the first-class season usually begins in early October, with the current curtain raiser being a match for the Irani Cup between the winners of the previous season's Ranji Trophy and an eleven drawn from rest of India. In 1992/93 there was an experiment with the Duleep Trophy during August and September, as a trial for finalising the tour party to South Africa. However, the pitches were under-prepared as the rains were still persisting, and the seamers flourished in the bowler-friendly conditions.

The domestic season in India draws to an end during the third week or so of April with the final of the Ranji Trophy. By this time temperatures are often in excess of 30°C, but by starting in the post-monsoon period, the Indian cricketers do not have to endure first-class matches throughout the hot period.

A similar pattern exists in Pakistan, with both the Quaid-E-Azam Trophy and PCB Patron's Trophy being played from early October until the first week of March. However, in Sri Lanka, a different climatic pattern exists. As Table 39 shows, April, May and June are wet months, whilst the later withdrawal of the monsoon means that October and November are also damp. This helps to explain why Sri Lanka is the home of the wettest international venue in Colombo, where 2,345 mm of rain falls each year. The increasingly complicated international schedules have also played a role, and consequently a different pattern often develops compared with their Indian neighbours. More domestic games are played during July and August, with for example, a Super Tournament during July 1992, primarily as a means of giving match practice to the leading players prior to a tour by Australia from early August until late September.

TABLE 39
MONTHLY AND ANNUAL PRECIPITATION FIGURES FOR SIX CRICKET VENUES
IN THE INDIAN SUB-CONTINENT (mm)

Venue	J	F	M	A	M	J	J	A	S	O	N	D	Total
Lahore	22	24	21	13	19	35	127	117	57	8	3	9	455
Delhi	23	18	13	8	13	74	180	173	117	10	3	10	642
Calcutta	10	31	36	43	140	297	325	328	252	114	20	5	1,601
Bombay	3	3	3	1	18	485	617	340	264	64	13	3	1,811
Madras	36	10	8	15	25	48	91	117	119	305	356	140	1,270
Colombo	9	69	147	231	371	224	135	109	160	348	315	147	2,345

Source: Online weather: http://www.onlineweather.com

In 1993/94 the South Africans also made a tour in August and September, and this followed a visit to Sri Lanka by the Indians. Their tour actually began in July; rain intervened to give Kandy the distinction of staging the shortest ever Test match, as just 12 overs were bowled in the match, all in a mere 49 minutes on the second day of the first Test between Sri Lanka and India. During the 1990s, the major domestic first-class competition – the P. Saravanamuttu Trophy – was staged between October and December, but in recent times it has been switched to run from early

January until ending in the last week of April, or the first week of May.

Whilst the climate has allowed Test matches in Sri Lanka during July and August, the withdrawal of the monsoon has not allowed any to be played in India until September or October at the earliest. As Table 40 shows, between 1932 and 1989, there was a pattern for most Tests to be staged during December and January. Even so, there are some subtle regional variations, largely influenced by the later withdrawal of the monsoon in the southern part of the sub-continent. In the north, Delhi and Kanpur have tended to stage Tests during November and December, whilst in the south, Tests have been held at Madras in January or February. Even so, some Tests have been staged at the Chepauk ground in Madras at the very end of the monsoon season. In 1979/80, it staged a match in the series between India and Australia which began on 11 September, whilst in 1982/83 India drew with Sri Lanka in a Test at Madras which began on 17 September.

TABLE 40
MONTHLY DISTRIBUTION OF TESTS PLAYED BY INDIA, 1932–89

Venue	Sept	Oct	Nov	Dec	Jan	Feb	Mar
Delhi	–	3	4	14	1	3	1
Kanpur	–	2	2	6	2	4	–
Calcutta	–	2	1	5	13	3	1
Bombay	1	2	9	10	3	4	1
Madras	2	2	1	3	16	5	-
Others	3	2	4	3	2	–	2
Total	6	13	21	41	37	19	5

Note: Tests have been staged at more than one ground in some cities.

Neither of these games was severely affected by rain or bad light, but the Indian authorities were not so fortunate in 1995/96 when they staged a three-Test series with New Zealand between mid-October and early November. To an extent, they were restricted as to the timing of this series by the World Cup that was starting some three months later. But they questionably opted to play the games in three venues in southern India – Bangalore, Madras and Cuttack – which were still being influenced by the final phases of the monsoon. No surprise then that the second Test staged on the Coromandel Coast at Madras between 25 and 29 October saw only 71.1 overs being bowled, and it went down in Indian cricket history as the shortest Test in terms of actual playing time ever staged in the country.[5] Ten days later the two teams met up again at Bombay for the final match of the rubber, and to their collective horror, the rains intervened again, with monsoonal storms sweeping in off the Bay of Bengal, causing the further loss of two days' play.

As well as precipitation, the amount of daylight is another restriction on the playing of cricket in the sub-continent. This has been particularly the case in one-day Internationals staged during the post-monsoon period, with venues in the south of India having up to three-quarters of an hour more daylight than locations further north. For example, at Bangalore (at latitude 12°58′N), there is daylight for about 11 hours and 50 minutes during October, whilst at Peshawar (at latitude 34°N), the length of day drops to around 11 hours and 15 minutes. In both localities, the angle of the sun's rays falls below 30° for 90 minutes at both dawn and dusk, giving a further three hours of diffuse light. Therefore, if floodlights are not being used, there are only around eight and a half hours when the light is good enough in which to stage a limited overs contest.[6]

Indeed, the reduced amount of daylight explains why in 1987, when India and Pakistan staged the World Cup, the allocation of overs per innings was reduced from 60 to 50, as it had been in the three previous World Cups in 1975, 1979 and 1983. In order fully to utilise the decent light, the contests began at 9 am although at this time in the early morning there was a risk that the early morning dew might assist the bowlers. However, this never actually happened, and out of the 27 fixtures, 19 were won by the side batting first, with the bowlers finding little to exploit.[7]

The sub-continent hosted the World Cup again in 1996, and this time the event was held between mid-February and mid-March. The difficulties posed by bad light were overcome by several of the games being day–night encounters, with floodlight pylons being erected for the first time at some of the Indian grounds. Before the introduction of artificial lights, the shortage of daylight played a subtle role in some one-day contests, and even led to allegations of gamesmanship and deliberately slow bowling rates, with fielding sides knowing that the bad light might come to their aid. Consequently, some one-day competitions in the sub-continent have seen the levying of substantial fines, and in the 1987 World Cup, the organisers levied fines of £1,200 for every over in the innings that was not bowled within the three and three-quarter hour allocation.

Even so, there was still the problem that in the hot and humid conditions, regular drinks breaks were needed to prevent fielders from dehydration, and the bowlers in particular found it difficult to maintain a fast over rate in the sweltering conditions. As a result, some one-day matches have fallen short of the 50 overs 'standard' now recognised by the Test-playing nations. For example, none of the matches in the six match series between India and Australia in 1986/87, saw the side fielding first bowl their full quota of 50 overs.

The likely temperature later in the day turned out to be a factor which captains took into account during the 1987 World Cup. Many teams may prefer to chase totals in limited overs competitions, but in the 1987 World

Cup many captains opted to bat first, so that opponents had to field first in the oppressive conditions. Indeed, in several matches the batsmen of the side chasing a target, made uncharacteristic mistakes, probably as a result of being exhausted after fielding, and duly lost their wickets and ultimately the game after panic had set in.[8]

Just what the doctor ordered

Australia is another cricket-playing nation where there are strong links between the playing of the game and meteorology, and it was where one Test match – the third Test of the 1970/71 Ashes Series at Melbourne – was abandoned without a ball bowled. Indeed, two of Australia's leading sporting academics, Ric Cashman and Ray Webster, believe that 'the Australian climate has played an important part in Australian cricket. The combination of heat and rain has produced wickets that are mostly hard, true and with good bounce. Australian wickets, unlike the low and slow wickets of New Zealand, the subcontinent and England, have always encouraged cricketers to play their shots with confidence, particularly square of the wicket.[9] Even so, there are marked climatic differences across Australia, which climatologically has a mix of temperate, sub-tropical and tropical regions. As Table 41 shows, the January temperatures in Australia's main Test venues soar above 26°C, and on occasions cricket has been played in even warmer conditions. For example, in 1896 the heat was so great during the game between Victoria and New South Wales that the bowlers had to use sawdust in order to grip the ball and prevent it from slipping out of their sweaty palms. Similarly, in January 1898 the tea interval in the match between South Australia and New South Wales had to be extended to 40 minutes in order to allow the players to have a proper respite from the intense heat, whilst players placed damp cabbage leaves under their hats in order to combat the heat.[10]

TABLE 41
RAINFALL AND TEMPERATURE DATA FOR SIX AUSTRALIAN CITIES

City	January Temp °C	Annual Rainfall mm
Adelaide	28.5	553
Brisbane	29.2	1,189
Darwin	31.8	1,666
Melbourne	25.7	661
Perth	31.5	869
Sydney	26.3	1,220

Note: The January data refers to maximum temperatures.
Source: Australian Bureau of Meteorology. http://www.bom.gov.au/

These conditions were extremes, but even so, summers over the temperate parts of southern Australia are mostly dry and hot with coastal sea breezes, whilst the tropical regions of northern Australia experience a wetter summer as the monsoon moves in. During the wet months from October to April, north-westerly winds bring humid conditions with showers and thunderstorms.

These regional differences in annual rainfall, outlined in Table 41, help to explain why two of the main Test grounds (Adelaide and Melbourne) are in the drier south where annual rainfall totals rarely exceed 700 mm. In contrast, in Darwin to the north, the annual total is often nearer 1,700 mm as a result of the monsoonal influences. But as Table 41 shows, Tests are also staged in Brisbane, where rainfall totals are higher than in the south. Indeed, features of the summer weather along the east coast are the violent thunderstorms caused by the intense heat and humidity. Perhaps the most famous were in late November and early December during the first Test of the 1946/47 Ashes series. Australia recorded a remarkable victory by an innings and 332 runs after England had twice been faced with batting on a sticky wicket following a sequence of torrential thunderstorms, and all after Australia had batted first and scored 645, with Don Bradman making a majestic 187.

The storms started to brew towards the end of Australia's mammoth innings and the start of England's first innings. As *Wisden*'s correspondent reported, 'during lunch, the sky became overcast and thunder was heard when, with the second ball after the interval, Lindwall bowled Hutton playing back. Bad light and showers caused many stoppages, and the day ended with England 21 for one wicket. Late that evening a violent thunderstorm broke, and next day England on a nightmare pitch took their score to 117 for five wickets before another thunderstorm flooded the ground, with hailstones as big as golf balls. Contrary to expectations, the ground made a remarkable recovery next day in the brilliant sunshine, but the pitch proved more treacherous than ever and fifteen wickets fell in three and a half hours.'[11]

Indeed, the Gabba at Brisbane was famous for these sticky wickets in the days before pitches were covered, and during the 1930s and 1940s the heavy rains produced sticky wickets in four of the first seven Tests staged at the ground. On the 1936/37 tour, Australia was dismissed by England for just 58 in their second innings to record what was Australia's lowest score in the twentieth century. This tradition for sticky wickets is also not surprising given the fact that the Woolloongabba suburb of Brisbane was originally a swampy parkland, before being developed into a cricket ground by the Queensland Cricket Association. It was opened in 1896, and around this time matches were still arranged well into the autumn in an attempt to avoid any interruptions by thunderstorms, and the hazard of batting on a sticky wicket.

The Gabba has also hosted all three of the only Sheffield Shield matches to be completely abandoned without a single ball being bowled. Ironically, all three have involved Victoria, with the abandonment of their games at the Gabba from 31 January to 4 February 1931, 30 January to 2 February 1971 and 11 to 14 February 1972. In addition, Ric Cashman has shown how Queensland have lost more playing time through rain than any other State side. He calculated that they lost 40 days out of 701 days of play from 1926/27 until 1982, compared with Western Australia losing just four days out of 474 from 1946/47 until 1982.[12]

Another of the most intriguing meteorological influences in Perth is 'the Fremantle Doctor', a cool breeze that during the afternoon blows in from the south-west, up the Swan River to the city. It is a typical onshore breeze, generated by the differential rates of heating of the land and sea, so that a cool wind blows across the WACA ground, assisting the bowlers and soothing the sun-drenched spectators.

Bowlers, both fast and slow, have been assisted by the Fremantle Doctor. Genuinely quick bowlers, such as Dennis Lillee and Graham McKenzie, plus into-the-wind swing bowlers such as Ian Brayshaw and Terry Alderman, have used the 'Doctor' to get the ball to hoop and curve alarmingly when bowling from the northern end of the ground during the afternoon.[13] Indeed, Ian Brayshaw fully exploited the Fremantle Doctor in October 1967 to take 10 for 44 for Western Australia against Victoria. He claimed his first batch of wickets on the first afternoon, when the south-westerly was blowing, before taking the remainder the next morning when an easterly breeze blew in during the morning. Brayshaw changed ends during his spell and swung the ball alarmingly both with and against the breeze.

The legendary Dennis Lillee also has fond memories of when, as a novice fast bowler, he was drafted into the Western Australian side and given the use of the wind against the MCC in 1970/71. He remembers how 'the two things combined to bring a breath of fresh air into my life. I was on top of the world again and went into the game full of vigour and vitality. The first ball I bowled knocked Geoff Boycott's cap off. It was pretty fast and the first couple of overs were generally yards faster than I had bowled all season.'[14]

Slower bowlers, such as Tony Lock, Bruce Yardley and Greg Matthews, have also used the breeze to obtain useful drift, loop and curve, but from 1985 however, the influence of the Fremantle Doctor has been affected by a revamping of the WACA ground. The centre square was relocated by 11 degrees, and as Ken Casellas noted 'for a while, this affected the ability of seamers to swing the ball away from right-hand batsman when operating from the northern end into the Doctor. But most bowlers have made the necessary adjustments. The vaunted Doctor remains a valuable ally for bowlers.'[15]

The curse of El Nino

The weather overseas can also cause hazards, and these may increase in the future, thanks to the feature known as El Nino, when the ocean currents and pressure systems across the Pacific Ocean alternate dramatically in a cyclical way. High sea-surface temperatures occur in the Pacific and trigger a reversal in the normal westward flow of the Trade winds and ocean currents. Every three to eight years, this oscillation, known as El Niño Southern Oscillation (ENSO), results in a tongue of warm water reaching the coast of the Americas, followed by a return to normal, sometimes with a more pronounced colder current than usual, known as La Niña.

Scientists believe that this oscillation is a natural feature, G. Philander stating that 'to ask why El Niño or La Niña occurs is equivalent to asking why a bell rings. The Southern Oscillation is a natural mode of oscillation of the coupled ocean-atmosphere system.'[16] There is no disputing that El Niño can have devastating effects across many nations, including those where cricket is played, and this section looks at the way, El Niño has affected cricket recently, as well as considering how it might play a greater role in the future.

Since 1950 there have been seven strong El Niño events – in 1957/58, 1965/66, 1972/73, 1982/83, 1986/87, 1991/92 and 1997/98. Studies of the latter El Niño between June and December 1997 showed four main effects in areas where Test cricket is played:[17]

1. a weak summer monsoon circulation in the Indian sub-continent – Annamalai and Slingo have shown how ENSO caused a delay by up to eight days in the arrival of the summer monsoon, and a more uneven distribution of rain than usual, both in spatial and temporal terms, resulting in floods in Kerala and drought in Andhra Pradesh.[18] However, in terms of the overall amount of precipitation, the 1997 summer monsoon was 2 per cent above normal. Disturbances continued for the rest of the year, with heavier storms than usual occurring in December, resulting in the Duleep Trophy having to be shared for only the second time in its 37-year history after heavy rain had severely affected the final between Central Zone and West Zone at Chennai from 17 to 21 December. Central Zone were 36 for 5 in reply to West Zone's 384 after three days had been lost to the weather. As Central Zone's innings was not completed, West Zone could not claim a lead and the trophy was shared;

2. less rain in South Africa between November and March, but an extremely wet period in East Africa from September to December. Usually, complex air masses converge over the heated southern African land mass, triggering heavy storms, such as those which

affected the England side on their recent tour to the Cape in 1999/2000. However, as Lindesay has shown, in El Niño years, there is a change in pattern, resulting in less precipitation in South Africa, but above average rains in East Africa.[19] and these were the conditions that faced the England 'A' tourists on their visit to Kenya in January 1998. The matches in East Africa had been arranged during what normally is the dry season, but as a result of ENSO, incessant rain disrupted the tourists' practice, as well as the unofficial one-day Internationals and the three-day match with Kenya;[20]

3.   drought in the northern part of South America, and a suppressed hurricane season in the West Indies. Usually, there are tropical cyclones between June and October, with a peak in activity in August and September. Jones and Thorncroft showed how the El Niño of 1997 was a low activity year, with only seven tropical storms in the Caribbean, one major hurricane, and a prolonged drought in the northern parts of South America.[21] The England tour to the West Indies in 1997/98 took place at the end of this ENSO, and it was drought conditions that faced the England cricketers when they arrived at the Bourda ground in Georgetown, Guyana, for the fourth Test in February 1998. The outfield was arid and bone-hard, and the wicket deteriorated as the game progressed, allowing the West Indies to win by 242 runs. This was in stark contrast to the previous season, before ENSO was operating, when heavy rains badly interrupted the fifth Test between the West Indies and India. In fact, the Bourda ground was so soft that no play was possible between the end of the first day and the last session on the fourth day, with the match, not surprisingly, petering out into a draw. By the time the England cricketers had travelled to Barbados for the fifth Test of the 1997/98 series, there was a change to La Nina conditions and an end to the prolonged drought. However, it came just when England were at last on top, with a lead of 374, but as *Wisden*'s tour correspondent reported, 'that was the moment when the island's five month drought chose to let up. The rain began in the small hours of Monday morning, and by dawn the roads round Bridgetown had become more like rivers. It did not stop until lunchtime. The parched ground absorbed the moisture fast enough for play to begin at 1 pm, but after 18.3 overs, another cloud blew over the Kensington Oval and snuffed out England's hopes for good;'[22]

4.   cooler seas around Australia, so that the trade winds slacken, so that less moisture is fed into the Australian region. Consequently, the monsoonal rains in Northern Australia will be late, and there is the likelihood of Eastern Australia being drier than normal. However, it is the La Niña trends that might cause problems for cricket. During these periods, the seas around Australia are warmer than usual, leading to widespread

summer rain and flooding. An example was in January 1974 when Brisbane witnessed its worst flooding that century as tropical cyclone 'Wanda' brought torrential rain and flooding to the east coast.

It is therefore clear that cricket in various parts of the world has been affected by these meteorological fluctuations and natural variations which are currently operating as part of ENSO. What is intriguing is what will happen in the future, and whether the ENSO phases of the 1990s have been typical or atypical?

Coral records and other marine evidence show that El Niño and La Niña events are more prominent and energetic during some decades, and less so during others. Scientists are still unsure if these more vigorous ENSO during the 1990s are part of this natural variability or are modifications caused by global warming. If it is the latter, then the impact on international cricket could be very wide-ranging indeed. Even so, research is taking place to predict, in advance, the likely effects that an ENSO may bring, and if these variations can be predicted in advance then perhaps domestic and tour schedules can be modified if heavy rains are likely to be produced.

Global warming

Another important consideration is what will happen in the future to the El Niño and La Niña variations under global warming. During the past two decades, the notion of global warming has moved from science fiction to science fact, with global temperatures being 0.7°C warmer than a hundred years ago. The four warmest years globally have been 1999, 1997, 1995 and 1990, and many academics have suggested causal mechanisms. It is known that there are natural mechanisms for climatic variability, but many scientists consider this increase in the past few years to have been the result of human activity. Indeed, in 1996 the Intergovernmental Panel on Climate Change concluded 'the balance of evidence suggests that there is a discernible human influence on global climate'.[23]

Scientists believe that global warming could result in greater extremes, especially in El Niño and La Niña years. This could result in more severe tropical storms and an increase in the number of places where they occur. In Australia, meteorologists are predicting that an increase in sea surface temperatures by 2 to 3 degrees would result in hurricanes affecting areas as far south as Brisbane, and with greater intensity than in the past. Scientists also believe that over the next 30 years, inland parts of northern Australia will warm by between 0.4 and 1.4 degrees, whilst coastal areas will warm by between 0.3 and 1 degrees, resulting in greater convectional activity and probably heavier summer thunderstorms.

Another aspect of global warming that needs serious consideration is a rise in sea levels, brought about by the melting of glaciers and ice sheets, as well as the thermal expansion of water. There is evidence to suggest that sea level rise has already taken place during the twentieth century, with a rise by about 15 cm, and scientists are already predicting a further rise of 18 cm by 2030 and 41 cm by the 2080s. Clearly, many low-lying areas of the world are going to be vulnerable to this rise in sea level, including the deltaic environments of Bangladesh, who have recently acquired Test status.

More varied and violent El Niño and La Niña oscillations, alterations to the monsoon cycle over Asia and a rise in sea levels in Bangladesh are just three of the possible consequences that global warming during the twenty-first century might bring. It is clear therefore that cricket's administrators in many parts of the world cannot safely assume the same meteorological conditions as in the past when planning their future tours and domestic calendars.

Greenhouse Cricket: The English Game in a Warmer World

Are British summers getting warmer and drier?

After this brief look at global warming from an international point of view, it is now time to consider the likely impact of these climatic changes on the United Kingdom. There is already a mass of data to show how the trend for global warming has affected Britain – temperatures during the 1990s have been about 0.5°C warmer than the 1961–90 average, with four out of the five warmest years on record having occurred since 1988. The 1990s has also seen the greatest number of 'hot days', when mean temperatures above 20°C have been recorded. During this decade an average of 7.5 hot days were recorded each year, nearly twice the long-term average. In fact, 1995 alone saw 26 hot days – the highest total in 225 years of measurements.[1]

Several surveys have been undertaken looking at these climatic changes, specifically in the summer months. Julian Mayes analysed changes during the summer months between 1947 and 1996, at both the national and regional level, using Davis' index of summer weather which combined measures of precipitation, temperature and sunshine from 24 evenly distributed sites across the country.[2] As far as the national picture was concerned, the index rose from 711.9 during the first part of the study period between 1947 and 1971 to 730.5 after 1972. This confirmed that there had been an increase in the frequency of good summers with warm temperatures, long hours of sunshine and little rainfall.

The trend for drier summers was also noted by N. Wood who found that four of the driest summers from 1921 to 1987 in Plymouth occurred between 1975 and 1984, whilst six of the ten driest in London were from 1972 to 1984. In their UKCIP98 report, Mike Hulme and Geoff Jenkins also showed how mean summer precipitation had fallen in eastern England from 180 mm in 1901–30 to 172 mm in 1931–60 and to 165 mm in 1961–90. Wales had also seen a similar decrease from 264 mm in 1901–30 to 248 mm in 1931–60 and to 234 mm in 1961–90.[3]

Thus, one can agree with Mayes that 'the changing geography of summer weather has been characterised by a decrease in precipitation in July and August over England and Wales, accompanied by a rise in temperature. This does not prove a link with global warming, of course, though it should act as an incentive for us to monitor the effect on the present day environment as a potential analogue for possible future changes.'[4]

The UK climate in the future

Given the evidence for generally warmer and drier summers, the next question that needs answering is what will the future British climate be like over the next hundred years. A number of models have been produced, with perhaps the most comprehensive being produced by Hulme and Jenkins for the UK Climate Impacts Programme, or UKCIP.[5] They believe that human-induced climate change and greater knowledge about natural climate variability and oscillations caused by volcanic eruptions and solar output, has meant that future projections cannot be based solely on extending forward the patterns observed over the past 30 years or more. Hulme and Jenkins therefore drew on the second assessment report of the Intergovernmental Panel on Climate Change (IPCC), and the climate modelling experiments undertaken by the Hadley Centre. They also described four possible scenarios – low, medium-low, medium-high and high – based on a different range of emission scenarios and differing climate sensitivities over three 30-year periods – 2010 to 2039 (2020s), 2040 to 2069 (2050s), and 2070 to 2099 (2080s).

In each case, the rise in annual mean temperature over the United Kingdom during each period is slightly smaller than for the global average, but Hulme and Jenkins exploded the myth that Britain might have a more comfortable Mediterranean climate. There is also likely to be a difference between the changes in the south-east of England and the changes further north. Hulme and Jenkins estimate that by the 2080s annual temperatures in south-east England could be between 1.5 and 3.2 deg.C warmer than the 1961–90 average. In contrast in Scotland, annual temperatures might only be between 1.2 to 2.6°C warmer. Modest changes in mean annual precipitation are also likely, with an increase by the 2080s of up to 10 per cent over England and Wales, and between 5 and 20 per cent over Scotland.

However, extreme events will become more common, with more frequent daily precipitation events and a 10 per cent increase in the number of summer gales. Drought summers, with temperatures warmer than 1997, could occur every other year, and once in a century droughts, such as the one in 1976, will take place once a decade. There could also be twice as many very hot days by the 2050s, with temperatures above 25°C. Indeed, this could have a significant effect on convectional activity. Although they did not consider each type of precipitation, Hulme and

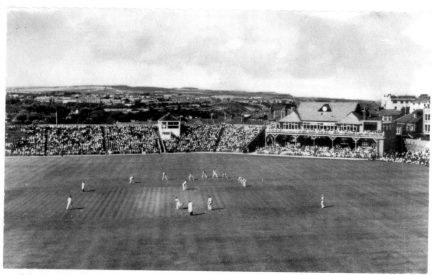

14. A postcard of the Scarborough ground during the famous Festival. The North Marine Road ground has hosted first-class cricket since 1874.

15. The New Road ground in April 1947 after the River Severn flooded, leaving the Worcester ground under four feet of water.

16. Snow stops play at Chester-le-Street, on the opening day of the 1999 Championship season during the match between Durham and Worcestershire. (Paul McGregor)

17. Tony Greig, the former England captain and now a television commentator, makes his pitch report alongside some interesting meteorological equipment at Sydney in 1991/92. (Patrick Eager)

18. Groundstaff at Worcester trying to dry the
New Road square during the Gillette Cup semi-
final between Worcestershire and Lancashire in
1974. (Worcestershire CCC)

19. The motorised covers installed by Warwickshire at the Edgbaston ground in
Birmingham. (Ken Kelly)

20. Perpetuating the rural mythology of cricket – the cover of a book on village cricket, published in 1938.

21. The groundstaff and volunteers help to mop up The Oval during the famous Ashes Test match in 1968. (Central Press Photos Ltd.)

22. A hailstorm interrupts play during the 1968 Test between England and Australia at Lord's. (J.G. Dunbar)

23. A postcard of youths playing cricket on the Village Green at Langton.

24. Lord's Cricket Ground – circa 1830. From a lithograph by C.Atkinson. (MCC)

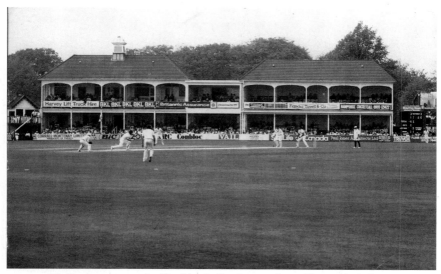

25. Southampton – the Northlands Road ground was Hampshire's home
from 1885 until 2000. (MORPHOT)

CHELTENHAM CRICKET FESTIVAL. GLOUCESTERSHIRE v. YORKSHIRE.

26. A packed enclosure in front of the College buildings during Gloucestershire's match against Yorkshire at the 1908 Cheltenham Festival. (Keith Hayhurst)

Jenkins looked at lightning frequencies, as related to convective thunderstorm activity. They suggested that by the 2080s the frequency of lightning will rise by about 20 per cent. The UKCIP98 report prepared by Hulme and Jenkins also included the regional patterns. Tables 42 and 43 show their estimates for the summers of the 2020s, 2050s and 2080s under each scenario for the following four regions of the country:

(a) the south coast belt including Kent, Sussex, Hampshire and Dorset,
(b) eastern England, the East Midlands and London,
(c) the south-west, the West Midlands and Wales,
(d) northern England and southern Scotland.

Table 42 shows the predicted rise in mean temperatures in June, July and August, whilst Table 43 indicates the estimates for summer rainfall. In each case, the south-east of England in region (a) was estimated as having a higher rise in temperature and less precipitation than northern parts in region (d).

TABLE 42
FORECAST INCREASE IN SUMMER MEAN TEMPERATURES
FOR THE 2020s, 2050s AND 2080s IN EACH REGION ACCORDING TO UKCIP98

2020s	(a)	(b)	(c)	(d)
Low	0.8	0.7	0.6	0.6
M-Low	1.4	1.2	1.0	0.9
M-High	1.6	1.4	1.3	1.2
High	1.8	1.5	1.4	1.3
2050s	(a)	(b)	(c)	(d)
Low	1.0	0.9	0.8	0.8
M-Low	1.8	1.5	1.4	1.3
M-High	2.6	2.2	2.1	1.7
High	3.1	2.5	2.4	2.0
2080s	(a)	(b)	(c)	(d)
Low	1.6	1.4	1.3	1.1
M-Low	2.8	2.4	2.2	1.8
M-High	3.5	2.7	2.6	2.1
High	3.9	3.0	2.9	2.4

Source: M. Hulme and G.J. Jenkins (1998), *U.K. Climate Impacts Programme Technical Report* No. 1.

At first, this trend for warmer summers might appear good news for county cricketers, but meteorologists have showed that global warming does not necessarily mean more golden summers. There are likely to be more rainfall events in a warmer world, and although many would occur during the winter months, increased convectional activity seems inevitable, especially in warm, urban areas. Indeed, models have been produced which show that the combined effect of global warming with a sunspot maxima will alter the 'normal' atmospheric processes, so that the cyclonic activity which usually brings storms to southern Europe will switch north towards Britain.

TABLE 43
FORECAST PERCENTAGE CHANGE IN SUMMER RAINFALL FOR THE 2020s, 2050s
AND 2080s BY REGION ACCORDING TO UKCIP98

2020s	(a)	(b)	(c)	(d)
Low	−4	−4	−3	+1
M-Low	−8	−6	−5	+2
M-High	−5	−3	−3	+2
High	−6	−4	−3	+2
2050s	(a)	(b)	(c)	(d)
Low	−3	−4	−1	0
M-Low	−5	−7	−2	+1
M-High	−19	−16	−13	−5
High	−22	−18	−15	−6
2080s	(a)	(b)	(c)	(d)
Low	−8	−8	−7	−3
M-Low	−14	−14	−12	−5
M-High	−24	−16	−13	+1
High	−27	−18	−14	+1

Source: Hulme and Jenkins, *UKCIP Technical Report* No. 1 (1998).

Other climate researchers have looked closely at how global warming will affect ocean currents, especially the Gulf Stream. This currently helps to bring mild weather to the United Kingdom, especially in the spring and early summer. A research team, led by Dr Peter Wadhams of the Scott Polar Research Institute at Cambridge has shown that global warming will reduce the amount of ice cover in Greenland and the Arctic Circle, thereby reducing the Odden Feature.[6] This is a huge natural pump, or thermohaline circulation, whereby each winter a vast tongue of ice forms to the south of Greenland which forces unfrozen, heavier and saltier water beneath it down to the ocean bed. This pressure creates a sea floor current of cold water which flows south off the west coast of Africa and Tropic of Cancer where it is warmed, rises and deflected by the Coriolis Force, so that the water returns towards the poles by flowing off the east coast of the USA. as the Gulf Stream. With a reduced Odden Feature and a less powerful Gulf Stream, the British climate is likely to become more variable and suffer more extremes. Wadhams and his team have noted a significant reduction in the Odden Feature since 1995 and it may be no coincidence that the United Kingdom had severe periods of cold weather and snow in the winter of 1995/96 and a damp, cool summer for much of 1998.

The effect of global warming on county cricket

The overall conclusion from this scientific research is that Britain's climate will become warmer, but at the same time more variable, with the chance of extremely hot summers, but also very cool and wet ones, especially if the Odden Feature is disturbed. This increased variability could severely affect both county and Test cricket, and it would be useful if, at the start of every season, each county, or even the ECB could accurately make a long-term prediction of the likely summer weather. But despite advances in technology and the capability of weather instruments, there is no likelihood of accurately predicting when extreme warm or wet summers will occur. Future researchers might show a link with the solar cycle, with the chance of exceptional conditions at solar maxima or minima, but even then there is no way of knowing if it is likely to be extremely hot or very wet.

Although long-term forecasting is impossible, it would still be possible for some form of forward planning, minimising the likelihood of weather interference under a warmer and more volatile climate. The most obvious area where work could be done would be improving the drainage at various grounds, especially those where water-retentive clays have been added to the soils. Indeed, the pedological aspects of county wickets merit close attention. In the past, there was a lot of local variability in the type of soil at each county ground, but since the 1960s, Surrey or Ongar loam has been added on many squares as a top dressing to a depth of 3 to 4 inches, whilst some county wickets have been completely reconstructed to a loam basis. As a result, these soils now have a clay content in the region of 30 to 35 per cent and have a better playing surface.

But should counties still be adding this loam in areas where a damper climate is likely in the future, especially as clay-based soils do not drain so freely.[7] The addition of clay could also affect those counties where the predictions are for a drop in summer rainfall. The result could be that the higher clay content will cause more cracking, creating drier and dustier wickets, favouring spinners rather than the swing bowlers, and the traditional English seam bowler.

Many counties may not want to change their wickets, as altering the playing surface could take time, and if things go wrong, there is the risk of losing points under the fining system in operation for counties who prepare substandard wickets. The counties might consider instead improved ground coverings. With some parts of the United Kingdom likely to become damper in the future, it seems crazy that so many grounds still use wheel-on covers and plastic sheets. We now live in an age of advanced technology, so more counties might wisely invest in improved and more rapidly deployable pitch coverings, such as the Brumbella at Edgbaston or the hover-cover recently installed at Lord's.

Many of the counties with a base in a large city could wisely consider such steps, as the rise in temperatures, forecasted by the UKCIP98 report could enhance the already existing urban heat islands. Indeed, higher air temperatures during the summer, combined with an increase in the emission of nitrogen oxides and hydrocarbons, will raise the tropospheric ozone concentration over built-up areas. With more particulates, condensation nuclei and warmer parcels of air with more water vapour, this could lead to greater cloud formation and increase the likelihood of rainfall events through convectional activity.

The results of work by Wood also indicate that these mechanisms might not only happen in mid-summer, as the increased variability associated with global warming in general, might be causing increased variability in the urban heat islands, causing disruption to games in the early and later parts of the season. Wood collated seasonal rainfall totals in London between 1921 and 1987 and, as shown in Table 44, produced a list of the ten driest and ten wettest seasons in the capital.[8] There was a slight trend to a decrease in summer rainfall, with three of the four driest summers occurring in the 1970s. But three of the four wettest springs and two of the four wettest autumns have taken place during the 1970s and 1980s. Indeed, Philip Bailey discovered that matches at Lord's were particularly disrupted during May, and all the evidence is suggesting that the urban heat island might increasingly disrupt play at other times of the year besides just mid-summer.[9]

TABLE 44
TEN DRIEST AND WETTEST SPRINGS, SUMMERS AND AUTUMNS IN LONDON, 1921–87
(rainfall, mm)

| | Driest | | | Wettest | |
Spring	Summer	Autumn	Spring	Summer	Autumn
1976–40	1921–34	1978–32	1979–270	1941–302	1974–331
1938–42	1976–46	1985–59	1983–208	1956–291	1960–315
1956–50	1972–50	1947–61	1964–206	1958–255	1976–284
1944–53	1975–56	1964–75	1981–203	1924–247	1940–268
1929–60	1983–73	1941–92	1947–195	1946–245	1939–261
1957–62	1949–79	1922–95	1932–192	1927–243	1987–255
1974–65	1955–83	1921–99	1978–190	1954–241	1970–229
1936–79	1984–83	1934–99	1951–182	1971–241	1984–226
1961–80	1959–84	1972–100	1967–182	1931–239	1924–225
1921–86	1979–93	1945–103	1975–176	1980–223	1935–225
					1946–225

Source: Research by Wood (1993).

As to whether the urban heat islands might become stronger under global warming, there is as yet no clear cut evidence. In fact, D.O. Lee found that the maximum temperature during the summer months in central London at St James' Park had actually decreased between 1962 and 1990.[10] In contrast, there had been a rise in the summer maxima at Wisley, in a more suburban location away from the centre of the conurbation. Lee accepted that care should be taken when interpreting his results, given the reasonably high level of variability and the relatively small sample of just two weather stations. But even so, it could be argued that at a time when average temperatures are rising, those in Central London were not necessarily behaving in the same way. This could be another function of the great complexities that characterise urban microclimates.

The increase in temperature at Wisley between 1962 and 1990 could also be an indication that London's urban heat island is now covering an even larger area, as urban sprawl and counter-urbanisation has taken place. This 'turning inside out' of urban land uses could also explain the slight fall in central area temperatures at St James' Park.

Whilst Wood's results suggests that urban microclimates are becoming more variable, further research clearly needs to be done to clarify for certain whether they respond in parallel with the larger regional climates. This attention to detail in urban areas is naturally too fine a level of analysis for the large UKCIP98 predictions and there remains much conjecture over what may happen. As far as any forward planning is concerned, it is going to be very important to know if rising temperatures at a regional scale will be translated into a more hot and humid climate at the city scale, thereby creating potentially more interruptions to matches, and the loss of valuable revenue. It would also be useful for cricket's planners to know whether there is a seasonal pattern to the build up of the urban heat islands, allowing forecasts to be made of suitable dates when games could be staged at these urban amphitheatres.

Indeed, looking closely at the timing of games would be another fruitful line of research, and the results of the UKCIP98 Report suggest that careful consideration should be given to extending the season further into September. The 'traditional' Championship season running from mid-April to early September is another of county cricket's inherited millstones. Before the mid-eighteenth century, games were tied to liturgical or agricultural calendars. From then, it broke free of the constraints of seasonal wake and parish festivals, but the arranging of fixtures was now at the whim of patrons and bookies. The weather imposed other constraints, but in the absence of leagues or national Championships, fixtures could be held in September or early October, as long as there was enough daylight.

The creation of the all-play-all Championships in the late 1890s led to an end to these autumnal challenges, yet festival games continued to be staged in mid and late September at the seaside grounds of Hastings, Torquay and Scarborough. Yet despite the demise of these festivals, the end of the Championship season has remained in early September. As global warming takes effect in the United Kingdom, it might make economic sense to consider extending the season.

There is already some evidence that an extension to the season could result in fewer interuptions due to rain. John Thornes attempted to see if more time was lost in some months during his survey of the 1974 season by looking at the monthly pattern of rain days during the so-called summer.[11] May was drier than average, but June and September were wetter than average, with the end-of-season fixtures across the country being severely affected by rain. Overall, few counties escaped the rain, whether at home or away, and overall 85 out of the 170 county matches were rain-affected in some way as a series of vigorous depressions crossed the country during June and in particular September.

My own survey of Championship matches in 1998 (so far, the warmest year on record) also showed that April/May and June were much wetter than July, August and September. The data in Table 45 show the monthly breakdown, and by 1 July the county clubs had lost 65.6 per cent of all time lost during the season. Duncan McLeish also undertook a temporal analysis of the abandoned county Championship matches between 1886 and 1997 to see which were the wettest months.[12] As Table 46 shows, May emerged as the wettest, probably as a result of fronts still being able to pass regularly across the country prior to the Azores high pressure cell building up and acting as a blocking anticyclone in July or August. September emerged as the month with fewest abandonments, although this is partly the result of staging fewer games than the other months, and only recently has the Championship season gone into the second or even third week of September.

TABLE 45
TIME LOST IN CHAMPIONSHIP CRICKET DURING EACH MONTH OF THE 1998 SEASON

	April/May	June	July	August	September
Hours lost	210.25	224.00	58.75	61.75	107.75
% of total time lost	31.74	33.81	8.87	9.32	16.26

Even so, the pattern is clear that April and May are the months when most weather interference takes place. Better weather generally occurs later in the season, and although September 1998 saw more interruptions than average, it would appear that a strong case could be put forward for counties playing more Championship games in August and September rather than April or May. The shorter amount of daylight could pose a slight difficulty, but at the present time, a way around the possible problems of bad light has been for Championship matches starting in September to start 30 minutes earlier. This would hardly be a major hardship for either the public or the players if it resulted in less playing time being lost overall during the whole season.

TABLE 46
ABANDONED CHAMPIONSHIP MATCHES BY MONTH 1886–1987

Month	No. matches	% of total
April/ May	46	32.62
June	30	21.28
July	28	19.86
August	28	19.86
September	9	6.38

Source: P. Bailey, 'Abandoned County Championship Matches 1886–1987', *The Cricket Statistician*, 78 (1990), 34–8.

Indeed, some interesting trends occur when the data on time lost at home games in 1998 is disaggregated into the wettest month for each county. As Table 47 shows, the southern counties, with the notable exception of Lancashire, lost most time in April and May, whilst the counties in the north, and the west and east midlands lost most time in June. For Glamorgan and Worcestershire in the west, the worst month in 1998 was September when vigorous frontal systems were sweeping in from the Atlantic. This was similar to Thornes' findings in 1974, although more data is going to be needed to see if these trends observed in 1998 are typical. Even so, they certainly hint at a north–south divide in the first two months of the season, with southern England gradually getting better weather before the midlands and the north, as the Azores high pressure becomes established.

TABLE 47
THE WETTEST MONTH, IN TERMS OF PLAYING TIME LOST, FOR EACH COUNTY IN 1998

April/May	Gloucestershire, Hampshire, Kent, Lancashire, Surrey, Sussex
June	Durham, Essex, Leicestershire, Middlesex, Northamptonshire, Nottinghamshire, Somerset, Warwickshire, Yorkshire
July	None
August	Derbyshire
September	Glamorgan, Worcestershire

If the UKCIP98 report is correct, these trends will be magnified in the future, with southern England becoming warmer and drier, whilst north-western and northern England become slightly damper as summer rainfall amounts rise above the current level. Mayes has already suggested a trend during the period 1981–90 for north-west England to receive more rain than counties further south. Despite a modification to the timing of fixtures, it is clear that some of the counties will be more prone to weather interference than others under global warming.[13]

Lancashire emerged as the wettest county in Llewellyn's survey between 1946 and 1968, and they were also the 'raining champions' of my 1998 survey. Under global warming they could be securing this unwanted title again in the future. The models are suggesting that the build-up of a high pressure cell over southern England and western Europe will push the rain-bearing fronts across northern and north-western England. Their passage over the south-east Lancashire conurbation and the Pennines already brings unwanted disruption at Old Trafford, and if the predictive models are correct, there will be an increased incidence of frontal and relief rainfall in the Manchester area, to say nothing of further localised convectional storms generated by the area's urban heat island.

All of this could pose a headache for the Lancashire committee, who not since 1934, have seen their county win the Championship. There might be an answer for them by looking at the geographical patterns of this rainfall. There are already orographic influences operating in the region itself, as the mountains of north Wales have a rain shadow effect on the Merseyside and Dee estuary area during south-westerly and westerly airflows. The shelter afforded by the Welsh mountains helps explain the localised differences in annual totals, with Bidston on the Wirral receiving 733 mm each year, compared with 808 mm at Manchester Airport and 996 mm in Macclesfield.

Perhaps a venue in the west of the county, close to the rain shadow of the Welsh Mountains, would mean less interference from relief and frontal rain, especially if under global warming the blocking anticyclone further south diverts more fronts towards the north. Another advantage in moving away from the built-up area to a more rural location would be that Lancashire would avoid the problems associated with the urban heat island and any enhanced convectional activity.

But a move away from a ground steeped in tradition like Old Trafford would be a huge wrench, and the players, spectators and sponsors alike would all incur extra travelling costs from their existing locations. Moving away from an excellent base of support to a smaller population base would also be a tricky decision. But if all of the estimates of climatic change are correct, the situation in a few years time might get even worse if nothing is done. Lancashire might not be the only club to be faced with the potential of increased frontal activity under global warming, and several county committees will have to carefully consider the precise geography of their county cricket in the twenty-first century. Some difficult decisions might inevitably have to be made, but clearly they, like Lancashire, would prefer to be the County Champions rather than the Raining Champions.

Redrawing the Boundaries

Place and Profit: geographical components of modern cricket

Sport, like other dynamic activities, is constantly changing and cricket is no exception. The county game has evolved over time with clear geographical patterns. Its entry into the modern era has seen a split into two, with the traditional county Championship fixtures played out over three, and more recently four days, alongside the junior version of limited overs games. In the eyes of Mike Marqusee,[1] the latter are the 'McDonalds of cricket – universally accessible, virtually pre-digested, quick and uniform'. Indeed, the one-day contests are entirely market-driven, and designed to appeal to the masses, either at the ground or watching their television sets at home.

This split in the modern calendar is therefore symptomatic of the move into the era of cheque book cricket, although money has always been in the game. In the eighteenth century, cricket fixtures were a form of gambling and challenges were often made in the form of wagers. Even in the golden age of amateur cricket, many people played for profit and the existence of 'shamateurs' highlighted the financial gains that could be made.

But in those so-called halcyon days, there were two important differences – firstly, it was personal rather than collective profit that was the main issue, and secondly, the location of games rarely entered the financial equation. It is a completely different situation today, when the staging of lucrative Test matches and One-Day Internationals and sharing the profits amongst the 18 first-class counties are at the top of the ECB's agenda. Counties themselves have had to look closely at where they play their matches, the capacity of their venues and the likelihood of attracting local sponsors.

Major changes have already taken place in the location of games at the international level. The globalisation of the game has seen One-Day Internationals being staged by Test playing nations in Sharjah, Singapore, Kuala Lumpur and Toronto. In the case of the latter, it was chosen by IMG, the world's largest sports promotion company, to host the Sahara Cup. It was a decision not made out of any altruistic motives to promote cricket in North America, but because playing at the Toronto Skydome would allow them to secure the television rights to games between India and Pakistan – a cricketing spectacle of vast commercial value in South Asia.

Traditional locations therefore matter less and less in a sporting world ruled by the corporate-media-sport conglomerates. To these multinational organisations, owned by media moguls such as Rupert Murdoch, it is where the game is broadcast to, that matters most. Place and profit, rather than place and people, are certainly the guiding influences on the international scale. Simon Heffer believes they have become a dominant influence in English cricket as well, commenting that 'spectators have long been irrelevant to the marketing men who run cricket – unless, of course, they happen at the time to be buying the videos, the souvenir books, the hats, the pyjamas and all the other panoply of trivia and junk that seems these days to be more important than the game itself'.[2]

Changes to the county calendar

Place and profit are therefore the two vital ingredients of the modern game, and this has recently necessitated important changes to the structure of the game and a re-drawing of the geographical boundaries of county cricket. During the early 1990s many people started to ask whether the county game needed reform. Indeed, Alan Lee of *The Times* believed that the county programme had degenerated into an unholy mess, and in the 1993 *Wisden Cricketers' Almanack* he commented that 'with each new year, it seemed, the schedulers were adopting baffling new variations with the glee of a creator of crossword puzzles producing heinously cryptic clues. It had become ever more obvious that the counties were playing too much cricket, most of it badly scheduled and designed to depress standards and discourage excellence.'[3]

There had been many calls for more radical reforms to the county calendar following the introduction of the Gillette Cup in 1963. Rowland Bowen, the eminent cricket historian had even suggested two-day county games played over weekends and on holidays, plus a two-divisional County Championship.[4] These cries for change were ignored until the late 1980s when the TCCB created a 'Structure Working Party' under the chairmanship of Mike Murray. Their brief was to identify the weaknesses in the baroque county programme, and to suggest how to rationalise the structure. Its recommendations were, at the time, amongst the most radical set of reforms the county game had ever seen, with the introduction of four-day Championship cricket, altering the Sunday League to a 50-overs contest and abolishing the zonal games in the Benson and Hedges. The rationale for change was that the experiments with four-day games, played since 1988, had produced more positive results and less contrived games than their three-day counterparts. The Murray Report therefore came down in favour of quality at the expense of quantity.

Another criterion for change was the need to produce a more competitive and successful Test side, and with four-day games scheduled to end on Mondays, it meant that international players would get two full days to prepare for Tests. Many traditionalists opposed the proposals, but in May 1992 the TCCB voted 11 to 8 in favour of the Murray Report and the changes were implemented in 1993 as the Championship became a 17 fixture competition with all counties playing each other once.

As the Murray Report had hoped, 105 out of the 153 games produced positive results compared with 104 out of 198 in 1992. But as the Editor of the 1994 *Wisden* commented 'about a fifth of all matches still finished inside three days – six of them in two days, thus ensuring that the amount of cricket available to county members dwindled even further than the TCCB intended when they framed the fixture list'.

The loss of five fixtures was inevitably going to affect the locational patterns, but the loss has been shared at both headquarters and outgrounds, and the changes have not seen the widespread loss of outgrounds as many feared. Although the festival at Weston-super-Mare has disappeared, most of the wandering counties have retained their lucrative festivals. However, there are more counties in Group B using two locations, and some of those in Group C have opted to rotate fixtures on a bi-annual basis between outgrounds.

The introduction of a 50-overs Sunday League, however, led to disquiet amongst the county professionals, who did not like having to play a longer limited overs game the day before the cut and thrust of the final day of a Championship match. Consequently, the 1994 season saw a return to the 40-overs format, but this did not mean an end to the calls for reform, and a working party was established under the chairmanship of Lord MacLaurin. They adopted a maximiser approach, aiming to create a virtuous circle of success to stimulate maximum public interest and to generate maximum revenue. This would allow the ECB to develop the best possible facilities, re-invest in cricket, improve the game at all levels, and creating a seamless progression for the most talented cricketers from school, through club into representative and international cricket.

As far as the county structure was concerned, the MacLaurin Report suggested reducing the number of domestic first-class fixtures to create a better balance between matchplay, recuperation and preparation, encouraging counties to become more financially independent, and having opportunities to stage a programme of cricket which has wide appeal. They believed that this would be possible by:

1. a three-conference County Championship with 12 fixtures and end-of-season play-offs. The counties would be divided into three groups – A, B and C, each with six teams and the teams for example in A playing against all those in B and C, but not those in A;

2. a two division 50 over National League, with promotion and relegation to supersede the AXA League and Benson and Hedges Cup. Several of these limited overs games could be floodlit encounters, whist counties with popular outgrounds could stage festivals of one-day cricket;

3. extending the NatWest Trophy with more minor counties getting the opportunity to play first-class sides.

Consideration was given to other suggestions, such as returning to three-day cricket on uncovered pitches in order to improve the techniques of batsmen and bowlers. However, the MacLaurin group rejected this, arguing that 'much has changed since the era of uncovered pitches in terms of the soils and grasses used for pitch preparation – a factor that could make three-day cricket on uncovered pitches problematic or even positively dangerous. Also it is highly doubtful whether uncovering pitches could be sustainable from a commmercial or public relations point of view.'

Their conclusions met with a mixed response from both counties and players alike, and it was subsequently agreed that the 1998 and 1999 Championships would remain in their present format, without any divisions or conferences. However, the top eight in the Championship would play in an early season Super Cup the following year, whilst the bottom four would play each other in the NatWest Trophy.

During 1998 more discussions took place over the idea of two divisions, as opposed to three conferences. This was initially out-voted as fears over elitism were raised, and questions were asked about whether the second division counties would get equal voting and financial treatment from the ECB. But by the end of the summer there was a growing consensus in favour of the two divisions, and in mid-October meetings were held by the ECB to look at further changes to the structure of the county game. In the words of Lord MacLaurin, 'no change was not an option. Cricket is a business. You can't go on looking at marketing information which gives you all the wrong signals and still say we will stay where we are. We have been singularly unsuccessful for too many years and we have to change things around.'[5]

The meetings at a London hotel led to further modifications being made to the domestic calendar, with the introduction from the year 2000 of seven Tests and ten one-day Internationals each season. A 16-match National League also began in 1999 with two divisions of counties playing each other on a home and away basis in 45-overs contests. In addition, the NatWest Trophy was redrafted as a 50-overs contest, with an FA Cup style approach, seeing the Minor Counties and County Board Elevens compete in the first two rounds, before the bulk of the first-class sides joined in the third round.

In December a further meeting of the First Class Forum resulted in a decision to split the Championship from the year 2000 into two divisions, and alter the bonus points system to make a draw more attractive relative to a win. The composition of the two divisions was based on the final placings in 1999, with the top nine going into a top division and the bottom nine going into the lower division. However, three sides each year would also be promoted or relegated, allowing a healthy interchange between divisions. Lord MacLaurin was naturally delighted at the news, describing it as 'an historic day for cricket in England and Wales. We can raise the profile of the game and improve the quality of the players by making this change, and I am confident that Team England will benefit from the introduction of a harder-edged competition.'[6]

Back in May, the Players Association had voted in favour of a split Championship, so it was no surprise that 15 counties were in favour of the changes, prefering two divisions rather than three conferences. Any fears about elitism and second division counties being unfairly treated were allayed as the ECB stated that second division counties would get equal financial treatment and voting rights with those in the top division. Some clubs had been worried that prolonged failure in the second division could lead to a club's extinction. But with three sides being promoted and relegated in the Championship, as well as a two-divisional National League, it would be very unlikely that a side would languish at the bottom end of the second division in both competitions for any length of time. The payout from the ECB would also help prevent the exodus of good players to top division teams, and in the words of Jim Cumbes, the chief executive of Lancashire, 'playing in a division where 30 per cent of teams will be promoted must have an advantage over an 18-team competition in which you might always be near the bottom'.[7]

Even so, some counties, most notably Glamorgan, felt that the Championship was competitive enough, whilst others such as Essex chairman David Acfield, argued that all the Championship needed was better marketing and more prize money. Indeed, the gate returns from Essex in 1998 showed some interesting trends, with more people going to watch their struggling Championship side than their more successful one-day team. Essex who finished bottom of the Championship had average home crowds of 6,827 per match, compared with 3,841 for the AXA contests.[8] Other critics feel that the existing 17 match all-play-all format is best left alone with the likelihood of England players being leased to the ECB for the greater part of the season to play in seven Tests and ten one-day Internationals.

Some of the county cricketers themselves were sceptical about the changes, and David Millns of Leicestershire, the 1998 County Champions, highlighted possible outcomes from interuptions by the weather. 'It only needs you to suffer a couple of wash-outs and lose a game or two, and suddenly you are chasing your tail. Then counties are going to start producing green flyers or dustbowls because they are under pressure to win games.'[9] The question of poor county wickets was also raised by leading cricket writer, Christopher Martin-Jenkins. Concerned that the new structure could provide even more temptation for counties to prepare pitches to suit their interests, he argued that 'the pitches have been the most important reason for England's international struggles in the last decade and more. Two-division cricket brings no guarantee that they will get better, rather the reverse . . . The effect of the changes will be to make the counties commercially more competitive in relation to rival sporting attractions, which is fine. What they will not do is to raise standards, which is what the real debate has been about in the light of England's reduced international status.'[10]

David Green, the former Lancashire and Gloucestershire batsman, also believes that 'two divisions is no more a solution than coloured clothing. Our redemption lies in a return to uncovering and a more significant reduction in our one-day cricket, but those are unlikely to occur because the marketing men don't like them.' Green also shrewdly points to the potential disruption from the weather, and the creation of more contrived and farcical games. 'An obvious objection to two divisions, is that in cricket, unlike soccer and rugby, there is no provision for games abandonment mid-way or completely called off, to be replayed. Ill fortune with weather could see strong sides unfairly demoted.'[11]

To Mike Marqusee, the headlong rush into the two-divisional structure is a microcosm of changes operating within Britain under New Labour. He believes that 'our New Labour elite offers national renewal through repackaging. And English cricket appears to be pursuing a parallel course, combining an upmarket economic base with a downmarket presentation – the worst of both worlds. In its preoccupation with individual and national success, and its assumption that English national identity can only thrive if the nation is seen to be beating other nations, it should fit in all too neatly with the elite vulgarity which is the hallmark of New Britain.'[12] Only time will tell whether the MacLaurin Report was the saviour of the county game.

Indeed, several commentators are questioning whether a top-down approach is the correct one, arguing instead that building strong counties should be at the heart of the argument. There are models from the 'development' arm of geography that show a bottom-up approach can be successful by thinking globally and acting locally. Indeed, Marqusee cites the success of the New York Yankees baseball side who won the 1998 World Series with a profit of £90 million. Their side included players from Cuba, the Dominican Republic, Puerto Rico, Japan and Australia, plus one native New Yorker, yet this cosmopolitan make-up did not affect the success or partisan loyalty to the Yankees. 'The fans expect their team to buy the best and to be the best, and its victories are seen as victories by and for New York and New Yorkers, wherever the players hail from. This suggests that some of the core assumptions guiding cricket's masters may be mistaken.'[13]

Despite all the recent changes to the domestic calendar, many counties have realised the importance of a bottom-up approach. Somerset and Glamorgan have recently constructed impressive indoor schools, whilst Leicestershire have established a scholarship programme with Oakham School and Loughborough University, whereby they sponsor a player each year. Together with their county board, Leicestershire CCC spend £100,000 each year on spreading the game throughout schools in Leicestershire. Other counties also have elaborate plans, and the ECB, to their credit, since 1999 have created Centres of Excellence at the universities in Bradford, Cambridge, Cardiff, Durham, Loughborough and Oxford (UCCE).

The dual economy of English cricket

To a large extent, a dual economy exists within the English game. This geographical concept is frequently applied to a Third World city, where there is a cycle of wealth and a cycle of poverty.[14] Both cycles operate independently to sustain the status quo – namely the wealth of the lucky few and the poverty of the vast majority. In applying this concept to the modern county game I am not trying to suggest that there are haves and have nots – at least not yet! Instead, there are examples of pluralism with two spirals operating in many facets of the first-class game.

There is pluralism in the way the county clubs still take for granted the possible interference from the weather, at a time when the modern game has become increasingly commercialised, with profit-maximisation being of supreme importance. Clubs, and the ECB itself, employ a vast number of commercial executives, marketing consultants and business managers, yet it is remarkable given the fundamental link with the weather, that they do not employ a meteorologist. Whilst ECB money is being poured into many aspects of the game, both on and off the field, not much research has gone to better 'mopping up' equipment, ground covering or indoor arenas.

So on the face of it, modern county cricket appears to be a money-making business, with profit-maximisation at the top of the agenda. Yet at the same time, the clubs still tacitly accept that the weather might halt play, and this is in many ways a throwback to the time when the county game was influenced by social, rather than economic, factors. Such a compromise between catering either for profit or precipitation is perhaps one of the game's most endearing and quaintly English features.

There is also a dichotomy in terms of the location of these games. As noted in Chapters 4, 5 and 6, there have been various arguments in favour of either centralising fixtures at a headquarters, or periodic marketing, by taking the game to outgrounds. Once again, many clubs have opted for a compromise, opting to play their Championship fixtures at a central base, but being quite prepared to take one-day matches to the outgrounds.

The whole structure of the county game since 2000 has had a strong element of pluralism following the creation of two divisions. Such a structure could result in a premiership mentality that might subsequently divide the previously harmonious 'family' of counties. Fears have already been expressed about a transfer system developing between counties in the First and Second Divisions. It would not be impossible for a two-tier system to emerge with a few elite clubs in the Premier Division, regularly skimming off talent from the Second Division. Mark Ramprakash's move from Second Division Middlesex to First Division Surrey might open the floodgates as the England batsman left a struggling county and joined the Champions of 2000.

There is an element of a dual economy in the actual playing labour, as since 1999 the ECB have a central core of elite players, contracted to the Board. Fears have been expressed over the impact the counties would face over the loss of their star players for a large proportion of the summer. Indeed, right at the top level of the game there are two contrasting arguments, namely should everything be geared up for Team England, or should it be for the benefit of the counties.

The debate over the nature of the fixture list is a microcosm of this pluralism, and the conflicting arguments over who comes first – Team England or the counties? Some feel that the balance of one-day and four-day cricket is weighted too heavily towards the limited overs game. Indeed, the ECB in 'Raising the Standard', had hoped to reduce the number of one-day games.[15] Yet during 1999, they announced a return to the early season, zonal format of the Benson and Hedges Cup in 2000, and also considered introducing a 25-overs short-form game played in June or July on a regional basis.

Mike Atherton is one of the modern generation of county, and Test, players who is genuinely concerned at the plethora of one-day cricket. He argues strongly that the chief purpose of county cricket is to prepare players for the Test arena, yet in 1999 'we prepared our team for the first Test by giving them no cricket at all or a week of Benson and Hedges Super Cup cricket. And usually after a Test match, you are dispatched to celebrate, or to mull over, by playing a knock-out one-day match for your county the next day.'[16]

One could ask, however, whether the English county game has ever not had a dual economy? Indeed, the pluralism has been allowed to develop, and to a large extent, it is an inherited feature in the 'brave new world' of a two-division Championship. As Chapter 2 showed, for many years the county game (and for that matter, the world game too) was ruled and run by the MCC, rather than by the counties themselves. Some of the antiquated, social divisions, such as Gentlemen and Players, have disappeared, but the rise of commercial interests and cheque book cricket has led to a rebirth in the polarisation of views. Many commentators on, and supporters of the English game feel that it is time to reduce this pluralism so that the counties and Team England both benefit.

Indeed, Chris Martin-Jenkins has highlighted the urgent need for 'a much better thought-out programme in county cricket – one which suits spectators and county members, and gives the players the best possible balance between first-class and one-day cricket, with sufficient breaks for practice and rest, but not the long gaps virtually devoid of first-class cricket which have appeared in the 1999 fixture list'.[17] However, there are some who believe that a much more radical reform is needed, with a major transformation of the format of the English game, away from the county unit.

Counties or regions?

As Chapter 2 showed, English cricket inherited the county system almost by default, and in recent years, a number of alternative playing units have been suggested. Morrison has put forward a scheme whereby the Benson and Hedges Cup would be replaced by three inter-regional matches, each played over five days to Test match rules. He divided up the first-class sides (then numbering 17) into the following four regions, each with a designated ground:

Midlands (at Edgbaston):	Leicestershire, Northamptonshire, Warwickshire, Worcestershire
North (at Old Trafford):	Derbyshire, Lancashire, Nottinghamshire, Yorkshire
South-east (at Lord's):	Essex, Kent, Middlesex, Surrey, Sussex
South-west (at Bristol):	Glamorgan, Gloucestershire, Hampshire, Somerset.

Morrison argued that 'regional pride is a strong force to be tapped, while at the moment, it is manifest mainly in a sense of aggrieved resentment at perceived or imagined selectorial bias'.[18] Eric Midwinter further developed this idea, with a competition to include these four regions, plus an overseas XI, drawn from registered county players not eligible for England, plus the main touring side of the summer. He argued that 'these six teams could play out a mini league with preference given to non-Test venues, so that the Worcesters and Hoves might feel the benefit of upper-grade cricket'.[19]

This lobby for regional cricket gained official recognition in one of the more radical suggestions from the initial publications of the MacLaurin Group. This would have involved a top tier of first-class cricket based on a regional rather than a county structure, involving the best players from each county as a means of refining the feeder system into Test Match cricket.[20] The Group suggested the following six groupings:

South-east	Middlesex, Essex, Surrey
South	Kent, Hampshire, Sussex
West	Glamorgan, Gloucestershire, Somerset
West Midlands	Warwickshire, Worcestershire
East Midlands	Derbyshire, Nottinghamshire, Northamptonshire, Leicestershire
North	Lancashire, Yorkshire, Durham.

Many objections were raised about this idea, chiefly that it would devalue the County Championship and increase both the playing time and travelling time of the top players. But many cricket writers, most notably Chris Martin-Jenkins have long advocated a regional focus with an annual tournament in April and May involving the cream of county talent from these six groupings (with Northamptonshire moving into the West Midlands to provide a balance of three counties per region).[21] This would be a very radical change to the geography of English cricket, which as the previous chapters have shown, has evolved in a rather haphazard way around the county unit. But other countries, such as Australia and South Africa, have teams drawn from larger area units. These nations have a smaller population density, never mind a different climatic system, and it is open to question whether a change to regional teams would help English cricketers compete at the highest level.

Even so, during 1998 the ECB modified their suggestions for a regional format, as outlined above, in favour of an early season tournament between the six regions, running parallel with the Championship. The regional sides would contain the cream of county talent, and in their absence promising youngsters would get an early chance to secure a place in the county side. It would also add interest to the first month of the season, and with England places up for grabs, and a chance to attract the selector's eye, the regional competition could see intense games.

Moreover, such a regional format would provide the sort of stepping stone up from county level to Test cricket that many current and recent England players have been calling for. With an apparently wide gulf between playing for your county and country, an inter-regional competition in May would be the ideal preparation for potential England players. It could also assist the established stars during the weeks leading up to an Ashes series or an intense series with the West Indies or South Africa. Former England captain Mike Atherton is a staunch supporter of regional cricket, believing that 'an advantage would be to keep these players hungry, knowing they have to play very well to get in the team and even better to keep their place. As these games would effectively be Test trials there would certainly be plenty of interest for the players themselves and then hopefully for the public.'[22] Regarding public support, there would be great interest in these regional fixtures, although members of the county not staging these fixtures might not attend and adopt a watching brief from afar, preferring instead to support their own county side in their Championship or National League encounter. Some people find it difficult to associate with a somewhat composite regional eleven, in the same way that some of the divisional games in rugby union have attracted smaller crowds than club matches. But if the bottom line is producing a more competitive and successful England side, then perhaps such a regional competition merits introduction, especially as it nestles alongside the Championship, which remains largely in place, appeasing both the county committees and the England hierarchy.

Nevertheless, there are some critics of the regional concept, including Vic Marks, formerly of Somerset and England, and now the cricket correspondent of *The Observer*. He argues that the regional games would result in 'the odious sight of professional cricketers earnestly playing for themselves rather than their team, in pursuit of international recognition'.[23] The former all-rounder is not totally against the concept of regional sides, but he feels that a more palatable alternative would be regional elevens for games against the touring sides. Indeed, there would be plenty of opportunity for assembling such teams, given the increase in Test and one-day Internationals. They could also be used to reward counties for a good performance the previous summer by allocating such fixtures to the headquarters of the county in each regional grouping that had the best Championship placing (or number of victories) or rotating the venue between counties every three years or so.

Games with touring teams would therefore gain a higher profile, and avoid the situation, as at present, when many county teams rest players during tourist games. Under the two divisional system, with promotion or relegation at stake, some counties have been more tempted to rest key players for non-Championship fixtures, resulting in even more one-sided games against the touring teams. Such regional elevens against touring sides would have all the added benefits expressed above by Atherton, and in Marks' view 'the easiest way to create another stratum of first-class cricket without disrupting the integrity of the domestic competitions'.[24]

New international grounds

Another facet of the pluralism within the English game is the way in which, over time, a powerful group of counties that stage Test matches has built up. For many years, the other group of counties who currently do not stage international games have tried to break this monopoly, and in 1999 the ECB gave them a golden opportunity – they decided to increase the number of Tests each summer from seven, and the number of One-Day Internationals to ten. Consequently, from 2000 England staged its international matches on more grounds, and those that currently only host county fixtures.

The county grounds at Cardiff, Bristol, Canterbury, Chelmsford, Worcester, Chester-le-Street and Hove were on the shortlist of new venues for these England games. Even so, some of the chief executives at the existing Test grounds were a little bit critical of the shortlist. For example, Jim Cumbes, Lancashire's chief executive said 'it is essential we experiment, but why does the south-west need games at Cardiff and Bristol? The dilemma is should the ECB be looking to make money or spread the gospel of the game? But the real issue is whether the facilities at these new venues are up to it. Safety is a big issue and experience should count for a lot.' [25]

To a large extent, the existing cartel of county clubs hosting international games did not want to lose its influence, especially as they have had a virtual monopoly, with no new Test venues in England for 97 years. Their relations with the non-Test match clubs were painted in some sections of the media as strained. There is no doubting, however, that the 1999 World Cup whetted the appetite of the smaller venues for staging international cricket. During the World Cup, every county hosted at least one game and Sussex claimed to have cleared around £100,000 from the India–South Africa fixture at Hove.

The economic factors would appear to be persuasive, but there are a number of key geographical factors which merit close attention, especially the arguments over taking international cricket to the West of England, which as Chapters 7 and 8 showed can be more prone to weather interference than grounds to the east. However, the time slot that the ECB were looking at for these one-day Internationals was June or July, and by that time of year, the western grounds tend to lose less time than earlier or later in the season. This is clear from the data in Table 48 for Sophia Gardens between 1995 and 1999, with the Cardiff ground losing just three hours of Championship play during July over this five year period.

The ECB 'western vote' eventually went to Bristol for 2000, with Cardiff staging the game between Australia and Pakistan in 2001.

TABLE 48
HOURS OF PLAY LOST EACH MONTH BY GLAMORGAN IN COUNTY CHAMPIONSHIP
MATCHES STAGED AT SOPHIA GARDENS, CARDIFF, 1995–99

	1995	1996	1997	1998	1999
April/May	1.00	3.00	19.00	12.50	4.00
June	2.50	–	1.00	16.00	–
July	–	3.00	–	–	–
August	–	7.50	–	–	12.25
September	6.50	–	3.00	24.25	11.50

The ECB also allocated one-day Internationals to Chester-le-Street and Canterbury for the 2000 season, with each ground staging matches in a triangular series involving England, West Indies and Zimbabwe. Then in November 2001, the ECB announced that Chester-le-Street would stage a Test match in 2003. This news was very well received in the north-east where a vast amount of money and careful planning have taken place in establishing initially Durham as a first-class county, and now Chester-le-Street as a venue worthy of Test status. But as Table 49 shows, compared with Bristol in the south-west and Canterbury in the south-east, the Durham ground consistently lost time to the weather in 1998 and 1999, except for July. Things could get worse in the future because the UKCIP98 forecast for north-east England in general suggests an increase in summer precipitation by between 1 and 2 per cent by the 2020s. Taking international cricket into Durham will surely be welcomed by the sporting public in the north-east, but it would not appear to be a venue where fine weather could be guaranteed. In the 2000 Triangular Series players taking part in the match at the Riverside ground in Chester-le-Street complained privately about the chilly conditions, whilst the match in the 2001 series was abandoned without a ball bowled – perhaps a foretaste of things in the future!

TABLE 49
HOURS OF PLAY LOST EACH MONTH IN COUNTY CHAMPIONSHIP MATCHES AT
BRISTOL, CHESTER-LE-STREET AND CANTERBURY, 1998, 1999

	Bristol		Chester-le-Street		Canterbury	
	1998	1999	1998	1999	1998	1999
April/May	5.25	–	8.00	12.25	15.50	–
June	5.00	22.50	16.00	12.00	3.00	–
July	–	6.00	–	–	–	–
August	1.75	8.50	1.25	9.50	5.25	10.50
September	4.00	0.50	10.25	1.00	5.50	9.25
Total hours lost	16.00	37.50	35.50	34.75	29.25	19.75

The ECB also announced in December 2001 that Hampshire's new ground, the Rose Bowl, will stage One-Day Internationals from 2004, and that over the next ten years, a total of eleven venues including the traditional Test grounds, plus Chester-le-Street, Southampton, Canterbury, Cardiff and Bristol would host international matches. It certainly makes economic sense for the counties concerned and the ECB to have a long-term blueprint and calendar, but perhaps in addition to allocating games to new venues, the ECB should also look closely at its existing venues. Given the findings in Chapters 10 and 11, a question mark could loom over the future of Old Trafford as a Test ground. Research by Mike Hulme has also shown how, in a survey of Test matches between 1979 and 1988, it was the dampest of England's grounds.[26] Hulme found that Old Trafford had an average loss of over eight hours per Test, whilst the Edgbaston ground in Birmingham was the least affected venue with under 90 minutes play lost per match. To an outsider, it seems a paradox that at a time when England's administrators are appealing for more sponsorship and investment, they opt to stage five days of Test cricket, plus one (or even two) One-Day Internationals each year at the ground whose county tends to lose more time each season at their home games than any other.

Supporters of Lancashire and the county's officials would blanch at the thought of losing Test cricket, and in Old Trafford's defence, perhaps more care should be taken in the precise timing of international matches in Manchester. Indeed, in his survey of weather-affected Test matches, Hulme tried to find optimal periods for each venue. This is linked to the theory of 'singularities', first put forward by Barry and Perry, that there are particular times of the year with a high tendency for certain weather types. Hulme suggested that at the national level, the periods of likely good weather during which Tests should be played are mid-July (8–18), late July to early August (23 July–2 August), and late August to early September (27 August–4 Sept). The wetter periods to avoid are 18–28 June and 14–24 August.[27]

Hulme drew up an optimal sequence for each venue during a six Test series. These are shown in Table 50, with ideal starting dates for each Test venue to minimise weather interference. The fact that the ECB will now be scheduling seven Tests per season, suggests that such an optimal sequence is unlikely. Indeed, Table 50 also shows the actual dates for the allocation of games to these venues in the 2000 season. The Edgbaston Test fitted perfectly, perhaps by chance, but all other England matches were being staged in non-optimal, and damper periods.

Another solution, of course, would be a back-to-back sequence of One-Day Internationals in September, along the lines of similar contests held in January in Australia. This would necessitate a major overhaul of the calendar for each season, but at a time when the English Cricket Board have devised plans to boost the game, it would greatly benefit the authorities to closely analyse these meteorological patterns. Hulme's work has already suggested a fruitful line of research, especially if the rescheduling of the Old Trafford Test to June, rather than July or August, could reduce the probability of losing a full day's play from 40 to 20 per cent. Hulme believes that this in turn would mean a monetary return over a five year period of one day's takings, in the region of £14,000. Whilst many seats are pre-booked in advance, there are longer term spin-offs, since someone who has had a good day watching England is likely to re-book the next year. Someone who has spent all day sheltering under an umbrella, or in the pavilion watching re-runs of old games, may not want to risk it again in the future, and in this modern era of cheque book cricket, these economic arguments are very persuasive.

TABLE 50
HULME'S OPTIMAL STARTING DATES FOR TESTS COMPARED WITH ACTUAL
STARTING DATES OF 2000 SERIES WITH ZIMBABWE AND WEST INDIES

Test match venue	Optimal starting date	Actual starting date(s)
Headingley	1 June	17 August
Edgbaston	15 June	15 June
Lord's	13 July	18 May, 29 July
Trent Bridge	27 July	1 June
Old Trafford	24 August	3 August
The Oval	7 September	31 August

Source: M. Hulme (1989), 'Match of the Day', *Guardian*, 19 May.

Changing the calendar

No matter how many reforms are made to the nature of the teams, the format of the competitions, and the number of Test and One-Day Internationals each year, cricket will still be, as it has always been, at the whim of the weather. Cricketers, whether they be representing their country, a county, a region or another areal unit, may not even venture on to the pitch if it rains heavily. Some interesting patterns emerged from the study of rain affected matches in Chapter 10, and the monthly totals of time lost in 1998 were compared with Hosking's monthly totals for the 1989 season.[28] Table 51 shows how less time has been lost recently in matches during September, whilst over half the time lost still occurs in April, May and June.

TABLE 51
PERCENTAGE OF PLAYING TIME LOST BY MONTH IN
CHAMPIONSHIP CRICKET, 1989, 1998

	April/May	June	July	August	September
1989	40.54	16.22	10.81	8.11	24.32
1998	31.74	33.81	8.87	9.32	16.26

Source: K. Hosking, *The Cricketer* (February 1990).

These are the results from just two seasons and more research is badly needed to see if these are becoming distinctive trends. A study in greater detail of the amount of time lost and the pattern of affected matches could yield huge dividends, especially if the loss of play affects attendances and the lucrative television coverage by Channel Four and Sky Television. Neither channel will want to play re-runs of old matches over and over again, or have lengthy interviews with famous players, interspersed with shots of the pitch under covers!

A further aspect that needs more investigation, and maybe alteration, is the length of both the matches and the county season itself. Evidence was presented in Chapter 10 to suggest that an extension of the season into September would be sensible if Britain is going to have a warmer and more variable climate. Warmer Septembers and Octobers would allow the season to be extended, assuming that the weather in April allows a prompt start in the middle of the month. If April and May become wetter, then the season will inevitably have to roll on later into September.

If the season can continue to start at its traditional time in mid-April, there are other possibilities to be gained by playing later in September. Not least that there are more days available for the ECB to squeeze seven Test and ten one-day Internationals into the calendar. Having more days available could also lead to the introduction of reserve days for Championship cricket, should there be significant interruption caused by long periods of rain or bad light. Already the major limited overs games have reserve days, as with the 1998 NatWest Trophy final at Lord's, when rain prevented the match being completed in one day. If the climate is going to become hotter and damper, then perhaps such reserve days are going to be needed also in Championship fixtures.

Such a scheme might not be needed, if the ECB were to plan carefully when county fixtures took place. Enough meteorological data now exists to help the ECB in drawing up the fixture list for county matches, and enough daily rainfall data exists to allow a long-term picture of rainy days to be drawn up since 1960. Hulme believes that a model could be devised for optimal fixture periods, by date and venue, as well as a worst case scenario, based on a 'look-up' table of rainfall probabilities. He believes that 'the benefits of using such a scheme over a number of years to minimise the rainfall hazard are clear: matches will be less likely to be interrupted or abandoned, thereby reducing the frustration of players and spectators alike; clubs will benefit from a reduced loss of takings and television and sponsors will have a surer, objective basis upon which to decide which matches to support'.[29]

Under the current capitalist culture of profit maximisation, there is some merit in looking at Berry and Parry's pattern of singularities and finding out when there are optimal periods for Championship matches. Scheduling rest days during the traditionally wetter periods would also be worth investigating. But there is a major stumbling block in the complexity of the county calendar itself, which ironically has been made even more complicated by the introduction of two separate divisions in both the Championship and the National Cricket League. Finding a perfect arrangement of fixtures would be very difficult, especially for those counties whose grounds are used both for international cricket as well as the bread and butter county fixtures. No doubt, the counties like Warwickshire or Surrey would cry foul if they felt that they were disadvantaged into playing games at Edgbaston or The Oval during wetter times, whilst non-Test counties such as Northamptonshire or Leicestershire had greater flexibility in the use of their grounds.

Extending the season later into September would give more opportunities of finding drier slots and reducing the inevitable timetable clashes over the use, for example of Trent Bridge for a Test match by England or by Nottinghamshire for an all-important County Championship fixture. To overcome this club or country argument, the ECB would have to use grounds devoted solely to international cricket, and this would be perhaps the biggest change in English cricket's long and turbulent history.

The only caveat in this line of argument is that the records of the recent past may not actually help such forward planning by the ECB mandarins. Indeed, in their UKCIP98 Report, Hulme and Jenkins concluded that 'we no longer have confidence that the climatic statistics of the recent past will provide us with an adequate description of the climate in the future. No longer is a 30-year sequence of past weather data – the conventional period used to describe climate established earlier this century by the World Meteorological Organisation – sufficient to define the probabilities of certain weather extremes occurring in the future.'[30]

In view of Hulme and Jenkins' report, it might therefore be best at the moment if the only change is an extension of the season later into September. Any modification of the Championship and Test calendar based on the rainfall patterns since 1960 would be very unwise. The predictions in the UKCIP98 report will bring subtle changes to the patterns, and once the picture becomes clearer, say in 2010, then the ECB administrators could start to devise optimal periods for county matches, although it is conceivable that the climate may become drier and there would be no need to change things.

County cricket: urban or rural?

There are other pressing issues to be resolved in the short and medium term, not least with the optimal location for fixtures – the real locational geography of county cricket. The question of whether county cricket should continue to be staged in large built-up areas is very important, given the long-term impact of an increase in temperature, as predicted by Hulme and Jenkins for the United Kingdom Climate Impacts Programme. The trend for a warmer climate could be magnified in urban areas, where a more complex and volatile micro-climate has already had an impact on the summer game. The rain which preceded England's famous win over Australia in 1968 might have been the warning sign that metropolitan grounds could suffer from greater interruptions by the weather.

Chapter 10 showed how distinctive micro-climates have become established in urban areas, whilst the UKCIP98 report outlined in Chapter 11, is suggesting an increase in temperature in the region of three or four degrees by 2080. Thus, it could be argued that further disruption might take place if county fixtures are still centralised in enormous urban amphitheatres. Finding cooler and drier locations for cricket would be a huge benefit for all concerned – player, county official, spectator, sponsor, TV watcher and armchair follower.

One solution might involve the counties moving their headquarters to an out-of-town location, possibly on a greenfield site, similar to the way Hampshire moved at the end of the 2000 season from their quaint and archaic ground in Northlands Road, Southampton out to a new purpose-built ground outside the city at West End in the Meon Valley. Such a move out from town centres would certainly find support from some environmentalists, concerned at the way an increase in traffic has resulted in the rise in pollutants and a deterioration in the air quality in urban areas. Cricket is just one of a number of summer sports, attracting a high volume of car-borne spectators. The high number of vehicles travelling to some of the key fixtures could be contributing to increased pollution and the occurrence of photochemical smogs, so prevalent in the summer under a blocking anticyclone when the descending air traps the pollutants. The United Kingdom government has started investigating ways of reducing the volume of traffic in an attempt to improve the quality of the atmosphere and to make urban roads safer places on which to drive. Taking cricket out of the central areas could be one way of reducing the problems during the summer months.

Therefore, the counter-urbanisation of cricket would appear to be preferable from an urban transport point of view. But if Lee's work is correct and urban heat islands are becoming larger and more complex than previously thought, great care would have to be taken over the choice of the precise location in the rural–urban fringe, avoiding where possible the already built-up complexes.[31] A site close to an urban ring road or motorway, preferably adjoining an urban park or green wedge, would be ideal, allowing easy access for players and spectators alike. But it still might be folly to think that a shift some 10 or 15 miles out from the centre would completely escape the vicissitudes of heavy rain or thunderstorms. Whilst convectional activity can be extremely localised in nature, a site on the edge of a built-up area, could still be prone to rainfall interruptions triggered by the urban, or even suburban heat island.

Another alternative for the headquarters would be to abandon the large urban complexes altogether and retreat to smaller towns, lower down the urban hierarchy. Whilst this would be a return to the inter-war pattern outlined in Chapter 6, from a purely practical point of view, the nature of many town grounds is still incompatible with the needs of modern county cricket. Whilst such locations as Abergavenny or Bath have a quaint and old world charm, they do not have the necessary infrastructure to even be considered as regular venues for county fixtures. It could be argued that wise and careful investment could transform some of these charming grounds into commercially viable locations, capable of housing a large crowd, droves of sponsors, and having enough decent wickets to stage up to two dozen games. But creating a large concrete amphitheatre might not find favour with the cautious town planners, ever mindful of preserving the urban fabric, and the thought of tens of thousands of spectators and sponsors descending on these small towns might be an unacceptable proposition.

For each county to have a group of smaller outgrounds might be another alternative, which in the eyes of many, would be a long overdue return to the days when many counties favoured a periodic marketing policy rather than centralisation. This quasi-nomadic format was shunned by many clubs when the costs became too prohibitive, but perhaps the time is ripe for the ECB to assist this process of taking cricket back to the people, by subsidising the costs of marquees and having a regional pool of mobile scoreboards, covers, seats and portable toilets. Scyld Berry of the *Sunday Telegraph* is a strong advocate of this 'roadshow' approach, and he believes that it could also help to raise playing standards. 'The variety in pitches and conditions that outgrounds can supply, will not only attract spectators and bring spice to the domestic game, but help the England Test cricketer adjust to environments overseas more successfully than he does.'[32]

His colleague, Michael Henderson of the *Daily Telegraph*, is also a supporter of this outground lobby – 'fund them to go back to Buxton and Chesterfield, Harrogate and Ebbw Vale, Folkestone and Weston-super-Mare. Let the battle cry be: bring back Ashby-de-la-Zouch! That would be real missionary work and possibly rewarding. Players may not like it, because they don't like playing on club pitches, which they often condemn in their minds before they have even set foot on them. But they can't be any worse than some of the pitches prepared on county and, dare one say it, Test grounds.'[33]

So one option for county cricket's decision makers in the twenty-first century might be to leave the large, urban areas and head back to the smaller centres. As the opening chapters showed, cricket is a game with its roots firmly in rural areas, so at a time when a changing climate could enhance the urban or suburban heat islands, perhaps the game should go back to the countryside. The answer might be purpose-built arenas, outside the city or town boundaries, surrounded by fields and trees, rather than brick and concrete.

The MCC's attempt to develop Shenley in rural Hertfordshire as an overspill ground for matches at Lord's might have been a stroke of pure genius. It could point the way for the future, but moving away from an urban site, steeped in heritage and full of tradition, is bound to be a very difficult decision, and a somewhat radical one for county committees, many of whom are renowned for their conservative decisions.

Many commentators have noted how history has acted as a millstone around the necks of cricket makers, and Mike Marqusee has described the Championship as 'a relic, saturated with nostalgia, its contestants festooned with the traditional emblems of communities which no longer exist'.[34] Now is the time to escape from this urban prison and to move the county game forward. The warning signs are clearly there, and unless vast amounts of money are spent on pitch coverings and improved drainage, it might be a huge gamble to stay in a central urban area under a warmer climate.

Place and Profit will continue to be the fundamental aspects of the game, even under a warmer and wetter climate, but if the spirit of profit maximisation is to be fully embraced, the clubs and the ECB must give serious consideration to the role of the weather. Geography, as an academic subject, covers the interaction between the human and physical environment, and it is time that county cricket's decision makers adopt a similar approach. Failure to do so would be a lie to cricket's most fundamental geographical characteristic, namely the link between playing and the weather.

Epilogue: The Future Geography of English Cricket

Many of the changes suggested in the previous chapter might be too radical for some of those involved in a game that is renowned for its conservatism. The cry that 'it's not cricket' might go up from the traditionalists if the counties were to be replaced by regions, or more Test matches were to be staged away from the traditional venues. But English cricket, both domestic and international, can ill afford to wallow in nostalgia and ignore the fundamental changes to the geographical environment, both physical and human, in which the games are played.

Changes have already taken place in Australia, where between 16 August and 20 August 2000 an inaugural series of indoor one-day Internationals took place under the retractable roof of the Colonial Stadium in Melbourne. In a competition called the 'Super Challenge 2000' Australia and South Africa played each other in three 50 overs contests, watched by an aggregate of 95,000 people.

Judging by the favourable comments these matches received, cricket historians of the future may come to regard 16 August 2000 as important a date in the game's development as the start of overarm bowling or the first inter-county match. Not only was it the first proper game staged indoors, but it was on a wicket prepared outside, on pallets under natural and normal conditions, before being transported inside the Colonial Stadium. Portable wickets had been used in Australia before, under the Packer era of the late 1970s and early 1980s, but this was the first time that One-Day Internationals took place on an artificial surface.

Playing the game indoors obviously negates the prospect of any interruption from the weather, and if county games in the United Kingdom were to be staged at complexes with retractable roofs, the phrase 'rain stops play' would be a thing of the past. There are at the moment few stadia in England and Wales which are of a suitable size to stage One-Day Internationals, or county matches, but the Millennium Dome in London's Docklands might not be the 'white elephant' that many believe Peter Mandelson's brainchild to be.

Since its closure, the complex has lain empty with its future very uncertain, but perhaps the complex should be converted into an indoor sporting arena. How different the scenario might be if the cricket-loving

John Major had still been Prime Minister. The former Prime Minister has
already devoted much of his energy into the redevelopment plans at The
Oval, and if he were still in office in Downing Street, then the Docklands
Dome might have already staged an indoor international on this prime site
in the capital city and easily accessible by both public and private
transport. Consideration is being given to using portable wickets at Lord's,
with Lord Alexander, the President of the MCC, announcing a plan in the
autumn of 2001 to improve several aspects of the famous ground,
including floodlights, better drainage, and portable wickets. But when
talking about the latter, Lord Alexander said 'of the three, it is the most
imaginative proposal, and the least urgent'.

Having said this, several counties are seriously considering creating
indoor arenas with portable wickets, with Warwickshire possibly
developing a purpose-built ground outside Birmingham with floodlights
and a retractable roof. According to their Chief Executive Dennis Amiss,
'there is no point in the county committing itself to an expensive stadium
and having it full for only six days a week. That involves putting pitches
in trays, installing floodlights and putting a roof over the ground to ensure
there is play even when it rains.' There are other advantages as well for
counties to consider using portable wickets, as it would help to 'free up'
the counties, allowing them to stage matches at venues which at the
moment do not have a good enough wicket, or indeed where one could not
be prepared to a suitable standard.

However, staging county games away from the club's traditional
headquarters and on drop-in wickets might seem too revolutionary for
some people. But should the counties be inhibited by these 'historical'
arguments? Perhaps a complete overhaul is needed of the root and branch
of English cricket, rather than just a little pruning. One quite radical
solution would involve the counties being re-invented into 'city-region'
teams allowing a new-style organisation to evolve overtime that could
raise the amount of cash needed to create indoor complexes. The
sportscape of twenty-first century Britain is an urban one and surely the
time has come for professional cricket to shed the millstone of having
outmoded names for its competing teams, so that they can represent areas
that are crystal clear both on the ground and in people's minds.

TABLE 52
RENAMING THE COUNTY TEAMS AND INVENTING CITY-REGION SIDES

'Old' county names'	New city-regions
Derbyshire County Cricket Club	Derby Region Cricket Club
Durham County Cricket Club	Durham Region Cricket Club
Essex County Cricket Club	Chelmsford Region Cricket Club
Glamorgan County Cricket Club	Cardiff Region Cricket Club
Gloucestershire County Cricket Club	Bristol Region Cricket Club
Hampshire County Cricket Club	Southampton Region Cricket Club
Kent County Cricket Club	Canterbury Region Cricket Club
Lancashire County Cricket Club	Manchester Region Cricket Club
Leicestershire County Cricket Club	Leicester Region Cricket Club
Middlesex County Cricket Club	North London Region Cricket Club
Northamptonshire County Cricket Club	Northampton Region Cricket Club
Nottinghamshire County Cricket Club	Nottingham Region Cricket Club
Somerset County Cricket Club	Taunton Region Cricket Club
Surrey County Cricket Club	South London Region Cricket Club
Sussex County Cricket Club	Brighton Region Cricket Club
Warwickshire County Cricket Club	Birmingham Region Cricket Club
Worcestershire County Cricket Club	Worcester Region Cricket Club
Yorkshire County Cricket Club	Leeds Region Cricket Club

Table 52 shows how all 18 of the existing first-class counties could be re-named by using the concept of a city-region which highlights the settlement at the top of the local settlement hierarchy and the one that most people in the counties gravitate towards for their services. In the case of Derby, Leicester, Northampton and Worcester, the word 'shire' could just be dropped from the county names. Other changes might be more contentious, especially in the case of Yorkshire and Lancashire, but should tradition stand in the way of progress?

There are huge economic benefits for the counties by having a makeover in terms of their name, as it could allow a merger with other sporting organisations within the urban area, with the creation of urban-based sporting conglomerates such as 'Sport Leicester', 'Sport Bristol' or 'Sport Cardiff', allowing sponsorship and financial support to be shared by the city's rugby, football and cricket clubs. Each would still have their own stadia, with a separate identity, and from the cricket teams point of view they would still have the regional identity that their name provides. There might also be international spin-offs for these city-based teams, especially if a transnational competition is organised along the lines of that proposed by Ian Preston, Stephen Ross and Stefan Szymanski. In a paper entitled 'Seizing the Moment: A Blueprint for Reform of World Cricket', presented at the ESRC Study Group Conference in December 2000, the three academics floated the idea of an international club competition involving city-based teams from Australia, South Africa, India, Pakistan and England.

The Professional Cricketers Association in England have already taken a small step in the direction of holding games between city-based teams, with the players' organisations masterminding the 'Zone Six City Challenge' at Bristol on 10 July 2001. Six teams were chosen, from an amalgam of county teams, representing London, Bristol, Birmingham, Leeds, Southampton and Manchester. However, rain intervened, allowing just 20 overs to be bowled before the contest was abandoned at four o'clock.

The abandonment was a salutary reminder that no matter what changes occur to the 'human' side of the game, the 'physical' factors can still intervene and disrupt even the best of ideas. It seems a paradox that in a society where we can clone sheep and identify our genetic make-up, cricket still falls foul of the weather, and surely it is time to start planning how these city-region teams could play indoors. The ECB could devise a plan for the development of portable wickets, whilst by linking up with other sporting organisations in these cities, the individual city-region teams could gain the sort of financial support and the economies of scale that would allow them to invest in covered grounds.

Some objections would inevitably be raised, especially about the potential demise of outgrounds if fixtures were concentrated at these covered arenas. But the outgrounds would still have a role to play in this brave new world of cricket, as by July and August, the weather could, even under global warming be more settled, so that each city-region side could play at open-air grounds, both for one-day and Championship fixtures. The grounds at Scarborough, Swansea, Southend and Cheltenham need not therefore disappear from the county calendar, especially if meteorologists are consulted.

The super-computers at the Met. Office headquarters have an enormous amount of data that could be used to determine the optimum dates in these months when rain was unlikely to fall at a certain outground. Even then the odd shower might still occur, but if the ECB had invested in an enhanced set of portable covers that were taken around the country and covered the whole of the playing area, an effort would have been made to prevent the amount of weather interruptions.

Another advantage that covered stadia provide is that the calendar can be modified without fear of weather interruptions. Games could take place in early April without the risk of players and supporters alike dodging the showers or donning extra sweaters as the hailstones fall and the cold wind blows. Matches could also take place in late September and early October, and by extending the season by three to four weeks, more time would be available for players to have proper rest periods and meaningful practice. All four competitions could be preserved, and there is the potential for more floodlit games to be staged, involving both the city-region and international sides.

With more time available, a regional competition could also be incorporated into the calendar, and an early-season competition, along the lines of that suggested by Christopher Martin-Jenkins, could provide the sort of showcase the selectors require when choosing the squad of centrally contracted players for the international contests that summer.

With the prospect of a true wicket and no hold-ups for the weather, spectators would surely flock in to these covered grounds to watch the games staged at these new cricketing centres. Club membership would rise and youngsters would be eager to take up the game and emulate the feats of their heroes. There are huge marketing and media spin-offs as well, with corporate involvement already being assisted by an affiliation to an urban sporting conglomerate. All of this would boost the coffers of the clubs, allowing all 18 of the sides – city-regions in name, but counties in spirit – to survive.

Apart from the quite recent change from three to four-day matches and the creation of two divisions, the County Championship has barely changed since its inauguration in 1890. Yet the geography of the United Kingdom, both physical and human, has changed. No longer is Britain the workshop of the world, with heavy industry dominant and sprawling industrial centres with densely populated residential areas. The settlements and the industries they spawned have dramatically changed, with light industries, retailing and leisure complexes, plus multinational conglomerates having all replaced the old smokestack industries.

If the predictions in the UKCIP reports are correct, the physical environment will also be dramatically changing over the next decades with even greater consequences than a shift to a service-based economy. The geography of the twenty-first century is therefore fundamentally different from the one of the eighteenth and nineteenth centuries when county cricket began. The time has surely come for the game to get rid of the outdated trappings from the past and to adapt to the new geography, both physical and human, of the modern era.

In 1997 the ECB produced the document 'Raising the Standard', but after considering all of these issues covered above, perhaps what is really needed is a report on 'Redrawing the Boundaries', looking at the locational aspects at the real heart of the professional game, especially within a more variable and volatile climate.

Perhaps it is time to stop thinking about rain stops play!

Notes

Series Editor's Foreword

1. Henry Newbolt, *Poems: New and Old* (London: John Murray, 1912), p.78.
2. See the obituary of Jack Mendl, *Daily Telegraph*, 27 December 2001, 27.
3. Graham Greene, *Stamboul Train* (Harmondsworth: Penguin Books, 1963), p.118.
4. J.C. Snaith, *Willow the King: The Story of a Cricket Match* (London: Ward, Lock and Co., 1891), p.21.
5. A.G. Macdonell, *England, Their England* (London: The Reprint Society, 1941), p.101.

Introduction

1. *Daily Telegraph*, 4 Sept. 1998.
2. *Wisden's Cricketers' Almanack* for 1999, pp.1464–5.
3. N. Cardus, *Cardus on Cricket* (London: Souvenir Press, 1977).
4. A. Sampson, *Grounds of Appeal* (London: Robert Hale, 1981).
5. W.A. Powell, *The Wisden Guide to Cricket Grounds* (London: Stanley Paul, 1992).
6. G. Plumptre, *Homes of Cricket: The First-class Grounds of England and Wales* (London: Queen Anne Press, 1988).
7. R. Bowen, *Cricket – A History of its Growth and Development Throughout the World* (London: Eyre and Spottiswoode, 1970).
8. P. Wynne-Thomas, *The History of Cricket from The Weald to The World* (London and Norwich: HMSO, 1996).
9. See for instance D. Birley, *Playing the Game: Sport and British Society – 1910–45* (Manchester: Manchester University Press, 1995); P. Bailey, *Leisure and Class in Victorian England* (London: Routledge, 1978); D. Birley, *A Social History of English Cricket* (London: Aurum Press, 1999) and D. Underdown, *Start of Play – Cricket and Culture in Eighteenth-Century England* (London: Allen Lane, The Penguin Press, 2000).
10. R. Sissons, *The Players: A Social History of the Professional Cricketer* (London: Kingswood Press, 1988).
11. K.A.P. Sandiford, 'The Professionalization of Modern Cricket', *British Journal of Sports History*, 5 (Dec. 1985), 270–89; K.A.P. Sandiford and W. Vamplew, 'The Peculiar Economics of English Cricket before 1914', *British Journal of Sports History*, 6 (Dec. 1986), 311–25.
12. J. Williams, *Cricket and England: A Cultural and Social History of the Inter-war Years* (London and Portland, OR: Frank Cass, 1999).
13. R.J. Holt, 'Cricket and Englishness: The Batsman as Hero', *International Journal of the History of Sport*, 13, 1 (March 1996).
14. J. Bale, *Sport and Place – A Geography of Sport in England, Scotland and Wales* (London: Hurst and Co, 1982), pp.68–92.
15. M. Hulme, 'Match of the Day', *Guardian*, 19 May 1989.
16. J.E. Thornes, 'Rain Starts Play', *Area*, 8 (1976), 105–12.
17. T. Mason, *Association Football and English Society, 1863–1915* (Brighton: Harvester, 1980).

18. J.A. Mangan, *Athleticism in the Victorian and Edwardian Public School* (Cambridge: Cambridge University Press, 1981).

19. A. Gattrell and P. Gould, 'A Micro-geography of Team-games: Graphical Explanations of Social Relationships', *Area*, 11 (1979), 275–8.

20. J. Rooney, *A Geography of American Sport from Cabin Creek to Anaheim* (Massachusetts: Addison-Wesley, 1974).

21. Bale, *Sports Geography* (London: E. & F. Spon, 1989).

22. Bale, *Sport and Place*.

23. J. Rooney, 'Sports from a Geographic Perspective', in D.W. Ball and J. Loy (eds.), *Sport and Social Order: Contributions to the Sociology of Sport* (Massachusetts: Addison-Wesley, 1975)

24. Bale, *Sport and Place*.

25. Bale, *Sports Geography*.

Chapter 1

1. A. Haygarth, *Frederick Lillywhite's Cricket Scores and Biographies of Celebrated Cricketers*, vol. 1, 1746–1826 (Kennington: Lillywhite's, 1862). This excellent series has been reproduced in facsimile by Roger Heavens (1996).

2. R. Brooke, *A History of the County Championship* (Enfield: Guinness Publishing, 1991).

3. R. Bowen, *Cricket – A History of its Growth and Development throughout the World* (London: Eyre and Spottiswode, 1970).

4. M. Marqusee, *Anyone but England: Cricket, Race and Class* (London: Two Heads Publishing, 1998). First published as *Anyone but England: Cricket and the National Malaise* (London: Verso, 1994).

5. E. Midwinter, *The Illustrated History of County Cricket* (London: Kingswood Press, 1992).

6. Bowen, *Cricket – A History*.

7. England and Wales Cricket Board, *Raising the Standard* (London: ECB, 1997).

8. J. Bale, *Landscapes of Modern Sport* (Leicester: Leicester University Press, 1994). See also J. Bale, 'Rustic and Rational Landscapes of Cricket', *Sport Place*, 2 (1991), 4–16.

9. J. Arlott and N. Cardus, *The Noblest Game* (London: Harrap, 1969).

10. G. Boyes, *The Imagined Village: Culture, Ideology and the Folk Revival* (Manchester: Manchester University Press, 1984); A. Howkins, 'The Discovery of Rural England' in A. Colls and R. Dodd (eds.), *Englishness: Politics and Culture 1880–1920* (Beckenham: Croom Helm, 1986).

11. *Daily Telegraph*, 1 May 1999.

12. P. Wynne-Thomas, *Nottinghamshire Cricket Grounds* (Nottingham: Nottinghamshire CC, 2001).

13. *Wisden Cricket Monthly*, News Register for June 1999.

14. Ibid.

15. R. Matusiewicz, *Financial Survey of Cricket 1999* (CD-ROM produced by Ambition Management, Nottingham, 1999).

16. *Sunday Telegraph*, 27 June 1999.

Chapter 2

1. C. Brookes, *English Cricket: The Game and its Players Throughout the Age* (London: Weidenfield and Nicolson, 1978).

2. J. Pycroft, *The Cricket Field* (London: Longman Green, 1851).

3. R. Bowen, *Cricket – A History of its Growth and Development Throughout the World* (London: Eyre and Spottiswode, 1970).
4. P. Wynne-Thomas, *The History of Cricket from The Weald to The World* (London and Norwich: HMSO, 1996).
5. See the series of articles by Peter Wynne-Thomas in *The Club Cricketer* magazine during 1988 on cricket's origins.
6. In 1611 two young men were fined for playing cricket on Sunday in Sidlesham in West Sussex.
7. Wynne-Thomas, *The History of Cricket*.
8. Ibid p.6. See also D. Terry, The Seventeenth Century Game of Cricket: A Reconstruction of the Game. *Journal of the British Society of Sports History*, 20 (2000), 33–43.
9. *Post Boy*, 28–30 March 1700.
10. C. Brookes, *The Game and its Players*.
11. M. Marqusee, *Anyone but England: Cricket, Race and Class* (London: Two Heads Publishing, 1998). First published as *Anyone but England: Cricket and the National Malaise* (London: Verso, 1994).
12. The scorecard for the match between Kent and Surrey in 1709 can be found in A. Haygarth, *Frederick Lillywhite's Cricket Scores and Biographies of Celebrated Cricketers* (Kennington: Lillywhite, 1862). See also Wynne-Thomas, *History of Cricket*.
13. Wynne-Thomas, *The History of Cricket*, especially pp.12–13.
14. Ibid.
15. A. Mote, *The Glory Days of Cricket – The Extraordinary Story of Broadhalfpenny Down* (London: Robson Books, 1997).
16. J. Nyren, 'Cricketers of My Time', quoted in J. Arlott, (ed.), *From Hambledon to Lord's* (Barry Sherlock, 1948) pp.26–7.
17. For a scorecard of the match in 1731 between Sevenoaks and Eleven Gentlemen of London, see Haygarth, *Frederick Lillywhite's Cricket Scores*.
18. Wynne-Thomas, *The History of Cricket*.
19. *Hereford Journal*, 31 July 1783.
20. A.K. Hignell, *A 'Favourit' Game* (Cardiff: University of Wales Press, 1992).
21. See for example the notice in the *Hereford Journal* for 5 May 1785, advertising a cricket meeting in Swansea.
22. A.R. Lewis, *Double Century* (London: Hodder and Stoughton, 1987).
23. Wynne-Thomas, *The History of Cricket*.
24. A.R. Lewis, *Double Century*.
25. The entries for 1811 and 1812 in Haygarth, *Frederick Lillywhite's Cricket Scores*.
26. E. Midwinter, *The Illustrated History of County Cricket* (London: Kingswood Press, 1992).
27. Ibid.
28. The scorecard of the 1825 contest between Kent and Sussex can be found in Haygarth, *Frederick Lillywhite's Cricket Scores*.
29. J. Bale, 'Cricket in pre-Victorian England and Wales', *Area*, 13 (1981),119–22.
30. Quoted in A.V. Pullin, *Talks with Old English Cricketers* (Blackwood, 1900).
31. Hignell, *A 'Favourit' Game*.
32. Wynne-Thomas, *The History of Cricket*.
33. A.A. Thomson, 'Lord's and the Early Champions, 1787–1865', in E.W. Swanton (ed.), *Barclay's World of Cricket* (London: Collins, 1980)
34. D.T. Smith, *The South Wales Cricket Club 1859–1886* (published privately, 1986).
35. For a detailed account of Monmouthshire's match with the All-England Eleven, see Hignell, *A 'Favourit' Game*.
36. D.T. Smith, *South Wales Cricket Club*.
37. A. Jacks (ed.), *Chepstow C.C. – The First 150 Years, 1838–1988* (Chepstow: Cricket Club, 1988).

38. *Cardiff and Merthyr Guardian*, 24 July 1852.
39. *The Cambrian*, 5 March 1869.
40. J. Marshall, *Sussex Cricket – A History*, (London: Heinemann, 1959); P. Wynne-Thomas, *The History of Nottinghamshire County Cricket Club* (London: Christopher Helm, 1992); J.M. Kilburn, *Yorkshire County Cricket* (London: Convoy, 1950).
41. D. Lemmon, *The Official History of Surrey County Cricket Club* (London: Christopher Helm, 1989); J. Kay, *A History of County Cricket – Lancashire* (London: Arthur Barker, 1974).
42. D. Moore, *The History of Kent County Cricket Club* (London: Christopher Helm, 1988).
43. R. Brooke, *A History of the County Championship* (Enfield: Guinness Publishing, 1991).
44. E.W. Swanton, 'The County Championship', in E.W. Swanton (ed.), *Barclay's World of Cricket*.
45. C. Brookes, *The Game and its Players*.
46. *John Wisden's Cricketers' Almanack* for 1895 (John Wisden, 1895).

Chapter 3

1. See M.G. Bradford and W.A. Kent, *Human Geography: Theories and their Application* (Oxford: Oxford University Press, 1977). Torsten Hagerstrand's work was first published in Swedish in 1953, and was translated into English by A. Pred in *Innovation Diffusion as a Spatial Process* (Chicago: University of Chicago Press, 1967).
2. G.B. Buckley, *Fresh Light on Pre-Victorian Cricket* (Cotterell, 1937); A. Haygarth, *Frederick Lillywhite's Cricket Scores and Biographies of Celebrated Cricketers*, vol. 1, 1746–1826; vol. 2, 1827–1840 (Kennington: Lillywhite's, 1862).
3. *The Cambrian Daily Leader, Monmouthshire Merlin, Hereford Journal, Cardiff and Merthyr Guardian, The Welshman, Carmarthen Journal, Swansea Journal, Bristol Gazette, South Wales Press, Monmouthshire Mercury, Swansea and Glamorgan Herald, South Wales Daily Press, Western Mail,* and *South Wales Daily News*.
4. J. Bale, 'Cricket in pre-Victorian England and Wales', *Area*, 13, 119–22.
5. P. Wynne-Thomas, *The History of Cricket from The Weald to The World* (London and Norwich: HMSO, 1996).
6. *Monmouthshire Merlin*, 26 July 1844.
7. Ibid., 27 June 1845.
8. Ibid., 31 August 1839.
9. *The Cambrian*, 16 September 1853.
10. Quoted in 'Bygones relating to Wales and the Border Counties, 1891–92', as referred to in H.M. Waddington, *Games and Athletics in Bygone Wales* (Transactions of the Honourable Society of Cymmrodorion, 1954), pp.84–100.
11. G.O. Pierce, 'Nonconformity and Politics', in A.J. Roderick (ed.), *Wales Through the Ages,* vol.2 (Llandybie: Christopher Davies, 1960), pp.168–76.
12. K.O. Morgan, *Rebirth of a Nation* (Oxford: Oxford University Press, 1981).
13. Quoted in K.E. Kissack, *Victorian Monmouth* (Ledbury: Bosbury Press, 1986), p.184.
14. *Western Mail*, 29 August 1874.
15. *The Cambrian*, 6 September 1850.
16. Quoted in D.T.W. Price, *A History of St David's University College, Lampeter* (Cardiff: University of Wales Press, 1977). vol.1, ch.7.
17. For a history of Cowbridge Grammar School, see I. Davies, *A Certaine Schoole*, (Cowbridge: Brown and Son, 1967). References to the school's matches at Merthyr Mawr can be found in *The Cambrian*, 4, 19 September 1857.

18. *The Star of Gwent*, 14 September 1867.
19. For information on E.U. David see A.K. Hignell, *100 Greats: Glamorgan County Cricket Club, 1888–1991* (Stroud: Tempus Publishing, 2000).
20. Their ground is clearly marked on the 1839 tithe map – Raglan Tithe Apportionment, D/Pa 36–17, Gwent Record Office.
21. *Monmouthshire Merlin*, 15 July 1834.
22. R. Purday, *One Hundred Years of the Phoenix: the Story of Panteg Cricket Club: 1876–1976* (The Club, 1977).
23. *Pontypool Free Press*, 6 May 1865.

Chapter 4

1. Walther Christaller first produced his theory in 1933. It was translated by C.W. Baskin in *Central Places in Southern Germany* (Prentice-Hall, 1966). For a concise outline of his theory, see M.G. Bradford and W.A. Kent, *Human Geography: Theories and their Application* (Oxford: Oxford University Press, 1977).
2. G.K. Zipf elaborated on the Rank-Size Rule initially in 1941, and subsequently in *Human Behaviour and the Principle of Least Effort* (Cambridge: Cambridge University Press, 1949). Also see M.G. Bradford and W.A. Kent, *Human Geography*.
3. A. Spearman's Rank Correlation co-efficient value was calculated as +0.47.
4. E. Midwinter, *The Illustrated History of County Cricket* (London: Kingswood Press, 1992).
5. Ibid.
6. R. Roberts, *Sixty Years of Somerset Cricket* (London: Westaway, 1952).
7. D. Foot, *Sunshine, Sixes and Cider – The History of Somerset Cricket* (Newton Abbot: David and Charles, 1986).
8. P. Wynne-Thomas, *The History of Lancashire County Cricket Club* (London: Christopher Helm, 1989).
9. J. Kay, *A History of County Cricket – Lancashire* (London: Arthur Barker,1974).
10. Ibid.
11. J. Marshall, *Old Trafford* (London: Pelham Books, 1971); M. Lorimer and D. Ambrose, *Cricket Grounds of Lancashire* (Nottingham: Association of Cricket Statisticians, 1992); Wynne-Thomas, *History of Lancashire*.
12. R. Brooke, *Cricket Grounds of Warwickshire* (Nottingham: Association of Cricket Statisticians, 1989); J. Bannister, *The History of Warwickshire County Cricket Club* (London: Christopher Helm, 1990); L. Duckworth, *The Story of Warwickshire Cricket* (London: Stanley Paul, 1974).
13. D. Cannadine, *Lords and Landlords: The Aristocracy and the Towns* (Leicester: Leicester University Press, 1980). See also D. Cannadine, *Patricians, Power and Politics in 19th Century Towns* (Leicester: Leicester University Press, 1982).
14. J. Bale, *Sport and Place – A Geography of Sport in England, Scotland and Wales* (London: Hurst and Co, 1982), pp.80–5.
15. D. Frith, *The Golden Age of Cricket* (Guildford: Lutterworth Press, 1978).
16. G. Cornwallis-West, *Edwardian Hey-Days* (London: Hodder and Stoughton, 1930).
17. D. Moore, *The History of Kent County Cricket Club* (London: Christopher Helm, 1988).
18. Ibid.

Chapter 5

1. K.A.P. Sandiford and W. Vamplew, 'The Peculiar Economics of English Cricket before 1914', *British Journal of Sports History*, (Dec. 1986), 311–26.

2. *John Wisden's Cricketers' Almanack for 1902; 1922; 1950* (Sporting Handbooks, London).

3. P. Wynne-Thomas, *Cricket Grounds of Nottinghamshire* (Nottingham: Association of Cricket Statisticians, 1984).

4. S. Draper, *Cricket Grounds of Yorkshire* (Nottingham: Association of Cricket Statisticians, 1995).

5. D. Moore, *The History of Kent County Cricket Club* (London: Christopher Helm, 1988).

6. G. Parker, *Gloucestershire Road – A History of Gloucestershire County Cricket Club* (London: Pelham, 1983).

7. D.M. Green, *The History of Gloucestershire County Cricket Club* (London: Christopher Helm, 1990).

8. I. Hall, *Cricket at Scarborough – A Social History of the Club and its Festival* (Derby: Breedon Books, 1992).

9. Ibid.

10. The value for the Spearman's Rank Correlation Co-efficient rose from +0.58 to +0.65 by 1921.

11. G. Plumptre, *The Golden Age of Cricket* (London: Macdonald Queen Anne Press, 1990).

12. C. Bray, *Essex County Cricket* (London: Convoy, 1950); L. Newnham, *Essex County Cricket 1876–1975* (Colchester: Vineyard Press, 1975).

13. E.E. Snow, *Cricket Grounds of Leicestershire* (Nottingham: Association of Cricket Statisticians, 1987); D. Lambert, *The History of Leicestershire County Cricket Club* (London: Christopher Helm, 1992).

14. D. Lemmon, *The Official History of Worcestershire County Cricket Club* (London: Christopher Helm, 1989).

15. L. Hatton, *Cricket Grounds of Worcestershire* (Nottingham: Association of Cricket Statisticians, 1985).

16. D. Lemmon, *Official History of Worcestershire*.

17. The Spearman's Rank Correlation co-efficient had strengthened to +0.69.

18. C. Bray, *Essex County Cricket*.

19. R. Bowen, *Cricket – A History of its Growth and Development Throughout the World* (London: Eyre and Spottiswode, 1970).

20. L. Duckworth, *The Story of Warwickshire Cricket* (London: Stanley Paul, 1974).

21. D. Lemmon, *The Official History of Surrey County Cricket Club* (London: Christopher Helm, 1989).

22. *John Wisden's Cricketers' Almanack* for 1938 (Sporting Handbooks, London).

23. M. Engel and A. Radd, *The History of Northamptonshire County Cricket Club*, (London: Christopher Helm, 1993).

24. D. Foot, *Sunshine, Sixes and Cider – The History of Somerset Cricket* (Newton Abbot: David and Charles, 1986).

25. Ibid.

26. J.M. Kilburn and N. de Mesquita, 'County Grounds of England' in E.W. Swanton (ed.), *Barclay's World of Cricket* (London: Collins, 1980) pp. 492–500.

27. Findlay Commission, Schedule VII.

28. J. Williams, *Cricket and England: A Cultural and Social History of the Inter-war Years* (London and Portland, OR: Frank Cass, 1999).

29. *The Cricketer*, Spring Annual for 1954.

Chapter 6

1. *Cricket Quarterly*, (1963), 49.

2. J. Laker, *One Day Cricket* (London: Batsford, 1977).

3. T.E. Bailey (ed.), *John Player Cricket Handbook* (London: Queen Anne Press, 1973).

4. R. Brooke, *A History of the County Championship* (Enfield: Guinness Publishing, 1991).

5. Ibid.

6. P. Wynne-Thomas, *The History of Cricket from The Weald to The World* (London and Norwich: HMSO, 1996).

7. J. Laker, *One Day Cricket*.

8. Ibid.

9. J. Laker, 'The Effects of One Day Cricket' in T.E. Bailey (ed.), *John Player Cricket Yearbook* (London: Queen Anne Press, 1973).

10. The Spearman's Rank correlation co-efficient value remained high at +0.64.

11. D. Lambert, *The History of Leicestershire County Cricket Club* (London: Christopher Helm,1992); E.E. Snow, *Cricket Grounds of Leicestershire* (Nottingham: Association of Cricket Statisticians, 1987).

12. R. Brooke, *Cricket Grounds of Warwickshire* (Nottingham: Association of Cricket Statisticians, 1989).

13. J. Bannister, *The History of Warwickshire County Cricket Club* (London: Christopher Helm, 1990).

14. J.H. Morgan, *Glamorgan County Cricket* (London: Convoy, 1952).

15. A.K. Hignell, *Cricket Grounds of Glamorgan* (Nottingham: Association of Cricket Statisticians, 1985).

16. *John Wisden's Cricketers' Almanack* for 1934 (Sporting Handbooks).

17. A.K. Hignell, *The History of Glamorgan County Cricket Club* (London: Christopher Helm, 1988).

18. A.K. Hignell, *The Skipper – A Biography of Wilf Wooller* (Royston: Limlow Books, 1995).

19. A.K. Hignell, *Cricket Grounds of Glamorgan*.

20. *John Wisden's Cricketers' Almanack* for 1970 (Sporting Handbooks).

21. I. Hall, *Cricket at Scarborough – A Social History of the Club and its Festival* (Derby: Breedon Books, 1992).

22. J. Laker, *One Day Cricket*.

23. T.E. Bailey, 'The County Championship – Relic or Relevant' in *John Wisden's Cricketers' Almanack* for 1990 (John Wisden and Co.), 75–80.

24. *John Wisden's Cricketers' Almanack* for 1981 (London: Queen Anne Press).

25. P.G. Carling, 'The Continuing Struggle for Survival' in *John Wisden's Cricketers' Almanack* for 1983 (London: Macdonald Queen Anne Press), 100–103.

26. D. Lemmon, *One Day Cricket* (London: Century Benham for Marks and Spencer, 1988).

27. E. Midwinter, *The Illustrated History of County Cricket* (London: Kingswood Press, 1992).

28. R. Matusiewicz, *Financial Survey of Cricket 1999* (CD-ROM produced by Ambition Management, Nottingham, 1999).

29. M. Marqusee, *Anyone but England: Cricket, Race and Class* (London: Two Heads Publishing, 1998), originally published as *Anyone but England Cricket and the National Malaise* (London: Verso Books, 1994).

30. G. Plumptre, *Homes of Cricket – The First-Class Grounds of England and Wales* (London: Macdonald Queen Anne Press, 1988).

31. W.A. Powell, *The Wisden Guide to Cricket Grounds* (London: Stanley Paul, 1992).

32. C. Sexstone (Chief Executive of Gloucestershire CCC) personal communication.

33. K.A.P. Sandiford, 'The Professionalization of Modern Cricket', *British Journal of Sports History* (Dec. 1985), 270–89.

Chapter 7

1. M. Hulme and E. Barrow (eds.), *The Climate of the British Isles: Present, Past and Future* (London: Routledge, 1997).
2. R.J. Reynolds, 'Wickets and Weather in 19th Century Cricket Seasons', *The Cricket Statistician*, 99 (1997), 33–7.
3. D. Jeater, 'Cricket season weather 1890 – 1993', *The Cricket Statistician*, 89 (1995), 26–9.
4. J. Kitchin, '1903 – The Wettest Summer of Them All ?', in *John Wisden's Cricketers' Almanack* for 1986 (London: John Wisden, 1986), pp.77–80.
5. Ibid.
6. H.S. Altham, *The History of Cricket* (London: Allen and Unwin, 1926).
7. R. Webber and K.M. Arnott, *Glamorgan 1921–1947* (Hunstanton: The Cricket Book Society, 1949).
8. *John Wisden's Cricketers' Almanack* for 1959 (London: Sporting Handbooks, 1959).
9. *John Wisden's Cricketers' Almanack* for 1960 (London: Sporting Handbooks, 1960).
10. For a report on Underwood's performance, see *John Wisden's Cricketers' Almanack* for 1969 (London: Sporting Handbooks, 1969), pp.316–18.
11. *John Wisden's Cricketers' Almanack* for 1981 (London: Queen Anne Press, 1981).
12. Letters by K Hosking in *The Cricketer* magazine for November 1988 and November 1989.
13. P. Eden, 'Cricket and the Weather, 1998', in *John Wisden's Cricketers' Almanack* for 1999 (London: John Wisden, 1999), pp.146–65.
14. P. Crofton, 'Weather Conditions', *The Cricket Statistician*, 91, 15–16.
15. J. Kitchin, 'The Wettest Summer'.

Chapter 8

1. G.J. Llewellyn, 'The Weather and Post-War English Cricket', *The Cricketer* (Winter Annual 1969/70), 32–3.
2. J.E. Thornes, 'Rain Starts Play', *Area*, 8 (1976), 105–112. See also the reply by R.P.C. Morgan, ibid., 257–8.
3. D. McLeish, 'Abandoned (Weather) Matches in the County Championship', *The Cricket Statistician*, 80 (1992), 33–5. The list of abandoned Championship matches on which Duncan McLeish largely based his work was initially produced by Philip Bailey in 'Abandoned County Championship Matches 1886–1987', *The Cricket Statistician*, 78 (1990), 34–8.
4. Thornes 'Rain Starts Play'.
5. The Duckworth–Lewis method of recalculating targets in rain-affected matches is explained in F. Duckworth *et al.*, *Your Comprehensive Guide to the 'Duckworth–Lewis' Method of Resetting Targets in One-Day Cricket* (Bristol: University of the West of England, 1999).
6. Taken from an article by John Mace, the Gloucestershire CCC statistician in the club's Yearbook for 1986.
7. Quoted by A. Lewis in 'Reverse Swing', *The Cricketer* (May 1993).
8. Ibid.
9. Quoted in G. Plumptre, *Homes of Cricket* (London: Macdonald Queen Anne Press, 1988).
10. I.A.R. Peebles, 'Dawn of the Modern Age, 1900–14' in E.W. Swanton (ed.), *Barclay's World of Cricket* (London: Collins, 1977), pp.19–26.
11. J. Arlott, *John Arlott's Book of Cricketers* (London: Lutterworth Press, 1979).

12. A.K. Hignell, *The Skipper – A Biography of Wilf Wooller* (Royston: Limlow, 1995).
13. *John Wisden's Cricketers' Almanack* for 1975 (London: Sporting Handbooks, 1975).

Chapter 9

1. R.G. Barry and R.J. Chorley (eds.), *Atmosphere, Weather and Climate* (London: Routledge, 1992).
2. J.W. King, 'Solar Radiation Changes and Weather, *Nature*, 245 (1973), 443–6.
3. Similarly, out of the 62 occasions when no play was possible on a day in Test cricket in England between 1880 and 1974, 41 were in such years of the solar cycle.
4. J. Kitchin, '1903 – The Wettest Summer of Them All?, in *John Wisden's Cricketers' Almanack* for 1986 (London: John Wisden, 1986), pp.77–80.
5. D. Jeater, 'Cricket Season Weather 1890–1993', *The Cricket Statistician*, 89 (1993), 26–9. See also K. Hosking's letter regarding a Weather Index in *The Cricketer* magazine (February 1983).
6. Jeater, 'Cricket Season Weather 1890–1993'.
7. B.W. Atkinson, 'Precipitation' in K.J. Gregory and D.E. Walling (eds.), *Human Activity and Environmental Processes* (Chichester: John Wiley & Sons, 1987), pp.31–50.

Chapter 10

1. T.J. Chandler, *The Climate of London* (London: Hutchinson, 1965).
2. G. Nagle, 'Urban Microclimates', *GeoFactsheets* 50.
3. B.W. Atkinson, 'A Preliminary Examination of the Possible Effect of London's Urban Area on the Distribution of Thunder Rainfall, 1951–60', *Transactions of the Institute of British Geographers*, 44, pp. 97–118; and B.W. Atkinson, 'Precipitation', in K.J. Gregory and D.E. Walling (eds.), *Man and Environmental Processes* (Chichester: John Wiley and Sons, 1987), pp.23–37.
4. T.R. Oke (1978) op.cit.
5. P. Bailey, 'Abandoned County Championship Matches 1886–1987', *The Cricket Statistician* 78, 34–8.
6. L. Tufnell, 'North-West England and the Isle of Man', in D. Wheeler and J.C. Mayes *Regional Climates of the British Isles* (London: Routledge, 1997) pp.181–204.
7. S. Gregory, 'Weather and Climate', in W.A. Smith, *Scientific Survey of Merseyside* (Liverpool: University Press of Liverpool, 1953); see also P.R. Crowe, 'Climate' in *Manchester and Its Region*, *Manchester Statistician*, 78, 34–8.
8. E.C. Barratt, 'Local variations in rainfall trends in the Manchester Region', *Transactions of the Institute of British Geographers*, 35, 55–72.
9. J.D.C. Webb, 'Hailstorms and intense local rainfalls in the British Isles', *Journal of Meteorology*, 18, pp. 313–27.
10. A.K. Hignell, 'Crowds, Clouds and the Raining Champions: A Locational Review of County Cricket in England and Wales', *Culture, Sport, Society*, 2, 2 (Summer 1999), 58–81. See also A.K. Hignell, 'Rain Stops Play – How's That?' *Weather*, 55 (2000), 150–6.
11. Taken from a note by J. Mace in the 1986 *Gloucestershire CCC Yearbook*.
12. Taken from notes in the 1981 and 1986 *Gloucestershire CCC Yearbook*.
13. Taken from a note by J. Mace in the 1986 *Gloucestershire CCC Yearbook*.
14. Taken from an article by W.J. Adams in the 1986 *Gloucestershire CCC Yearbook*.
15. *Wisden Cricket Monthly* (October 2001), 19.

Chapter 11

1.   M. Manley, *A History of West Indies Cricket* (London: André Deutsch, 1988).
2.   B. Stoddart, 'Cricket and Colonialism in the English-speaking Caribbean to 1914: towards a cultural analysis' in H. Beckles and B. Stoddart (eds.), *Liberation Cricket: West Indies Cricket Culture* (Manchester: Manchester University Press, 1995).
3.   M. Bose, *A Maidan View – The Magic of Indian Cricket* (London: George Allen and Unwin, 1986).
4.   T.F. Kennedy and T.O. Newnham, *Asia – The Monsoon Lands* (London: Heinemann, 1971).
5.   *Wisden's Cricketer's Almanack for 1997.*
6.   See D. Shimwell, *The Cricketer* (June 1987), 22–3.
7.   W. Frindall (ed.), *Playfair Cricket World Cup Guide* (London: Headline, 1996).
8.   S. Berry, *A Cricket Odyssey: England on Tour 1987–8* (London: Pavilion Books, 1988).
9.   R. Cashman (ed.), *The Oxford Guide to Australian Cricket* (Oxford: Oxford University Press, 1996), pp.570–1.
10. Ibid.
11. *Wisden Cricketers' Almanack* for 1948 (London: J. Wisden).
12. R. Cashman (ed.), *Oxford Guide*, p.440.
13. K. Casellas, 'The Fremantle Doctor' in R.Cashman (ed.), *Oxford Guide*, p.202.
14. D.K. Lillee, *Back to the Mark* (London: Stanley Paul, 1974).
15. K. Casellas, 'Fremantle Doctor'.
16. G. Philander, 'Learning from El Nino', *Weather*, 53 (1998), 270–3.
17. K. Wolter and M.S. Timlin, 'Measuring the strength of ENSO events: How does 1997/98 rank?', *Weather*, 53 (1998), 315–23.
18. H. Annamalai and J. Slingo, 'The Asian summer monsoon, 1997', *Weather*, 53 (1998), 284–6.
19. J.A. Lindesay, 'South African rainfall, the Southern Oscillation and a Southern Hemisphere semi-annual cycle', *Journal of Climatology*, 8 (1998), 17–30.
20. *Wisden's Cricketers' Almanack* for 1999, pp.1053–6.
21. C.G. Jones and C.D. Thorncroft, 'The role of El Nino in Atlantic tropical cyclone activity', *Weather*, 53 (1998), 324–36.
22. *Wisden's Cricketers' Almanack* for 1999, pp.1043–5.
23. See for instance J.T. Houghton *et al.*, *Climate Change: The Intergovernmental Panel on Climate Change Scientific Assessment* (Cambridge: Cambridge University Press, 1992).

Chapter 12

1.   M. Hulme and G.J. Jenkins, 'Climate Change Scenarios for the U.K.: Scientific Report', *U.K. Climate Impacts Programme Technical Report* No. 1 (Norwich: Climate Research Unit, 1998), p.7.
2.   J.C. Mayes, 'Recent Trends in Summer Rainfall', *Weather*, 46 (1998), 190–6; N.E. Davis, 'An Optimum Summer Weather Index', *Weather*, 23 (1968), 305–17.
3.   N.L.H. Wood, 'Rainfall Variability at London and Plymouth', *Weather*, 44 (1989), 202–9; M. Hulme and G.J. Jenkins, 'Climate Change Scenarios'.
4.   J.C. Mayes, 'Recent Trends'.
5.   M. Hulme and G.J. Jenkins 'Climate Change Scenarios'.
6.   Wadhams' work is covered in general terms by an article in the *Daily Mail*, 19 February 1996.
7.   My thanks to Dr David Thornton of UWIC, another Glamorgan supporter, and Dr Bill

Adams of Aberystwyth University for their help with various matters relating to the soil science of cricket squares.

8. N.L.H. Wood, 'Rainfall Variability at London and Plymouth 1921–87', *Weather*, 37 (1993), 202–8.
9. P. Bailey, 'Abandoned County Championship Matches 1886–1987', *The Cricket Statistician*, 78 (1990), 34–8.
10. D.O. Lee, 'Urban Warming? – An analysis of recent trends in London's heat island', *Weather*, 40 (1995), 50–6.
11. J.E. Thornes, 'Rain Starts Play', *Area*, 8 (1976), 105–12.
12. D. McLeish, 'Abandoned (Weather) Matches in the County Championship', *The Cricket Statistician*, 80 (1992), 33–5. Where a three-day game spanned two months, it was allocated to the month in which two of the days were to have been played. Fortunately, none of the four-day games that were abandoned spanned two months.
13. J.C. Mayes, 'U.K. Summer Weather over 50 Years – Continuity or Change?', *Weather*, 53 (1998), 2–11.

Chapter 13

1. M. Marqusee, *Anyone but England: Cricket, Race and Class* (London: Two Heads Publishing, 1998), originally published as *Anyone but England: Cricket and the National Malaise* (London: Verso Books, 1994).
2. *The Cricketer* (March 1993), 21.
3. A. Lee, 'The Murray Report – The Case in Favour', *John Wisden's Cricketers' Almanack* for 1993 (London: John Wisden and Co., 1993), pp.26–7.
4. R. Bowen, *Cricket – A History of its Growth and Development Throughout the World* (London: Eyre and Spottiswode, 1970).
5. *Daily Telegraph*, 4 December 1998.
6. Ibid.
7. *The Independent*, 4 December 1998.
8. *Daily Telegraph*, 13 October 1998.
9. *Independent*, 4 December 1998.
10. *Daily Telegraph*, 5 December 1998.
11. *The Cricketer* (January 1999).
12. M. Marqusee, *Anyone but England*.
13. M. Marqusee, 'Planet Waves' in R. Steen (ed.), *Universal Stories: The New Ball*, vol. 2 (Edinburgh: Mainstream Publishing, 1998).
14. See for instance R. Potter, *Urbanisation in the Third World* (Oxford: Oxford University Press, 1992).
15. England and Wales Cricket Board, *Raising the Standard* (London: ECB, 1997).
16. *Sunday Telegraph*, 18 July 1999. See also the article by Christopher Martin-Jenkins in *The Times* 12 July 1999.
17. *The Cricketer* (August 1999).
18. *The Cricketer* (October 1988), 16.
19. *The Cricketer* (May 1990), 38.
20. EWCB, 'Raising The Standard'.
21. *The Times*, 9 May 2001.
22. *Sunday Telegraph*, 10 October 1998.
23. *The Cricketer* (December 1998).
24. Ibid.
25. *The Sunday Times*, 13 June 1999.
26. M. Hulme, 'Match of the Day', *Guardian*, 19 May 1989.

27. R.G. Barry and A.H. Perry, *Synoptic Climatology: Methods and Applications* (London: Methuen, 1973).

28. *The Cricketer* (November 1989), 18.

29. M. Hulme, 'Match of the Day'.

30. M. Hulme and G.J. Jenkins (1998), 'Climate Change Scenarios for the UK: Scientific Report', *U.K. Climate Impacts Programme Technical Report* No. 1 (1998).

31. D.O. Lee, 'Urban Warming? – An analysis of recent trends in London's heat island', *Weather*, 40 (1995) 50–6.

32. *Sunday Telegraph*, 2 May 1999.

33. *Daily Telegraph*, 12 July 1999.

34. M. Marqusee, *Anyone but England*.

Appendix 1

Grounds in the United Kingdom used for first-class and limited overs games since 1801

Location	Ground Name	First Game	Most Recent	Status
Aberdeen	Mannofield Park	1930	1957	FC
		1983	1985	Lim
Abergavenny	Pen-y-Pound	1983	1997	FC
		1981	1982	Lim
Aberystwyth	Vicarage Field	1977	1989	Lim
Aldershot	Officers Club Services Ground	1905	1964	FC
Alton	Municipal Ground	1904	1904	FC
Amersham	Shardeloes	1972	1977	Lim
Arundel	Arundel Castle	1990	2001	Lim
		1972	2001	FC
Ashby-de-la-Zouch	Bath Grounds	1912	1964	FC
Ashton-under-Lyne	Ashton Club Ground	1865	1865	FC
Aston Rowant	Butt's Way, Kingston Blount	1994	1996	Lim
Attleborough	Old Buckenham Hall	1912	1921	FC
Aylesford	Preston Hall Ground	1846	1847	FC
Ayr	Cambusdoon	1958	2000	FC
Banstead	Recreation Ground	1984	1984	FC
Barnes	St Ann's Ground	1890	1890	FC
Barnsley	Clarence Ground	1862	1862	FC
	Shaw Lane	1975	1978	Lim
Barrow	Abbey Road	1997	2001	Lim
Barwell	Kirkby Road	1946	1947	FC
Basingstoke	May's Bounty	1906	2000	FC
		1967	2000	Lim
Bath	Lansdown Cricket Club Ground	1844	1884	FC
	Recreation Ground	1969	1996	Lim
Batley	Mount Pleasant	1883	1883	FC
Beaconsfield	Wilton Park	1992	2001	Lim
Beckenham	Foxgrove Road	1886	1905	FC
Bedford	Goldington Bury, Church Lane	1968	1991	Lim
	Bedford School Ground, Burnaby Road	1971	1982	Lim
Beeston	Meadow Road	1870	1870	FC
Belfast	Ormeau	1926	1999	FC
		1996	1999	Lim
Benenden	Hensted Park	1843	1843	FC
Bexhill	Manor Ground	1896	1896	FC
Billericay	Toby Howe Cricket Ground	2000	2000	Lim
Birkenhead	Oxton Cricket Club Ground	1985	1989	Lim

FC = First-class match

Lim = Limited overs match (involving at least one side recognised as a first-class team)

Data correct to the end of the 2001 season

Compiled with the assistance of Philip Bailey of the Association of Cricket Statisticians and Historians

Birmingham	Aston Park	1861	1861	FC
	Aston Lower Grounds	1879	1884	FC
	Edgbaston	1886	2001	FC
		1964	2001	Lim
	Mitchell's and Butler's Ground	1931	1961	FC
Bishop's Stortford	Cricket Field Lane	1872	1872	FC
Blackburn	Alexandra Meadows	1932	1935	FC
Blackheath	Rectory Field	1887	1971	FC
		1968	1972	Lim
Blackpool	Stanley Park	1905	1997	FC
		1976	2001	Lim
Blackwell	Miners Welfare Ground	1909	1913	FC
Bletchley	Manor Fields	1980	1983	FC
		1976	1983	Lim
Bolton	Back o' the Bank	1871	1871	FC
Bourne	Abbey Lawn	2001	2001	Lim
Bournemouth	Dean Park	1897	1992	FC
		1963	2001	Lim
Bournville	Bournville Cricket Ground	1910	1911	FC
Bowdon	South Downs Road	1984	1999	Lim
Brackley	Brackley Cricket Club Ground	1971	1975	Lim
Bradford	Great Horton Road	1863	1874	FC
	Horton Park Avenue	1880	1996	FC
Bramshill	Bramshill Park	1823	1826	FC
Bray	Woodbrook Cricket Club Ground	1907	1912	FC
Brecon	Christ College	1993	1995	FC
Brentwood	Old County Ground	1922	1967	FC
		1965	1967	Lim
Brighton	Royal New Ground	1814	1847	FC
	Lillywhite's Ground	1839	1842	FC
Bristol	The Royal & Sun Alliance County Ground,	1889	2001	FC
	Nevil Road	1963	2001	Lim
	Greenbank	1922	1928	FC
	Imperial Athletic Ground	1957	1966	FC
		1971	1979	Lim
	Ironside Lane, Brislington	1969	1970	Lim
Brockhampton	The Park	1999	2001	Lim
Bromley	Phillip's Field	1840	1840	FC
	White Hart Field	1841	1842	FC
Burton-on-Trent	Town Ground	1840	1841	FC
	Burton-on-Trent Cricket Club Ground	1914	1937	FC
	Ind Coope Ground	1938	1980	FC
		1969	1988	Lim
	Bass Worthington Ground	1975	1976	FC
Bury St Edmunds	Town Ground	1830	1847	FC
	Victory Ground, Nowton Road	1981	2001	Lim
Buxton	Park Road Ground	1923	1986	FC
		1969	1986	Lim
Byfleet	British Aerospace Company Ground	1970	1979	Lim
Camberley	Royal Military Academy Ground	1938	1938	FC
Camborne	Roskear	2001	2001	Lim
Cambridge	Parker's Piece	1817	1864	FC
	University Ground	1821	1830	FC
	F.P. Fenner's Ground	1848	2001	FC
		1972	2001	Lim
Canterbury	Beverley Ground	1841	1846	FC
	St Lawrence Ground	1847	2001	FC
		1967	2001	Lim
Cardiff	Cardiff Arms Park	1910	1966	FC
		1963	1966	Lim

	Sophia Gardens	1967	2001	FC
		1969	2001	FC
Carlisle	Edenside	1996	2000	Lim
Castleford	Saville Park	1967	2000	Lim
Catford Bridge	Private Banks Sports Ground	1875	1921	FC
Catterick	Army Ground	1954	1954	FC
Chatham	New Brompton	1862	1862	FC
	Nore Command Cricket Ground	1926	1929	FC
Chatteris	Town Ground	1832	1832	FC
Cheadle	Tean Road Sports Ground	1973	1987	Lim
Cheam	Cheam Cricket Club Ground	1999	2001	Lim
Checkley	Uttoxeter Road	1991	1991	Lim
Chelmsford	County Ground	1925	2001	FC
	Ransome, Hoffman and Pollard Sports and Social Club	1959	1961	FC
		1969	1969	Lim
	County Ground	1969	2001	Lim
Cheltenham	College Ground	1872	2001	FC
		1969	2001	Lim
	East Gloucestershire Cricket Club Ground	1888	1903	FC
	Victoria Park	1923	1986	FC
	Dowty Arle Court	1992	1992	Lim
	Hatherley and Reddings CC	1999	2000	Lim
Chesham	Amy Lane	1970	1978	Lim
Chester	Chester Boughton Hall	1972	2001	Lim
Chesterfield	Saltergate Ground	1874	1875	FC
	Queen's Park	1898	1988	FC
		1966	1997	Lim
Chester-le-Street	Ropery Lane	1992	1994	FC
		1967	1993	Lim
	Riverside Ground	1995	2001	FC
		1995	2001	Lim
Chichester	Priory Park Ground	1852	1950	FC
Chippenham	Hardenhuish Park	1964	2001	Lim
Chislehurst	West Kent Cricket Club Ground	1822	1838	FC
Chiswick	Chiswick Park	1886	1887	FC
	Civil Service Sports Ground	1927	1927	FC
Cirencester	Cirencester Cricket Club Ground	1879	1879	FC
Clacton-on-Sea	Vista Road Recreation Ground	1931	1966	FC
Cleethorpes	Sports Ground	1980	1990	FC
		1972	2000	Lim
Clifton (Bristol)	Durdham Down	1870	1870	FC
	Clifton College Close Ground	1871	1932	FC
Coalville	Fox and Goose Ground	1913	1914	FC
	Town Ground	1950	1950	FC
	Snibston Colliery Ground	1957	1982	FC
		1970	1970	Lim
Coatbridge	Langloan	1980	1980	FC
Colchester	Castle Park Cricket Ground	1914	2001	FC
		1974	2001	Lim
	Garrison 'A' Cricket Ground	1924	1972	FC
		1970	1972	Lim
Coleraine	Lodge Road	1987	1987	FC
Colwall	Stowe Lane, Colwall	2000	2000	Lim
Colwyn Bay	Rydal School	1929	1929	FC
	Rhos Ground, Penrhyn Avenue	1930	2001	FC
		1972	2001	Lim
Comber	North Down Cricket Club Ground	1995	1995	Lim
Copdock	Old London Road	2001	2001	Lim
Cork	Mardyke	1947	1973	FC

Cove	Grasmere Road, Cove	2000	2000	Lim
Coventry	Bulls Head Ground	1903	1992	FC
		2001	2001	Lim
	Rover Ground	1925	1930	FC
	Morris Motors Ground	1931	1932	FC
	Courtaulds Ground	1946	1982	FC
		1972	1983	Lim
Cowbridge	The Broadshoard, Cae Wyndham	1931	1932	FC
Cowes	J.Samuel White's Ground	1956	1962	FC
Cowley	Morris Motors Sports Ground	1970	1975	Lim
Cranbrook	School Field	1850	1851	FC
	Swifts Park	1862	1863	FC
Croydon	Whitgift School	2000	2001	Lim
Crystal Palace	Crystal Palace Park	1864	1906	FC
Darley Dale	Station Road	1975	1975	Lim
Darlington	Feethams	1992	2000	FC
		1964	2000	Lim
Dartford	Bowman's Lodge	1806	1809	FC
	Hesketh Park	1956	1990	FC
		1978	1981	Lim
Derby	County Ground	1871	2001	FC
		1969	2001	Lim
	County Ground	1969	2001	Lim
Dewsbury	Dewsbury and Savile Ground	1867	1933	FC
Dinton	Dinton Cricket Club	2001	2001	Lim
Dover	Crabble Athletic Ground	1907	1976	FC
		1970	1975	Lim
Downpatrick	Strangford Road	1983	19893	FC
		1990	1990	Lim
Dublin	College Park	1895	1961	FC
	Rathmines	1912	1998	FC
	Castle Avenue	1964	1999	FC
		1981	2000	Lim
	Sydney Parade	1965	1965	FC
	Malahide	1991	1997	FC
Dudley	Tipton Road	1911	1977	FC
		1969	1971	Lim
Dumfries	Nunholm	1988	1988	FC
Dundee	Forthill	1924	1999	FC
Dunstable	Lancot Park	2001	2001	Lim
Dunstall	Deer Park	1999	1999	Lim
Durham	Durham University Ground	1992	1999	Lim
		1979	1994	Lim
East Challow	Vicarage Hill	2001	2001	Lim
East Molesey	Hurst Park Club Ground	1890	1890	FC
		1983	1983	Lim
Eastbourne	Ashford Road	1867	1873	FC
	The Saffrons	1896	2000	FC
		1970	2000	Lim
Ebbw Vale	Eugene Cross Park (The Welfare Ground)	1946	1990	FC
Eccles	G.P.Codie's Ground	1857	1858	FC
Edinburgh	Raeburn Place	1905	1998	FC
		1998	1999	Lim
	Myreside	1982	1990	FC
		1985	1996	Lim
Eglinton	Woodvale Road	1979	1993	FC
		1995	1996	Lim
Enfield	Lincoln Road	1982	1982	Lim
Epsom	Epsom Down	1816	1819	FC
Evesham	Evesham Cricket Club Ground	1951	1951	FC

Exeter	County Ground	1927	1928	FC
		1980	1980	Lim
Exmouth	The Maer Ground	1986	2001	Lim
Faversham	Mount Field	1876	1876	FC
Finchampstead	Memorial Ground	1988	2000	Lim
Finedon	Dolben Cricket Ground	1986	1989	Lim
Folkestone	Municipal Ground	1925	1995	FC
		1969	1995	Lim
Forfar	Strathmore County Cricket Club, Lochside Park	1991	1998	Lim
Frome	Agricultural Showgrounds	1932	1961	FC
		1970	1970	Lim
Gainsborough	Rose Brothers Ground	1931	1937	FC
Galashiels	Mossilee	1911	1911	FC
Gateshead Fell	Eastwood Gardens	1992	1994	FC
		1992	2000	Lim
Gillingham	Garrison Stadium	1937	1968	FC
		1971	1972	Lim
Glasgow	Hamilton Crescent	1911	1994	FC
		1983	1999	Lim
	Titwood	1963	1986	FC
		1980	1995	Lim
	Shawholm	1965	1979	FC
Glastonbury	Morlands Athletic Ground	1952	1973	FC
		1969	1978	Lim
Glossop	North Road Ground	1899	1910	FC
Gloucester	Spa Ground	1882	1923	FC
	Wagon Works Ground (Tuffley Park)	1923	1992	FC
		1969	1982	Lim
	Archdeacon Meadow, King's School Playing Fields	1993	2001	FC
		1993	2001	Lim
Godalming	The Burys	1821	1830	FC
	Broadwater Park	1854	1854	FC
	Charterhouse School	1972	1972	Lim
Godmanchester	The Parks, Fox Grove	2000	2001	Lim
Goodwood	Goodwood Park	1814	1814	FC
Grantham	Gorse Lane	2000	2000	Lim
Gravesend	Bat and Ball Ground	1849	1971	FC
Greenock	Glenkpark	1926	1972	FC
Guildford	Woodbridge Road	1938	2001	FC
		1970	2001	Lim
Halesowen	Seth Somers Park	1964	1969	FC
Halifax	Thrum Hall	1888	1897	FC
Hambledon	Stoke Down	1806	1806	FC
	Broad Halfpenny Down	1908	1908	FC
Harlow	Harlow Sports Centre	1970	1970	FC
		1969	1982	Lim
Harrogate	St George's Road	1882	1996	FC
		1970	2000	Lim
Hartlepool	Park Drive	1992	1997	FC
		1992	2000	Lim
Hastings	Central Recreation Ground	1865	1989	FC
		1973	1989	Lim
	Horntye Park	2000	2001	Lim
Hawkhurst	Hawkhurst Moor	1825	1826	FC
Heanor	Town Ground	1987	1987	FC
		1976	2000	Lim
Hellesdon	Manor Park	2001	2001	Lim
Hereford	Racecourse Ground	1919	1983	FC
		1983	1987	Lim

		1983	1987	Lim
Hertford	Balls Park	1999	2001	Lim
High Wycombe	London Road	1970	1987	Lim
Hinckley	Ashby Road	1911	1937	FC
	Coventry Road	1951	1964	FC
	Leicester Road	1981	1991	Lim
		1984	2001	Lim
Hitchin	Hitchin Town Cricket Club Ground	1966	1989	Lim
Holbeck	Recreation Ground	1868	1889	FC
Hornsey	Tivoli Road	1959	1959	FC
Horsforth	Hall Park Ground	1885	1885	FC
Horsham	Warnham Court	1853	1855	FC
	Cricket Field Road Ground	1908	2001	FC
		1971	2001	Lim
Horton	Horton House Cricket Club Ground	1976	1977	Lim
Hove	Royal Brunswick Ground	1848	1871	FC
	New County Ground	1872	2001	FC
		1963	2001	Lim
Hoylake	Ellerman Line Sports Club	1964	1964	Lim
Huddersfield	St John's Ground	1873	1955	FC
		1969	1982	Lim
Hull	Town Cricket Club Ground	1875	1879	FC
	The Circle	1899	1974	FC
		1969	1990	Lim
Hunslet	Woodhouse Hill Ground	1869	1872	FC
Ilford	Valentine's Park	1923	2001	FC
		1969	2001	Lim
Ilkeston	Rutland Recreation Ground	1925	1994	FC
		1970	1994	Lim
Ipswich	School Ground, Ivry Street	1966	1966	Lim
	Ransomes and Reavals	1978	1978	Lim
Islington	Cattle Market Ground	1864	1868	FC
Jesmond	Osborne Avenue	1965	1974	FC
		1971	2001	Lim
Kendal	Netherfield CC	1984	1999	Lim
Kennington Oval (London)	Kennington Oval	1846	2001	FC
		1964	2001	Lim
Kettering	Town Ground	1923	1971	FC
		1970	1973	Lim
Kidderminster	Chester Road North Ground	1921	2001	FC
		1969	2001	Lim
Kingsland	Luctonians CC	2001	2001	Lim
Kingston-upon-Thames	Leyland Motors Ground	1946	1953	FC
Kington	The Recreation Ground	1999	1999	Lim
Knowle (Bristol)	Knowle Cricket Club Ground	1926	1928	FC
Knypersley	Victora and Knypersley Social Welfare Centre	1985	1990	Lim
Lancaster	Lune Road Ground	1914	1914	FC
Leamington Spa	Parr and Wisden's Ground	1849	1850	FC
	Leamington Cricket Club Ground	1905	1910	FC
Leatherhead	St John's School	1969	1972	Lim
Leeds	Headingley	1890	2001	FC
		1969	2001	Lim
Leek	Highfield	1986	1995	Lim
Leicester	Barker's Ground	1836	1846	FC
	Grace Road	1894	2001	FC
		1964	2001	Lim
	Aylestone Road	1901	1962	FC
Lewes	Dripping Pan	1854	1860	FC
Leyton	County Ground	1886	1997	FC
		1969	1977	Lim

Lincoln	Lindum Sports Club	1969	1969	FC
		1974	2001	Lim
Linlithgow	Boghall Cricket Club Ground	1996	1999	FC
		1998	2001	Lim
Liverpool	Wavertree Road Ground	1859	1872	FC
	Aigburth	1881	2000	FC
		1970	2001	Lim
Llandarcy	B.P. Oil Refinery Ltd Ground	1971	1971	FC
Llandudno	The Oval, Gloddaeth Avenue	1925	1928	FC
		1969	1969	Lim
Llanelli	Stradey Park	1933	1965	FC
		1988	1993	Lim
Londonderry	Beechgrove	1963	1963	FC
Long Eaton	Recreation Ground	1887	1887	FC
	Trent College	1975	1979	Lim
Lord's (London)	Lord's Old Ground	1801	1810	FC
	Lord's New Middle Ground	1811	1813	FC
	Lord's	1814	2001	FC
		1963	2001	Lim
	Lord's Nursery Ground	1903	1903	FC
Loughborough	Tyler's Ground	1875	1875	FC
	Park Road Ground	1913	1952	FC
		1970	1970	Lim
	College Ground	1928	1929	FC
	Brush Ground	1953	1965	FC
Lurgan	Pollock Park	1999	1999	FC
Luton	Wardown Park	1986	1977	FC
		1967	2001	Lim
Lydney	Recreational Trust Ground	1963	1969	FC
		1969	1975	Lim
Lytham St. Anne's	Church Road Ground	1985	1998	FC
Macclesfield	Macclesfield Cricket Club Ground	1966	1974	Lim
Maidstone	Mote Park	1859	2001	FC
		1969	2001	Lim
Manchester	Moss Lane	1844	1846	FC
	Botanical Gardens	1848	1854	FC
	Old Trafford	1860	2001	FC
		1963	2001	Lim
March	The Avenue Sports Club Ground	1975	2001	Lim
Margam	Steel Company of Wales Ground	1953	1963	FC
Margate	Clifton Villa Estate	1864	1864	FC
Marlow	Pound Lane	1990	1999	Lim
Melton Mowbray	Egerton Park	1946	1948	FC
Merthyr Tydfil	Hoover's Sports Ground, Pentrebach	1988	1989	Lim
Middlesbrough	Swatter's Carr, Linthorpe Road East Ground	1864	1867	FC
	Linthorpe Road West Ground	1882	1882	FC
	Acklam Park	1956	1966	FC
		1963	1995	Lim
Midhurst	Town Ground	1830	1830	FC
Mildenhall	Wamil Way, Mildenhall	2000	2001	Lim
Millom	St. George's Road	2001	2001	Lim
Milton Keynes	Campbell Park	2000	2000	FC
		1997	1999	FC
Moreton-in-Marsh	Moreton-in-Marsh Cricket Club Ground	1884	1914	FC
		1972	1996	Lim
Moulsey Hurst	Town Ground	1806	1806	FC
Neath	The Gnoll	1934	1995	FC
		1963	1994	Lim
Nelson	Seed Hill Ground	1925	1938	FC
		2001	2001	Lim

New Beckenham	Lloyds Bank Sports Ground	1954	1954	FC
	Midland Bank Sports Ground	1970	1970	Lim
Newark-on-Trent	Kelham Road	1856	1856	FC
	Elm Road	1966	1978	FC
		1970	1976	Lim
Newmarket	The Severals	1864	1864	FC
Newport, Isle Of Wight	Victoria Recreation Ground	1938	1939	FC
Newport, Mon	Rodney Parade	1935	1965	FC
		1964	1989	Lim
Norbury	J.W. Hobbs Ground	1888	1888	FC
North Perrott	North Perrott Cricket Club	2001	2001	Lim
Northampton	Racecourse Ground Promenade	1872	1872	FC
	County Ground, Wantage Road	1905	2001	FC
		1963	2001	Lim
Northrop Hall	Northrop Hall Cricket Club, Wrexham	1994	1994	Lim
Norwich	New Ground	1834	1836	FC
	Newmarket Road	1912	1986	FC
		1969	1998	Lim
Nottingham	The Forest New Ground	1827	1837	FC
	Trent Bridge	1840	2001	FC
		1965	2001	Lim
	John Player Ground	1970	1973	Lim
Nuneaton	Nuneaton Cricket Club Ground	1912	1914	FC
	Griff and Coton Ground	1930	1989	FC
		1969	1980	Lim
Oakham	Oakham School Ground	1935	2000	FC
		2001	2001	Lim
Oxford	Magdalen Ground	1829	1912	FC
	Bullingdon Green	1843	1843	FC
	Christ Church College Ground	1878	1961	FC
		1981	2001	Lim
	The University Parks	1881	2001	FC
		1973	1998	Lim
	New College Ground	1906	1907	FC
Pagham	Pagham Cricket Club Ground	1976	1979	FC
Paisley	Whitehaugh	1952	1960	FC
Pentyrch	Parc-y-Dwrlyn Ground	1993	1993	Lim
Perth	North Inch	1909	1970	FC
		1984	1989	Lim
Peterborough	Town Ground	1906	1966	FC
	Baker Perkins Sports Ground	1967	1969	FC
		1969	1974	Lim
Petworth	Petworth Park	1824	1826	FC
	Petworth Park New Ground	1844	1849	FC
Plymouth	Peverell Park	1972	1972	Lim
Pontarddulais	Pontarddulais Park	2000	2000	Lim
Pontypridd	Ynysangharad Park	1926	1996	FC
		1970	1999	Lim
Portsmouth	United Services Recreation Ground	1882	2000	FC
		1965	2000	Lim
Preston	West Cliff	1936	1952	FC
Prince's (London)	Prince's Cricket Ground	1872	1878	FC
Purfleet	Thames Board Mills Sports Ground	1969	1972	Lim
Radlett	Brunton Memorial Ground	1999	1999	Lim
Reading	Church Road	1981	1981	FC
		1965	1985	Lim
	Courage's Cricket Ground	1986	1986	Lim
	Reading Cricket Club, Sonning Lane	1991	2001	Lim
Reigate	Priory Ground	1909	1936	FC
Repton	Repton School Ground	1988	1988	Lim

Richmond	Old Deer Park	2000	2001	Lim
Rickmansworth	Clifford's Park	1803	1803	FC
Rochdale	Merefield Ground	1860	1860	FC
	Milnrow Ground	1876	1876	FC
	Sparth Bottoms Road Ground	1876	1876	FC
Roehampton	Bank of England Sports Ground	1967	1967	FC
Romford	Gidea Park Sports Ground	1950	1968	FC
Rotherham	Ferham Park	1880	1880	FC
Rushden	Town Ground	1924	1963	FC
Salford	Broughton Cricket Club Ground	1856	1863	FC
Sandgate	Sandgate Hill Ground	1862	1863	FC
Sawston	Spicer's Sports Ground	1964	1964	Lim
Scarborough	North Marine Road Ground	1874	2001	FC
		1969	2001	Lim
Scunthorpe	Scunthorpe and Appleby Frodingham Works CC, Bramby Hall	1975	1975	Lim
Selkirk	Philiphaugh	1963	1971	FC
Sevenoaks	Sevenoaks Vine Cricket Club Ground	1827	1829	FC
Sheffield	Darnall New Ground	1826	1829	FC
	Hyde Park Ground	1830	1853	FC
	Bramall Lane	1855	1973	FC
		1969	1973	Lim
	Abbeydale Park	1946	1966	FC
		1982	1999	Lim
Shenley	Denis Compton Oval	1996	1999	FC
		1996	1996	Lim
Sherborne	Sherborne School	1968	1968	Lim
Shifnal	Shrewsbury Road	2000	2001	Lim
Shireoaks	Steetley Company Ground	1961	1961	FC
Shrewsbury	London Road	1984	2001	Lim
Skegness	Richmond Drive	1935	1935	FC
Sleaford	London Road	1860	1864	FC
		1983	2001	Lim
Slough	Chalvey Road	1981	1986	Lim
Southampton	Antelope Ground	1842	1884	FC
	Itchen Ground	1848	1850	FC
	County Ground	1885	2000	FC
		1965	2000	Lim
Southborough	B.M. Close's Ground	1867	1867	FC
Southend-on-Sea	Southchurch Park	1906	2001	FC
		1977	2001	Lim
Southgate	John Walker's Ground	1859	2001	FC
		1991	2001	Lim
Southport	Trafalgar Road Ground	1959	1999	FC
		1969	1987	Lim
Southwell	Brackenhurst Cricket Ground	1846	1846	FC
St Albans	Clarence Park	1984	1990	Lim
St Austell	Wheal Eliza, Bethel	1995	1996	Lim
St Leonards-on-Sea	Old Racecourse	1857	1857	FC
Stevenage	Ditchmore Lane	1969	1969	Lim
Stockton-on-Tees	Portrack Lane	1858	1861	FC
	Grangefield Road	1992	1999	FC
		1992	1996	Lim
Stoke-on-Trent	New County Ground	1886	1929	FC
	Michelin Ground	1953	1953	FC
	Longton Cricket Club Ground	1959	1972	FC
		1971	1976	Lim
Stone	Lichfield Road	1973	1996	Lim
Stourbridge	Amblecote	1905	1981	FC
		1969	1982	Lim

Stourport-on-Severn	Chain Wire Club Ground	1980	1980	FC
Stratford-upon-Avon	Stratford-upon-Avon Cricket Club Ground	1951	1951	FC
		2000	2000	Lim
Stratton-on-the-Fosse	Downside School	1934	1934	FC
Street	Millfield School	1961	1961	FC
		1975	1977	Lim
Stroud	Erinoid Ground	1956	1963	FC
Sunbury-on-Thames	Kenton Court Meadow	1972	1974	Lim
Sutton	Cheam Road	1969	1969	Lim
Swansea	St Helen's	1912	2001	FC
		1966	2001	Lim
Swindon	County Ground	1967	1967	FC
		1970	1992	Lim
Taunton	County Ground	1882	2001	FC
		1964	2001	Lim
Telford	St Georges	1984	2000	Lim
Tewkesbury	Swilgate	1973	1973	Lim
Todmorden	Centre Vale	1874	1874	FC
Toft	Booth Park	2001	2001	Lim
Tolworth	Decca Sports Ground	1973	1973	Lim
Tonbridge	Angel Ground	1869	1939	FC
Torquay	Recreation Ground	1954	1994	FC
		1969	2000	Lim
Town Malling	Old County Ground	1836	1890	FC
Tring	Pound Meadows	1974	1991	Lim
Trowbridge	Trowbridge Cricket Club Ground	1990	1990	FC
		1987	1993	Lim
Truro	Boscawen Park	1899	1899	FC
		1970	2001	Lim
Tunbridge Wells	Higher Common Ground	1844	1884	FC
	Nevill Ground	1901	2001	FC
		1963	2001	Lim
Twickenham	Orleans Club Ground	1878	1883	FC
Uckfield	Sheffield Park	1881	1896	FC
Uttoxeter	Oldfields Ground	1907	1909	FC
Uxbridge	Royal Air Force Sports Ground	1964	1964	FC
	Uxbridge Cricket Club Ground	1980	1998	FC
		1985	1998	Lim
Wakefield	College Grove Ground	1878	1878	FC
Walsall	Gorway Ground	1986	2000	Lim
Walworth	Montpelier Gardens	1802	1802	FC
Warrington	Walton Lea Road, High Walton	1993	1993	Lim
Watford	Watford Town Cricket Club Ground,			
	Woodside, Garston	1977	1981	Lim
Welbeck	Welbeck Abbey Cricket Ground	1901	1904	FC
Wellingborough	Hatton Park	1874	1874	FC
	Town Ground	1929	1929	FC
	Wellingborough School Ground	1946	1991	FC
		1970	1991	Lim
Wellington	Orliton Road	1979	1979	FC
		1974	1999	Lim
Wells	Rowden Road	1935	1951	FC
Welwyn Garden City	Digswell Park	2000	2001	Lim
Wembley	Wembley Park	1896	1896	FC
West Bridgford	West Park	1932	1935	FC
West Brompton	Lillie Bridge	1871	1871	FC
Westbury	Town Ground	1890	1890	FC
Westcliff-on-Sea	Chalkwell Park	1934	1976	FC
		1970	1976	Lim
Weston-super-Mare	Clarence Park	1914	1996	FC

		1973	1996	Lim
	Devonshire Road Park Ground	1969	1970	Lim
Whalley	Station Road Ground	1867	1867	FC
Wimbledon	Wimbledon Cricket Club Ground	1999	1999	Lim
Winchester	Green Jackets Ground	1875	1875	FC
	Winchester College Ground	1875	1875	FC
Wirksworth	Derby Road Ground	1874	1874	FC
Wisbech	Queens Road	1867	1867	FC
	Wisbech Cricket Club Ground	1927	1927	FC
		1967	1997	Lim
Wolstanton	Porthill Park	2001	2001	Lim
Worcester	County Ground	1899	2001	FC
		1963	2001	Lim
Worksop	Town Ground	1921	1988	FC
		1970	1980	Lim
Worthing	Manor Sports Ground	1935	1964	FC
Wrecclesham	Holt Pound Cricket Ground	1808	1809	FC
Wrotham	Napps	1815	1815	FC
Yeovil	West Hendford	1935	1939	FC
	Johnson Park	1951	1967	FC
		1969	1970	Lim
	Westlands Sports Ground	1971	1978	Lim
York	Yorkshire Gentlemen Cricket Club Ground	1890	1890	FC

Appendix 2

Pre-1974 county boundaries (first-class counties shaded)

Index

(This does not include grounds mentioned in Appendix 1)